I CAN'T BREATHE
I CAN'T BREATHE
I CAN'T BREATHE
I CAN'T BREATHE
I CAN'T BREATHE
I CAN'T BREATHE
I CAN'T BREATHE
I CAN'T BREATHE
I CAN'T BREATHE
I CAN'T BREATHE

THE KILLING THAT STARTED A MOVEMENT

1 3 5 7 9 10 8 6 4 2

WH Allen, an imprint of Ebury Publishing,
20 Vauxhall Bridge Road,
London SW1V 2SA

WH Allen is part of the Penguin Random House group of companies
whose addresses can be found at global.penguinrandomhouse.com

Copyright © Matt Taibbi 2017

Matt Taibbi has asserted his right to be identified as the author of this
Work in accordance with the Copyright, Designs and Patents Act 1988

First published in the United Kingdom by WH Allen in 2017
First published in the United States by Spiegel & Grau in 2017

www.penguin.co.uk

A CIP catalogue record for this book is available from the British Library

Hardback ISBN 9780753548684
Trade Paperback ISBN 9780753548660

Printed and bound in Great Britain by Clays Ltd, St Ives PLC

Book design by Simon M. Sullivan

Penguin Random House is committed to a sustainable future for
our business, our readers and our planet. This book is made
from Forest Stewardship Council® certified paper.

I CAN'T BREATHE

MATT TAIBBI

To the family and friends of Eric Garner,
who told his story with love.
To Clementine Russ, who is still waiting.

Rock the V-Gooses, everything we wore was name brand
Sold three loosies, just to get on call plan . . .

—RAEKWON

CONTENTS

PART II THE PERPETUAL INJUSTICE MACHINE

PART I
LIFE AND DEATH ON BAY STREET

ONE IBRAHIM

Bang bang bang!

At about 2:45 P.M. on April 2, 2014, on a drizzly afternoon in Staten Island, New York, an aspiring music producer in his late thirties named Ibrahim Annan was sitting in his car when a noise outside startled him.

"Open the fucking window!"

Tall and slender, with a slim mustache, Annan, known as Brian or B or Bizzy B to his friends, was the son of two devout Muslim Ghanaian immigrants. On this afternoon, he was parked on private property, a muddy driveway in front of a friend's apartment building. The noise came from the driver's side of his spiffily maintained 2011 Toyota Camry.

Annan looked up and saw a white man with a hoodie obscuring most of his face, rapping on the window.

Bang bang bang!

"Open the fucking window before I break your fucking arm!"

Annan looked past his dashboard and saw another figure standing at about ten o'clock, also dressed in street clothes. This one was aiming a gun at him.

Annan froze. He was a regular visitor to this address, 100 Pierce Street, on the northern side of the island. It's a dull three-story apartment building, nestled in a sleepy mixed-race neighborhood of rundown one-family homes. He had a key to an apartment there belonging to his friend, a local DJ known as Icebox International. The two sometimes mixed music inside. He would later say he was there that day to visit his friend on the way back from the post office.

The police version of this story is different. They say Ibrahim Annan pulled into the parking spot and began ostentatiously playing around in his front seat with a giant baggie of weed, which they would describe in a criminal complaint as a "ziplock bag of marihuana."

This "ziplock bag" in the complaint was described as being "open to public view." By unsurprising coincidence, New York City police are not supposed to arrest people for marijuana possession unless the subject is "publicly displaying" the drug. If you're carrying it or even smoking it in private, it's just a ticket. But at the time, tens of thousands of New Yorkers were criminally arrested for pot possession every year, which either pointed to an epidemic of exhibitionist drug use or a lot of iffy police reports.

Bang bang bang!

"OPEN THE FUCKING DOOR!"

A dependable rule of thumb in police brutality cases is that the worst incidents are triggered by something the suspect says. A lot of these episodes are already running hot before they fully erupt. They often start with the police tackling someone, putting a knee in his or her back, hurling obscenities (to be fair, sometimes in retaliation for obscenities thrown at them). So it doesn't take much to raise the collective temperature beyond the bursting point. An F-bomb or two will usually do it.

Annan yelled back: "Get a fucking warrant!"

Boom! The inside of Annan's car exploded with glass as the officer in the hoodie used something—a nightstick maybe?—to shatter the driver's-side window. At the hospital later on, Annan would have glass fragments removed from his eyes.

Annan turned his face to the right to avoid the impact. But when he opened his eyes, he was immediately struck on the left side of his face with what he thought was an ASP, a kind of telescoping metal baton used by police all over the country.

Another policeman had opened the passenger-side door and was also striking him repeatedly with something. He heard the impact of steel on his skull before he felt it.

Meanwhile the original officer in the hoodie was yanking at his seat belt. The Toyota dealership would later have to replace the seat belt lock, which is designed to withstand car accidents. It was broken and ripped loose in the struggle.

After more than twenty blows to his face and head, Annan was pulled from the car and thrown to the ground. A police cruiser had driven up beside his car, and he was now facedown in the mud and glass, obscured in a narrow spot between two vehicles. Annan says he screamed for bystanders behind the cars to reach for their cellphones.

"Film them!" he screamed. "Film them!"

"Shut the fuck up!"

"Film them!"

Hands pulled behind his back, Annan felt a set of cuffs go on. Officers were raining blows down on him from all angles. He detected a strange sensation in his left leg and tried to protest.

"Yo, hey, the ankle cuff is too tight!" he gasped.

"What are you talking about?"

"The cuff on my ankle! It's too tight!"

In fact, there was no cuff on his ankle. Annan's left leg had been stomped on repeatedly, broken in three places, the damage so severe he would still be walking with a cane more than a year later.

Annan tried to focus. He looked down at the mud in front of him. The blows were coming so furiously that he began to worry that he would die here, in this coffin-sized space between two cars.

His legs and wrists were throbbing and now he also felt something, a hand maybe, sliding under his neck, preparing maybe for a headlock. In his panic he felt himself losing air and spoke three words destined to become famous in another man's mouth.

"I can't breathe," he said.

"Shut the fuck up."

"I'm serious. I can't breathe!"

One of the officers answered him: "You can fucking talk, you can fucking breathe."

In the ambulance a few minutes later, Annan was beside himself. He looked at his mangled left foot and nodded at the officer.

"Where do you live?" he shouted. "Identify yourself!"

The cop shook his head. Annan says he then leaned forward and punched Annan in the face.

The EMT in the front of the vehicle said nothing and kept driving.

The borough of Staten Island would later charge Annan seven hundred dollars for the ambulance ride.

Ibrahim Annan was well known to the staff of the Richmond University Medical Center. He and his sister both suffered from sickle cell anemia and had come there regularly for treatment their whole lives.

Now Annan was pushed through the door of the ER on a gurney. He was shouting, hysterically, at the top of his lungs.

"They attacked me and broke my leg! Don't let them hurt me! Don't let them hurt me!"

"Shut up," one of the officers muttered.

Annan's gurney was moved to a private room. Inside, the hospital staff implored him to keep his mouth shut. He was eventually hand-cuffed to his bed and then wheeled off to a far corner of the ER.

Much later in the evening, after word of his detention had finally reached his family, Annan's youngest sister, Mariama, wandered through the emergency room, looking for her brother.

Mariama caught a glimpse of him from afar, his face bloodied and his leg smashed. "I had never seen him like that before," she said. "It was awful."

The police wouldn't let her or anyone else in the family visit him or even learn exactly what had happened, so she had to steal a glance from a distance.

"The incident completely changed the way I think about everything—the government, the police, everything," she said later. "I didn't trust the nurses because they were following the police instructions. I was afraid to leave him there with any of them."

Annan's parents also tried to get access to Ibrahim. It took more than a full day and multiple trips back and forth to Staten Island's infamous 120th Precinct before the two slow-moving, elderly Africans were finally given a pass to see their son. As immigrants they had a poor instinct for the uglier nuances of American culture and were puzzled by every part of the process.

The deal for the pass had been brokered by Mariama. She recalls pleading with a desk sergeant at the 120th Precinct, an outpost that had for decades been the subject of horror stories within the island's nonwhite community, who refer to it darkly as the "One Two Oh."

On the street in certain parts of Staten Island, people believe the 120 is where they send all the reject cops from other precincts, especially the ones with too many abuse complaints. The precinct jailhouse in particular has a terrible reputation for, among other things, its smell and poor ventilation. Even hardened criminals go the extra mile to try to avoid landing there, even for a night.

Mariama remembers the moment when she got the pass. She was

standing in the precinct with her two parents when finally, the desk man shook his head and sighed.

"Okay, I'll give them a pass," he said. "But only because they're fucking old."

Mariama nearly fainted.

"I was afraid for my parents," she said later. "They were shocked by the language. These are elderly, proper people. They could have had a heart attack."

After a bedside arraignment in the hospital, Ibrahim Annan faced a litany of charges: menacing, criminal possession of marijuana in the fifth degree, obstructing government administration, unlawful possession of marijuana, assault in the second degree, and assault in the third degree, among others.

Annan's family later hired a tall, sharply dressed African American lawyer named Gregory Watts. He would grumblingly describe the charges of assaulting the police.

"They smashed the guy's car window, and one of them got a little cut after they beat his ass up," he said. "That's the assault."

The last charge was criminal possession of a weapon in the fourth degree. The police explanation for that charge is that when they banged on Ibrahim Annan's car window, the accused responded by holding up a lighter and an aerosol can and shouting at armed police from inside a closed vehicle, "IF YOU OPEN THE WINDOW I'M GOING TO BURN YOU." The officers used all caps in the complaint. Annan would later claim he never even read that part of the charges. "I said *what*?" he asked, incredulous.

The long list of charges slapped on Annan were part of an elaborate game police and prosecutors often play with people caught up in "problematic" arrests. A black man with a shattered leg has a virtually automatic argument for certain kinds of federal civil rights lawsuits. But those suits are harder to win when the arrest results in a conviction. So when police beat someone badly enough, the city's first line of defense is often to go on offense and file a long list of charges, hoping one will stick. Civil lawyers meanwhile will often try to wait until the criminal charges are beaten before they file suit.

It's a leverage game. If the beating is on the severe side, the victim has the power to take the city for a decent sum of money. But that's just money, and it comes out of the taxpayer's pocket. The state, meanwhile, has the power to make the losses in this particular poker game very personal. It can put the loser in jail and on the way there can take up years of his or her life in court appearances. As Annan would find out, time is the state's ultimate trump card.

Annan was in the hospital for more than three weeks. His ankle had to be reconstructed surgically.

When he finally went home, he was mostly immobile. It was spring outside, and he missed seeing the weather turn warm.

Feeling better one day in the beginning of May, however, he decided to get some fresh air. With the aid of a walker, he went outside and headed down toward Bay Street, near the water.

The big man in the doorway saw everything. He knew this part of the island like the back of his hand. Anything in this little crisscrossed city block that looked or felt out of place, he registered instantly.

If you judged this man by his clothes, you missed a lot. He looked a mess from the outside. He'd change T-shirts every day, but the giant XXL sweatpants were often the same smudged and stained pair from the day before. The big man suffered from sleep apnea and chronic allergies, which left his nose constantly running. A hundred times a day or more, he'd wipe his nose with his fingers, then wipe his fingers on those sweatpants.

Eric Garner's one recent concession to fashion was a pair of shell-toe Adidas sneakers, made iconic in New York by Run-DMC, a band he was crazy for as a kid growing up in Brooklyn. His sneakers were huge—size 16—and yet still too small for him, because he also suffered from diabetes and his swollen feet spilled out of his shoes.

One of his friends on the street called him "Elephant Foot." But it really wasn't that funny. The swelling from his illnesses left him in constant pain, which was a problem because his job required him to stand in place, rain or shine, hot summer or biting winter, for as much as ten or twelve hours a day.

His usual place of work was on a little stretch of Bay Street, on Staten Island's North Shore. He spent most of his time there, circling a small triangular patch of trash-strewn grass called Tompkinsville

Park. The park, which used to be nicknamed Needle Park, contains a dozen or so benches, a big red brick public toilet building long ago locked up by authorities, and a view of New York's Upper Bay. On most days it's also home to a collection of dope fiends, drifters, crack-heads, and alcoholics. They come here to hang out, get high, drink, argue, and trash-talk.

Just a hundred yards or so from this crowd, on the water side of the park, sits a new fifty-seven-unit condominium complex bearing the absurdly pretentious name "The Pointe at St. George."

"The Pointe" is part of a major Staten Island renewal project called the Bay Street corridor, an ambitious plan to invest nearly a billion dollars in a string of high-end residential buildings that would dot the waterfront leading to the Staten Island Ferry. A two-bedroom unit at the "luxury, full-service" condo complex sells for half a million dollars or more. A nice starter home for an entry-level Wall Street hustler, perhaps, who wants a water view at night and doesn't mind reading the *Financial Times* on a morning ferry ride to downtown Manhattan.

The condos looked like great investments but for one thing: the view across the street. Needle Park is an old-school New York street hangout—not too dangerous, but visually rough around the edges and definitely way too black for anyone who'd spend a half-million dollars to spell "Point" with an "e."

When this place was just a straight-up shooting gallery in the early 2000s, police hardly ever came by. But now that the park was on the edge of a billion-dollar real estate investment, the police were always coming around, mixing it up with the park's denizens over one thing or another. Nickel-and-dime stuff, mostly, what the police call "quality of life" arrests: drinking from open containers, peeing on the sidewalk, disorderly conduct.

Garner caught a significant share of that extra police attention, which grated on him. But he wasn't really part of the wine-and-dope crowd at Tompkinsville. It's more accurate to say he was in the service industry catering to that group. He sold tax-free cigarettes there, and he was good at it.

He'd arrived in Staten Island years before, an ex-con fresh out of prison on crack charges, and he didn't have a way to feed his kids. After struggling to find a square job, he broke down and at first considered selling drugs again. But those doors on Bay Street were closed at the time, so he turned to something a little less dangerous and a little more entrepreneurial.

There was an irony to the fact that Eric Garner eventually found himself making a living on the streets of Staten Island selling smuggled cigarettes. He was a symbol of the borough's bizarre history.

Staten Island was once the home of the world's largest landfill, an artificial mountain of filth that in the seventies and eighties began growing to fantastic dimensions. Fresh Kills, named for a nearby estuary, opened in 1947 but over the decades became a sore point for the mostly white citizens on the south side of the island, where all of that garbage from Manhattan and Brooklyn and Queens was unloaded.

Many of Staten Island's residents were middle-class white people who had fled to the distant borough from Brooklyn and Queens when the Verrazano-Narrows Bridge, then the world's largest suspension bridge, opened in 1964. Coincidentally, New York was ravaged by race riots that very year, after the shooting of a black teenager named James Powell by a white police officer. The fleeing white New Yorkers departed for Staten Island to get away from what locals to this day still euphemistically describe as "city problems." ("Come to Staten Island and you can still live in New York City without the 'city' problems!" is how the *Staten Island Advance* recently described the borough's pitch to potential residents.)

But having escaped the city itself, the new arrivals were still on the hook for those problems, at least when it came to paying taxes. The landfill therefore had enormous symbolic significance for many white Staten Islanders. They felt like they paid more than their fair share of taxes and got to babysit the troubled city's stinking trash for their trouble. Their resentment was real, as palpable as the smell of the city's largest dump.

So by the time 1993 came around, white Staten Island voted as a bloc to help elect Mayor Rudy Giuliani, who'd run on a law-and-order platform. Already "law and order" was proving to be a euphemism for something else. Rudy had been a successful prosecutor and portrayed himself as a friend of the police department and enemy of crime—but he'd proven himself among outer-borough white New Yorkers with stunts like marching with a mob of protesting police officers who burst across barricades and rumbled through lower Manhattan denouncing the city's then mayor, a black man named David Dinkins ("The mayor's on crack!" protesting cops chanted). The "law and order" candidate, in other words, wasn't so hung up on law or order, not exactly. But to the white ethnic voters who'd deliver him the mayoralty, he'd proven that he would take their side in a fight and put their enemies—the black and brown people who'd driven them to the outer boroughs and even taken over City Hall—back in their place.

After the election, Giuliani closed the Staten Island dump down and began sending thousands of tons of New York's garbage not to other white neighborhoods in the city but to the people of Virginia. Hilariously, Giuliani told Virginians they owed it to New York to take its garbage because Virginian tourists took in New York's great musicals and museums. We bless you with our culture, you take our garbage, that's the deal. It was, the mayor said, a "reciprocal relationship."

Virginia reciprocated the relationship all right. When New York imposed the country's highest cigarette taxes under its next mayor, Michael Bloomberg, adding almost six dollars per pack to retail prices within the city, smugglers began heading to other states. Virginia and other low-tax states of the South began flooding New York with cheap smokes brought in by canny street arbitrageurs, who undercut New York's tax laws one illicit trunkful at a time.

Eric Garner became one of those smugglers. He had several employees and regularly sent mules on runs to Virginia, where they filled their trunks with wholesaled cartons. He was shrewd with money and ran a tight ship. Fifty dollars plus expenses is what he supposedly paid his drivers. They never got caught and brought hundreds of cartons back to Staten Island every few months.

In Virginia, Garner was paying around five dollars a pack. In New York, the highly taxed cigarettes sold legally in stores at about fourteen dollars a pack. The low-tax policies of the South instantly created a booming pseudo-criminal trade in cities like New York, but that didn't seem to bother the southern pols who Giuliani had once insisted should be thankful for New York's great stage shows. Despite repeated calls from inside the state and out to raise cigarette taxes to help end the smuggling problem, the government of Virginia, for instance, would continually refuse to raise taxes by even a symbolic amount.

Garner would split the difference and sell packs for around nine bucks. And sometimes he would sell individual cigarettes, known as loosies, upping the profit margin even more—two for a dollar, a rate of ten bucks per pack. He sold a variety of brands in cartons and packs, but loosies were almost always Kools or Newports. It was a feature of the Garner brand.

When he sold loosies, he was always reaching into a pocket with those same fingers he had just used to wipe his runny nose with, then handing over the cigarettes. The dopers and wine-heads who were many of his customers would hesitate, then look up at the unsmiling big man and quickly take his cigs before he changed his mind. Garner's friends often doubled over laughing watching these transactions.

Garner was six foot three and weighed 350 pounds. He was serious and formidable to look at, but few people on the street had ever seen him truly angry. The one exception was when another young cigarette seller, also named Eric, called him "Big Dummy." It was a nickname from *Sanford and Son* some of Garner's friends used to throw at him to try to get a rise out of him.

He took the abuse from friends, but this younger Eric wasn't enough of a friend to get away with it, and when he tried, Garner went nuts. He took off after the kid but didn't get very far. Once a great athlete, Garner couldn't run anymore. Out of breath on sore feet, he gave up the chase.

In addition to the fact that he was well liked and rarely known to raise his hand to fight, there are two things the people on Bay Street almost all say about Eric Garner. They say he loved football, and he had a tremendous head for numbers.

Garner could calculate the price of six different cigarette deals simultaneously and never be off by a cent. He was a little like the Harlem bookmaker from *The Autobiography of Malcolm X,* West Indian Archie, who never wrote a number down because he could keep them all in his head. Eric Garner's skill ran in the family: Garner's mother, Gwen Carr, can rattle off addresses and phone numbers of distant relatives from fifty years ago.

His facility with numbers went well with his love of football. Garner was the kind of person who studied sports statistics like a rabbi studying the Talmud. If you asked him how many receptions Amani Toomer had in 2002, he wouldn't hesitate.

"Eighty-two," he'd say. "And for thirteen hundred and forty-three yards."

"He'd throw some number at you, and you'd be like, 'Uh-uh, fuck that, that can't be right,' " says one of his close friends, a tall street hustler from Brooklyn named John McCrae who spent months and years standing on the corner next to Garner. "And he'd look at you and with that deep voice of his, he'd say, 'Google that shit.' "

McCrae laughs at the memory. Almost everyone who knew Eric Garner does an Eric Garner impersonation. He had a unique voice. Some impersonations are more convincing than others. McCrae has clearly worked hard on his. He adjusts his voice downward to Teddy Pendergrass levels.

"*Google that shit.*" McCrae laughs again. "And then you'd google it, and he'd be right every time. Motherfucker was *always* right. You couldn't win an argument with him."

McCrae remembers another story. It was early May 2014. The name of Eric Garner was just over two months away from becoming known around the world. McCrae was standing on Bay Street with Garner when a figure came around the corner.

It was Ibrahim Annan, moving slowly with his walker. McCrae raised an eyebrow. Everybody on Bay Street knew Annan, the music man. McCrae himself knew him pretty well but hadn't heard from him in a while. He stared at the walker.

"B, man, what the fuck?"

"Cops beat me up," Annan said.

Annan stayed for a while and told his story of being stomped and choked and kicked. He even pulled out his cellphone to show an X-ray picture of his splintered ankle. Heads shook all around. McCrae and Annan both remember Garner listening to the story.

After a few minutes, Annan shook hands with everyone and moved on.

"Shit is fucked up," McCrae said to Garner.

Eric Garner nodded, staring off into the distance. He had other things on his mind.

TWO PINKY

Bored again?
Interested in a new way to meet people?
Just pick up the phone and dial . . . 1-976-8585! . . . IT'S THE PARTY LINE!

In the summer of 1987, a young woman with high cheekbones and long, ropelike black hair picked up the telephone. She was striking, and of mixed race, with a father who was Native American and a mother who was black and Jewish. Her name was Esaw, but everyone called her Pinky.

The story went that when she was born, the doctor was confused by the little girl's light skin and narrow eyes. He asked Esaw's mother, "Is the father Oriental?"

Her mother quipped, "No, but I ate Chinese food last night."

Mama Snipes was a performer who would still be doing raunchy stand-up comedy into her nineties. She looked down at her daughter's pink skin and what she called her "chinky" eyes and called the child Pinky.

Pinky was in an apartment on Twenty-Second Street in Manhattan's Chelsea neighborhood when she picked up the phone to call the Party Line that night. This was before the Internet, before chat rooms. The goofball TV ads for party lines were just about the most visible thing on the air in New York the late eighties, second only maybe to the schlock electronic-store ads put out by famed pitchmeister and con man "Crazy" Eddie Antar. The chat line wasn't expensive. It was a flat rate, three dollars per call. You could talk all night if you met someone.

Pinky put her ear to the phone.

"Hello?"

A deep voice answered. "Yeah, hello. How are you?"

"I'm all right. How are you?"

"I'm good."

"What's your name?"

"Eric. What's yours?"

"Pinky."

Eric said hi again. Things were going well, but then Pinky asked, "Eric, how old are you?"

"Eighteen." He was not quite seventeen.

"And I thought, 'He's too young,'" Pinky recalls today. "So I said, 'Next!' and left him behind."

She moved on and talked to a few more guys on the line, but none of them impressed her. There were even a few racist chatters, she remembers. "They were idiots," she says now, laughing. "So I said, 'Eric, are you still there?'"

"Yeah," he said.

"Well, you can take my personal number, and we can talk on our personal line."

Eric Garner brightened and took Pinky's number and called right back. He was living at his grandmother's high-rise apartment in the Coney Island Houses at the time. He always spent holidays and summers at his grandmother's project home near the famed beachfront amusement park.

He stayed on the phone with Pinky Snipes for hours that night, talking about all sorts of things, but mostly about his family. He spoke about his mother and about how, without his father in the house (Elliott Garner had died when Eric was five), he felt like he had to be the man in the place, the disciplinarian. He had a brother and a sister and also lived with two young cousins whose parents had died and who had moved in with Eric's mother.

"He talked a lot about that, about feeling the responsibility, being responsible before he was responsible, if that makes sense," she says. "He'd tell his little sister to do something, and she'd say, 'You're not my daddy!' And he'd say, 'But I'm your big brother. You've got to listen to me.'"

There is a story in family legend that Eric's little sister, Ellisha, once had a boy call the family's Brooklyn apartment while she was still in elementary school. Eric took the phone and hung up on him. When she ran to complain to her mother ("Eric hung up on my friend!"), her big brother snapped back.

"You shouldn't have boys calling you," he said. "You're still seeing a pediatric doctor!"

Eric went on and on to Pinky that night, about things that inter-ested her and things that didn't. He talked about cars. He wanted to be a mechanic and talked about going to a technical school in Ohio to study diesel engines.

Pinky for her part talked a little less. She didn't tell Eric right away that she had a baby daughter named Shardinee, or that she was sev-eral months pregnant with another child, from a man she'd already broken up with.

Their conversation went on so long that Eric's grandmother inter-vened. "Get off the phone!" Pinky heard her shouting.

Finally he said, "I want to take you on a date."

"Well," Pinky said, "I have a child."

Eric didn't hesitate. "Then we'll go somewhere kid friendly," he said.

Pinky didn't spend much time preparing for their first date. She met him straight after a shift scooping ice cream, her nine-month-old daughter in tow.

"I was working at that time at a Häagen-Dazs in Grand Central Station," she remembers. "So I had on a red Häagen-Dazs sweatshirt, jeans, and sneakers. When I get off the train at Coney Island, here comes Eric in dress pants, a dress shirt, and nice shoes."

She told Eric she didn't expect him to be so dressed up.

"I wanted to make a good impression," he told her.

They went to the kiddie park at Coney Island. It was a warm eve-ning and you could smell the ocean. They took her baby, Shardinee, on all the rides: the pony carts, the jumping motorcycles, the fire en-gines, and the dizzy dragons. After a little while Pinky got bored with the kid stuff. She decided to take Eric on some rides she wanted to go on, starting with the Tilt-a-Whirl.

Eric Garner as a teenager didn't yet have the health problems he would have later in life. He wasn't overweight. But he was a big, im-posing man, six foot three, well over two hundred pounds. And he was afraid of the Tilt-a-Whirl.

"I was shocked," Esaw recalls. "Big as he was, he was scared as hell of those rides. I convinced him to go on the Ferris wheel, and you know how they have the carts that swing and the carts that are still? He wanted to sit in one of the still ones."

She laughs. "I said, 'No way.' We got in the swinging one, and the whole way up, he was wailing like a bitch. I'm serious, he was like, *'I want my mommy!'* And I said, 'Big as you are, you're crying for your mother?' "

Still, she liked him. And she liked the way he was with her daughter. Eric Garner, by all accounts, from people who knew him as a young man and as an older one, was good with kids. Next to his love of football, it's the one thing almost everyone who knew him mentions.

Eric liked Pinky. Esaw says she was the first girl he ever brought home to his mother. Eric's mother, Gwen, was on her guard.

"She'd heard rumors that I was twenty-five and had three kids," Esaw recalls now. "And I said, 'No, I'm twenty and I have one.' "

Eric was still in high school when they met. Esaw remembers helping Eric with a paper that he wasn't terribly interested in writing. "It was something about Christopher Columbus, the *Niña,* the *Pinta,* the *Santa Maria,*" she says. "Something about Columbus and the three boats."

They separated for a while after that summer. Eric said he was going away to technical school in Ohio. Pinky was getting ready to have her baby. Eric asked if he could check in on her after she delivered. She said yes.

In January 1988, Eric called.

"What did you have?" he asked.

"A girl," Pinky said. "Her name is Dorothy."

They started seeing each other again. Eric had given up on technical school and was trying his hand at different jobs at the time. One was as a security guard at an A&P on Eighth Avenue in Chelsea, a few blocks from Pinky's place. One time, she remembers, one of her neighbors knocked on her door with a surprise.

"Pinky," she said. "There's a cop downstairs to see you."

"A *cop?*" she said. "What cop?"

She went downstairs and there was big, lumbering Eric, in his security guard uniform. "That was the cop," she says, laughing.

She fell for him. "It was the way he accepted me and my daughter," she says. "That's why I fell in love with him."

They got married on August 26, 1989, and went on to have four children. Erica was born in 1990, then came Emerald in 1991. Eric Jr. was born in 1994, and the youngest boy, Emery, was born in 1999.

One of the first places they lived was 2359 Southern Boulevard in the Bronx. It's an eccentric choice of location for a young family, right across the street from the Bronx Zoo. And not just any part of the Bronx Zoo, but the elephant cage. Kids love zoos, obviously, but there were other factors.

"We had the pleasure of smelling elephant dung for years," she said. "I used to fill the place with Renuzit packets just to try to fight the smell. All those years, we never once took the kids to the damn zoo."

It wasn't a perfect marriage, but in a weird way Esaw and Eric were a fit, personality-wise. Pinky was direct and had inherited her mother's sharp tongue. When she felt he needed it, she would get in Eric's face.

Garner, on the other hand, was a big fan of the path of least resistance. Although he liked to argue for fun, real confrontation was something he typically tried to avoid. Even as a child, he never talked back to his mother, preferring to wait her out rather than take her on. "Eric never, ever raised his voice at me, he never talked back to me," his mother recalls. She laughs. "In his mind, I guess he said, 'I wish she would shut up so I can get on doing what I got to do.'"

In the early years, they had what seemed on the outside like a pretty normal family life. Throughout most of his younger years, Eric Garner worked square jobs. After the security guard job he worked at the Greyhound terminal at the Port Authority Bus Terminal in Manhattan. Pinky remembers coming down from the Bronx on Eric's paydays, bringing little Erica in a baby carrier and holding her two little girls, Shardinee and Dorothy, by the hand. They'd meet up at Eric's job and then go out to Sizzler together. "Sizzler was a big thing back then," she says. "It was a family tradition."

Eric was a pretty good mechanic, but his skills became outdated quickly. "He was really good, until they came out with computerized cars," Esaw says. "He was lost in the computers."

Later, when the family moved away from the elephant cage to Brooklyn, Eric supposedly got another job, this one with the help of Pinky's mother, whose day job was in quality control at a pharmaceutical company. Garner, too, was there for a short while, until, she says, he took a nap during a break one day and didn't wake up in time to go back to his shift. He was fired.

Years later, Garner's friends on the streets of Staten Island would tell stories about how he worked such long hours on the street that he would sometimes fall asleep standing up. To this day, people on Bay Street do affectionate impressions of the great man snoring on his feet.

There was a reason why Garner was tired. He had a second life apart from the straight pharmaceutical job.

"I'm not going to sugarcoat shit," Esaw says. "He was a drug dealer."

Eric Garner hadn't grown up wanting. His mother, Gwen, was a hardworking and dedicated woman who put in long hours first for the telephone company, then later for the post office, and ultimately as a subway operator. Throughout Eric's childhood, there had always been food on the table, shoes on his feet.

But Garner wasn't even nineteen when he married a woman several years his senior with two children to feed, who also happened to have a taste for clothes and nice things. The reality of his financial situation at that moment hit the teenage Garner like a tidal wave. How did people live?

He knew that other kids in the neighborhood where he grew up were making lots of money dealing drugs and through other hustles, but Eric Garner had a problem. He wasn't a natural criminal.

According to family legend, right around the time he got married, Garner planned to commit a burglary. He targeted a pizza place in his neighborhood. But when he actually broke into the place at night, he went into the kitchen and cooked himself a pizza instead of going straight for the cash. He ended up starting a small fire and fleeing without a dime. That, legend has it, was the end of his career as a burglar.

Much later on in life, he would tell his kids that he turned to dealing crack cocaine at that time out of necessity. It was easy, it was there, and it was what everyone else did. And once he began to have his own children with Esaw, it became a way of life. He stopped questioning it.

"Eric didn't give a fuck," Esaw puts it bluntly. "He had kids and was going to make the money."

Eric may have watched his mother work from the time he was born, but from a young age he also became accustomed to being the man of the house, an archaic role even then, and tried to impose a patriarchal ideal onto his marriage that never quite existed in his childhood. He wanted to be the family breadwinner, which meant he didn't want his wife working outside the home. The implicit deal was that he would take care of the money while she would take care of him. In some ways, this worked out well because Esaw herself didn't particularly want to work.

"He didn't want me to have to work," Esaw says. "So I never had to."

When it came to how he was making his money, Eric made the drug dealer's usual argument. "You're against me selling drugs, but you don't mind spending the money," he'd say.

Esaw was paralyzed by that logic. "It was like a catch-22," she says. "I enjoyed the money, but the risk wasn't worth it. I told him that no matter what, he was never going to get rich doing this, that he would most likely end up dead or in jail."

And it's true, he didn't get rich from selling drugs, but over the years, Eric's family began to accumulate nice things. There was expensive furniture in the house and the kids would be dressed to the nines on the first day of school.

And they drove nice cars. Eric had a lifelong fondness for Cadillacs. He had a gorgeous tan one in the nineties, with a hood so long his kids remember not being able to see to the end of it from inside the car.

Garner didn't work out on the street, at least not that his family observed. What they saw of his business was in little glimpses before a bedroom door slammed shut. Garner loaded raw product into vials and from time to time would get paged. He would slip out, quietly, and make a delivery. Sometimes he'd be gone for more than a day. Back at home, he would load and unload money and product into a safe that nobody was allowed to watch him open, although the kids were sometimes instructed by Pinky to try to catch the combination.

He was making real money. But around that same time, he began to develop a quirk in his personality, one that would become a defining trait when he was a middle-aged man. Apart from the car, he spent all of his money on his wife and children, to the point where he wouldn't buy himself even the most basic things. He began, slowly, to ignore himself.

"Your sneakers have holes," Esaw would say.

"Yeah, but the kids need this and that."

"That's fine, but you can get yourself a pair of sneakers," she'd say.
But he'd tune her out and keep wearing the shoes with holes in
them. Even his pants started to deteriorate.

"In the nineties, he had one pair of jeans," Esaw remembers. "They
were split from the right knee up to the crotch. Believe me when I tell
you, he wouldn't throw those away."

Garner began to develop a mania for saving. He had little piles of
money stashed in different places for different things. He would keep
cash in the soles of sneakers, in holes in walls, in the trunks of cars.
He became phobic about spending and scrupulous about the way he
played the drug game.

"He never spent his re-up," is how his wife puts it. In other words,
he never touched the money he needed to buy the next package of
drugs.

Garner for the most part was mild mannered and soft-spoken. But
he had a few sensitive spots, and one of them was his family. As Esaw
remembers it, the one thing that was guaranteed to get her husband
truly angry was implying that he wasn't a responsible father. Eric was
part of a generation of young black men for whom the worst insult
was to be called a deadbeat, a word often thrown at black men of his
father's generation by white politicians, including New York's own
Senator Daniel Patrick Moynihan. These politicians and social scientists in the mid-sixties began to point fingers at the unemployed black
male as the root of much inner-city evil. "Deadbeat dad" was the
counter to Ronald Reagan's "welfare queen," an insult that cut to the
core, and Garner would have none of it.

"You could say anything to him, but if you called him a deadbeat
dad, he'd go crazy," Esaw says. "He'd say, 'I take care of my kids! I'll
take care of them from a jail cell!'"

As it turned out, he had to do exactly that. On July 13, 1994, Garner got arrested for selling crack cocaine. Even though it was his first
serious offense, and there was no violence in the charge, he was sen-
tenced to eighteen months to three years.

When Garner went away to prison, he and his wife fought. Their
phone calls were tense.

"One time, I was crying," Esaw remembers. "I said, 'Babe, I'm out
here, I'm alone, I don't have any money.'

"And he said, 'Baby, calm down. Go in the bathroom.'"

Esaw had noticed that the medicine cabinet looked separated from the wall, but she hadn't given it a second thought. Now Eric told her to move the medicine cabinet and stick her hand in the hole.

There was five thousand dollars in cash inside.

The money lasted awhile. But soon there was nothing left but promises and letters from jail.

After Eric came home from that first stint in jail, the family moved around for a while. Finally they settled for a time in a tough section of Brownsville, New York, in a little green four-story building on Mother Gaston Boulevard, between Liberty and East New York Avenues. The neighborhood landmarks were a junk pile in the alley next to the apartment building and a tire shop on the corner. There was a nearby public pool that stank of urine and was ringed with leering men out for a glimpse of little girls in bathing suits.

The building's stoop, situated behind a gate, was where people sat, smoked cigarettes, hung out, and sometimes drank a little, day and night.

The family spent much of the late 1990s and early 2000s in this spot, and it was a complicated time for them, filled with pain and tragedy, but also some powerful memories of a group of people who stuck together through the toughest of situations. What the Garner kids—four now, from preschoolers to middle schoolers—experienced there was a parody of family life. For instance, sometimes Eric would get up and announce he had to go to "work." All of his kids who were old enough to walk—Erica, Emerald, their little brother Eric Jr., sometimes even Esaw's daughter Shardinee—would wrap their arms around Garner's ankles, thighs, and arms and beg him not to go. They riffed on a running joke from the TV comedy *Martin* about Martin Lawrence's friend Tommy, who was always pretending to go off to a job he didn't have.

"You ain't got no *job*!" they'd say.

But it was no good. He was so big, he'd just drag all the kids with him out the door, where they'd reluctantly turn him loose to the world.

While Eric was home, the family had enough money for small luxuries—furniture, electronics, cars. But by now he was in and out of jail often, and the family's fortunes waxed and waned with his presence. When he went away, all of the material things would vanish.

The kids, for instance, all had TVs in their own rooms when Eric was home. When he went away to jail, the TVs would get sold and all of the kids would have to pile into Mom's room to watch cartoons. Sometimes the kids would come home and watch their family furniture being moved out, like the sofa that his daughter Erica remembers being relocated to the apartment of the drug dealer up the hallway.

When Garner wasn't incarcerated, he loved to be home, a sometimes fatal flaw in his line of work. If hustling drugs is a twenty-four-hours-a-day, seven-days-a-week job, Garner was short a day or two every week. The streets were where he reluctantly dragged himself to make money. On Sundays he didn't like to budge from the couch and would frown if anyone walked in front of the game on television. And he would not miss holidays with his children, a trait passed down from his mother, who always got away from work to celebrate the holidays with her family when Eric was a kid.

Esaw remembers one particular Halloween when they were living in East New York. The neighborhood had become too dangerous for trick-or-treating. So she went to the store and bought each of the kids a big bag of candy, and they had a pretend Halloween in the house.

"We would go rent scary movies," Esaw recalls now. "And we would all—we had a big king-size bed when we lived in Brooklyn, so we would all get up on the bed. It would be me, Eric, and all the kids.

"And I let them eat candy, and we'd sit there and watch all the scary movies together. He made it his business that every Sunday and every holiday he spent with the kids, no matter what."

She laughs. "I know how it sounds, but if somebody called up and ordered five thousand dollars' worth of crack, he would not leave the house. He would say, 'Nope, this is a family day, see me tomorrow.'"

Garner was no kingpin. He didn't have the stomach for what it would take to get there.

"He never killed anyone, and he wasn't thugged out, you know?" Esaw explains. "He was a good guy. He just felt that was the only way he could take care of all of the kids that we had."

Resentments built up over the years. Esaw had a way of getting under Eric's skin that no one else could match. He was the kind of person who would take a ribbing for a long while before bursting, and she picked at this particular characteristic. When Esaw would start in on

Eric, he would take it for a while, but eventually it would become too much. He'd put a fist through a wall, smash a television. "There was a lot of violence in the house," daughter Erica remembers.

Once, in the early 2000s, Eric went away to jail again. While he was gone, another neighborhood drug dealer, a man much younger than Eric, took an interest in his family, started to check in on his kids. When Esaw went out shopping, the young man would come by and help the girls with their homework, or so Erica remembers.

By all accounts, there was nothing romantic going on between this man and Esaw. To the girls he was too young even to be a father figure and was more like a big brother.

But when Eric got back from jail, he wasn't pleased to see another man involved with his children.

So one day the young man came by, expecting Esaw to be home and Eric out. But it was the other way around. He knocked on the door. Eric, back home now, leaped to his feet and yelled at the man through the door not to come around anymore. "Don't talk to none of my kids. Don't talk to my wife," he said.

At some point the door opened and an epic melee ensued just outside the apartment. The kids remember seeing their father coming back into the house with a hand wrapped in a towel, and there was blood everywhere.

The young man was very seriously hurt. Garner, considerably bigger than this younger man, had grabbed him by the head and pulled him so fiercely he yanked two of his dreads out.

When the fight was over, Garner walked in a trancelike state over to the bedroom and placed the two curls on Esaw's television. Then he sat, defeated and miserable, and waited.

Police came knocking shortly thereafter. All four of Eric's natural children—Erica, Emerald, Eric Jr., and even little baby Emery—were in the apartment. When he opened the door, Eric found himself staring at the barrel of a police officer's gun. The kids could see it, too.

Eric was taken away. He got two years.

Garner's daughters were furious that he had left them and gone away to jail yet again and began rebelling against him. He was only in Rikers Island, not far away, but they didn't visit as they had before. Instead they gave him an ultimatum: they wanted him to commit to being around more often or they would continue to withhold their presence from him.

Garner, in prison, responded in despair and fury. He wrote a devastating letter renouncing forever the children he felt had now betrayed him. Later, he regretted it and would work for years to repair things with his kids, but for a stretch of years in the mid-2000s while he served out his bid, the family was almost completely in schism and Garner was alone.

When he came home from jail after the assault case, they had a family conference, and Garner's children insisted that he give up drug dealing and commit to being in their lives full-time.

Weeping, he promised.

THREE PEDRO

In his childhood years, Pedro Serrano was easy to spot on the streets of the North Bronx. There was a hit new movie out in the early nineties called *Boyz n the Hood,* and Pedro was like a Puerto Rican version of Morris Chestnut's Ricky character, the kid carrying a football everywhere he went. And just like in the movie, he walked in a foursome, with friends nicknamed Freckle-Faced Ivan, Little Man Ivan, and Karate Pete.

But there were some sections of the North Bronx neighborhood where you weren't welcome if you weren't white. Pedro knew from very early on, for instance, that he and his friends weren't allowed on some stretches of 187th Street, in Bronx's Little Italy. He learned the lesson the hard way.

"I remember turning a corner on my bicycle and a whole group of white people coming out of nowhere, chasing me back in the other direction," he says. "You got good at running when you grew up around there."

As he got older, he was presented with a problem: how to go to junior high at MS 45 on 189th Street. He couldn't walk straight to class, because that would take him right through the Italian neighborhood. One day, he and his three friends walked past an Italian social club, one of those mysterious cafés with the blacked-out windows. A man Pedro assumed was the owner pulled a gun on him and his friends.

"Get in the fucking store," he said.

The man was drunk and apparently upset about an incident involving his daughter and some other Hispanic kids from a nearby neighborhood. That had nothing to do with Pedro, who was just a little kid. It didn't matter.

"He threatened us," he remembers. "He's like, 'I'm going to kill you.'" A door-to-door salesman came in and discovered the bizarre scene, allowing Pedro and his friends to escape.

He never forgot that day. From then on, in order to get to school, he took a long detour, traveling many blocks out of his way north to Fordham Road and heading west before turning south back to school.

"It was a racial divide," he says. "That's just the way it was."

Like a lot of the people who grew up in the Brooklyn neighborhoods of Eric Garner's youth, Serrano was raised in a world with rigid borders.

"I grew up with kids who didn't even know what it was to go six blocks away from home," he says now. "You paid a price for crossing the line."

In the early nineties, just as Eric Garner was settling into a career as a drug dealer, New York was ground zero for what would become a nationwide revolution in policing strategies. People like Pedro Serrano didn't know much about the new enforcement techniques, other than that they meant more contact with the cops.

The newspapers called the program "Stop, Question, and Frisk." Pedro didn't know what it was called, but he soon learned to accept a strict new street-interrogation program as an extension of the same dynamic he'd dealt with in childhood.

"Now if you went in the wrong neighborhood, a police car was coming by," he remembers. "Cops would jump out and say, 'Hey, what the fuck are you doing here? You don't belong here.'"

Then the Stop-and-Frisk ritual would start. The kids didn't know anything about how it was supposed to work, but they knew exactly how it did work, which was that the police would put you up against a wall and empty your pockets every time they saw you, especially if you were walking with friends.

It happened so often that Pedro and his friends learned to assume the position as the police car rolled up. The instinct to put hands up on the wall was so immediate that he often didn't have time to carefully put down whatever he was carrying, usually a football or a basketball.

"The football would go bouncing down the sidewalk, every time," he recalls. Then the cops, mostly all white, would start rifling through the kids' pockets in search of drugs or guns or whatever, feeding them attitude the whole way, swearing at them, calling them animals and other names.

A few times, Pedro talked back.

"Then they'd slap you on the back of the head and be like, 'Shut the fuck up, you little spic,' " he says. "They didn't even try to hide the fact that they were racist."

For Pedro, the new regime just put an official government stamp on neighborhood rules that he'd understood since his earliest childhood days. The streets may seem free and public, but they don't belong to you. You walk down them at someone else's pleasure, with someone else's permission.

"That's what's so crazy about it. It was the same thing in a lot of ways."

By the early 2000s, Serrano was out of school and looking for a career direction. As a younger man, he'd gone to LaGuardia Community College, had worked at the Hunts Point meat market, had loaded trucks and done some bookkeeping. None of these jobs excited him. Eventually he got a gig working in a Bally's gym in the Bronx.

There were a lot of cops and corrections officers at the gym, and Pedro started thinking about joining one or the other service. Obviously his prior experience with the police growing up in the Bronx was a serious issue for him—his memories didn't exactly predispose him to police work. But one of the gymgoers, a female corrections officer, urged him to join the police. She insisted that the best reason was that the institution needed to be reformed from within.

"There are plenty of minority officers in corrections," she said. "But the police department is highly racist. They need more good minority cops. You could change it from the inside."

So Serrano joined the NYPD at age thirty-four, just before the cutoff date of thirty-five. He went to the academy and built up a circle of friends, most of them other minority cops.

In school, the NYPD trainers were very explicit. Not only was racial profiling not allowed, but doing it, they said, might cost you your job.

Serrano was impressed. He believed the rap. When he and his friends graduated, they were all itching to get started. They all stayed in touch, anxious to hear what one another's experiences on the street were like.

Serrano's first assignment was a foot patrol in the Bronx, a little south of his old neighborhood. His job seemed a little dull at first, but pretty soon he was getting texts and calls from his fellow rookies all over the city, with fantastic stories.

"I'm standing on 149th Street and Third Avenue, and my friend calls me," Serrano recalls. "He says, 'What are you doing?' I said, 'I'm standing on a corner for eight hours. What are you doing?'

"He says, 'I'm in a van. You wouldn't believe what's happening. We're jumping out and tossing people at random. No rhyme or reason. We just go into their pockets. We're looking for drugs, and weapons, and arrests.'"

Serrano's friend started telling him about how the cops in his precinct—this was the Fifty-second, up in the northwest Bronx, a tough neighborhood that included "hot spots" like Bedford Park—were not just stopping people at random but strip-searching them. They had a term for it: "socially raping." Sometimes they'd yank a guy's pants down in the precinct, but other times they'd do it in the open air, right on the sidewalk.

"He's like, 'We're strip-searching people on the street!'

"And I'm like, 'Listen, man, what are you talking about?'

"He says, 'I'm telling you, I've seen a guy's penis, I've seen his ass, you can't believe what's going on here.'"

Even worse, after they'd search a guy, the cops in this unit would make the detainee thank the officers for not arresting him.

"It was intimidation," Serrano says. "It's like, 'You see me coming, you drop your pants. And when we're done, say thank you.'"

In certain precincts, Serrano learned, young academy recruits were being pressed by older lieutenants and sergeants to execute these mass searches. Then, if the recruits botched the searches—broke rules, violated rights—the elders would fix it for them.

"If a guy screwed up, they made it right," Serrano says. "He'd say, 'Oh, I found this gun in a trunk.' And they'd say, 'You're not supposed to search the trunk. But don't worry about it, kid. You found it in the backseat. And you saw the tip of the gun on the passenger side. It was right near you, remember? Okay, write it down. Now you're okay, guy.'"

Serrano pauses as he tells the story now. "It turns into that, you understand? You pull the guy over, you socially rape the guy. Then you search his trunk, then you find a gun and get a collar."

It got worse. In his first few years on the force, Serrano saw a mania for statistics that corrupted the entire mission of the police department.

There was an emphasis on generating arrests and summonses—what cops called "activity"—that turned the police department into a kind of industrial production scheme. As a textile company produces shirts, pants, and socks, the NYPD produced stops, arrests, and tickets (and with luck, but far less often, guns), mainly using young black and Latino males as the raw materials.

The police were also supposed to be deterring crime—preventing it from happening in the first place. The problem was that police were also in charge of reporting crime—that is, keeping account of the problem they were supposed to be eliminating.

These bureaucratic imperatives, Serrano saw, pushed the NYPD toward a pair of dovetailing data-massaging schemes.

The first was to generate stops, searches, and seizures in huge numbers. This was designed to show concrete effort in the fight against crime.

The second imperative was to suppress as many reports of felonies as possible. This was to show the result of all of that effort.

Serrano remembers that any attempt to write up a felony often got immediate attention from a supervisor. He tells a story of responding to a call in which a woman claimed her house had been burglarized. She insisted that her adolescent daughter left a window open before going to school and someone had come in through the window, stolen all of the liquor out of her liquor cabinet, and gone back out through the window.

"It's a burglary," says Serrano. "A felony. A bullshit felony, but a felony. And I tried to write it up that way. But my supervisor came on scene immediately and told me, 'Don't write it up. The daughter took it.'

"I'm like, 'Boss, she was in school, she couldn't have.'

" 'The daughter did it and that's that.' "

With this kind of pressure, a street cop like Serrano was now in an increasingly ridiculous position. On the one hand, he or she was discouraged from reporting real crime in the community, which had the effect of letting people know that police weren't interested in committing resources to their actual needs.

On the other hand, cops were pushed into the position of producing huge numbers of useless and antagonizing stops and summonses for the bosses.

So they couldn't do their jobs, but they couldn't leave people alone, either.

Serrano would ask his bosses, "We know who the drug dealers are, why don't we just surveil them until we can make a clean arrest?"

The answer he'd get was, "That takes too long. Faster just to toss them."

The only snag in the deal was that tossing random people is illegal if you don't have probable cause. For cops to generate searches fast enough to make the numbers work, they essentially had to prejustify every stop. You couldn't possibly wait for the legal standard of "reasonable suspicion" each time.

The problem was solved through every bureaucracy's secret power: paperwork. The form that police used to make records of their stops, called a UF-250, evolved over time to make generating a bogus reason for a stop and/or a search as simple as possible. In the 2000s, police checked boxes on a form indicating their reasons for "250" stops. These included:

- Inappropriate attire
- Furtive movement
- Actions indicative of engaging in violent crimes
- Suspicious bulge

Thus if you were standing in the wrong neighborhood at the wrong time of day, wrong day of the week, wrong season in the year, or you made a "furtive movement" or wore "inappropriate attire," you could be stopped.

When experts studied these forms, they found that the legally meaningless term "furtive movement" was listed as a reason for a stop in about half of all cases.

It was clear to anyone looking honestly at the numbers that police had been encouraged to lie on official forms millions of times. Even worse than this mass deception was the psychological reflex this process ingrained in police. In order to justify all of these stops, police had to be trained to see the young men they were tossing as deserving what they got, before they even did anything. They were taught to presuspect entire neighborhoods. It was a factory-style *Minority Report*.

Serrano describes riding around in cars with white cops, listening to them talk about the kids in the projects like they weren't even human, totally oblivious to the fact that Serrano himself had been one of those kids.

"Look at these fuckin' animals," they'd say. "Look at these savages."

Now when police rolled up to groups of teenagers hanging out on the street, Serrano saw that his fellow officers were already in confrontation mode before they even got on scene.

"They'd say, 'What the fuck are you doing here? Get the fuck out of here,' " he remembers.

"Now you're messing with [the kids'] pride," Serrano explains. "And in every group of three or four kids, there's always one that's a little unstable. Inevitably, that kid says something. Now it's an arrest: disorderly conduct, obstructing government administration, blocking pedestrian traffic, whatever. If there's a struggle, now it's assaulting a police officer."

He pauses.

"But the point is, you created the situation. You could have handled it differently, if all you wanted was to get them to move off the corner. You could say, 'Look, man, I've got a job to do, and you're scaring some people. If you take it somewhere else, everything's cool.' "

By the late 2000s and early 2010s, Serrano and multiple other (mostly minority) officers were fed up with the numbers game. They created a kind of secret union within the police union to discuss it. They had no choice: the actual police union was no help.

As Serrano soon learned, police unions not only didn't protest the numbers regime, they actually bargained with the NYPD over the number of illegal stops their members would have to make each year.

This came out, among other things, via a secret recording made by a Dominican officer named Adhyl Polanco. In a roll call meeting at the Forty-first Precinct, a Patrolmen's Benevolent Association rep addresses the troops and explains what the union has been negotiating with the department.

"I spoke to the CO for about an hour and a half on the activity, twenty-and-one," the PBA rep says. "Twenty-and-one is what the union is backing up."

"Twenty-and-one" meant twenty summonses and one arrest. Polanco had captured, on tape, proof of a quota system that the department and its union were complicit in building.

Just like Serrano, Polanco had been put in the position of writing
up innocent people. In one incident, he was forced to cuff a thirteen-
year-old Mexican boy, with his superiors telling him they'd figure out
the charge later. He even recounted being ordered to summons a guy
for having no dog license when Polanco couldn't even see a dog.

Inspired by Polanco, Serrano decided to tape his own bosses. He
had clashed with a deputy inspector of the Fortieth Precinct named
Christopher McCormack, a man nicknamed Red Rage for his pro-
pensity for full-throated screaming sessions. On one of the tapes, he
asked McCormack to explain what he was supposed to do with regard to his 250s.

"This is about stopping the right people, the right place, the right
location," McCormack seethed.

He told Serrano that in the Mott Haven neighborhood, where "we
have the most problems," his goal should be to stop young black
men.

"The problem was what?" McCormack said. "Male blacks. And I
told you at roll call, I have no problem telling you this, male blacks,
fourteen to twenty, twenty-one. I said this at roll call."

Serrano didn't realize it at the time, but he'd procured one of the main
pieces of evidence in the lawsuit that would ultimately put an end to
the Stop-and-Frisk program he'd been around since childhood.

The line about "stopping the *right people*" also perfectly summarized an increasingly ugly argument that America was having with
itself about race.

Open racism for the most part had vanished from mainstream debate since the civil rights era, replaced with a series of arguments by
proxy. Recalcitrant white America complained about things like "cul-
tures of dependency," "free stuff," and "income redistribution," but
the most passionate complaints were always about crime.

Fifty years after Selma, few Americans outside of extremist neo-
Nazi sites like Stormfront.org were willing to make the blunt eugenic
argument that nonwhite people were somehow predisposed to commit crimes.

What was offered up in more mainstream circles was a slight se-
mantic twist on the same take: minority neighborhoods are "where
the crime is," and any program designed to stop potential criminals
should target blacks and Hispanics as the "right people" to stop.

A version of this argument quietly took over the leadership of the
NYPD during the 1980s, 1990s, and early 2000s. Later, through the
bizarre spectacle of New York billionaire Donald Trump's presidential campaign, it would bleed into national presidential politics.
Trump would seize the Republican nomination and eventually the
presidency itself by promising to build a "big, beautiful wall" to keep
out rape-happy Mexicans, a lunatic ploy that defied actual crime rates
and that would never have worked had millions of people not believed in the inherent criminality of other races.

Like Trump's wall, New York's new policing regime was also a
form of border enforcement. It was about keeping "the right people"
off the streets, not through physical walls but through constant, de-
moralizing, physically invasive harassment.

The argument that raged in the city then, and nationwide later on,
went like this: Was this racism or simply effective law enforcement?

While conservatives and liberals sorted that out, minorities of all
descriptions who lived in big cities were caught up in the question of
who "the right people" were to keep off the streets. Were they hardened criminals, the "one" in the twenty-and-one quota who would
actually be arrested? Or were they complete noncriminals, the other
twenty who were just the wrong kind of people on the wrong corner
at the wrong time? Or were they people like Eric Garner, who in his
later years began to fall somewhere in between?

FOUR JOHN

By 2007, Eric Garner was home from jail and living in Staten Island, where his wife had moved while he was inside. His family was in shambles. Most of his children were in some version of state care, having been removed because of various problems in the home.

Still, committed to keeping his agreement with his family, Eric was trying to fly straight. Through a state program called Back to Work, he'd gotten a job with the Parks Department in Staten Island, picking up trash from median strips and parks.

But the job only paid about $68 every two weeks, and before long, Garner began to slip. One day in September of that year, he got arrested for dealing one last time, but it was a very different kind of arrest.

Garner didn't like to write. His mother used to pick on him for his handwriting, calling it a "chicken scratch." Nonetheless, from a jail cell in Rikers Island on September 12, 2007, where he was awaiting trial, yet again, Garner in painstaking scrawl described his last arrest for crack dealing, telling a story very similar to the one Pedro Serrano told about police field searches:

On September 1, 2007, at Approx 7:30 p.m. on the corner of Castalton Ave & Heberton Ave Officer William Owens and his team stopped me for reasons of there own. I was ordered to place my hands on the black SUV in which they were riding in. I compliyed with no problem. Officer William Owens then patted me down by ways of going through my pockets and socks and not finding anything illegal on my person. Officer William Owens then places me IN handcuffs and then performs an cavity search ON me by ways of "Digging his finggers in my rectum in the middle of the street" Officer William Owens also unzips my shorts and feels under my testicals in the middle of the street, all the while there are people passing back and forth.

I told Officer William Owens to stop and if he wanted to do a strip search I was willing to go to the police station because I had nothing to hide, my request was ignored. I then told Officer William Owens that I was fileing charges for him violating my civil rights, I was then hit with drug charges and told by Officer William Owens that "I don't deserve my city job because I'm a convicted felon on parole." (I work for the New York City Park Department)

Under "Injuries," Garner wrote the following:

The injuries I received were to my manhood in which Officer William Owens violated by ways of digging his fingers in my rectum and pulling my penis out in public so he can feel my testicals for his own personal pleasure. Officer William Owens violated my civil rights.

The suit went nowhere and Garner lost his criminal case. Originally accused of selling crack again, Garner had the charge knocked down to possession. He got a year.

Eric Garner did not do well in jail. While other men found ways to cope, for Garner confinement of any kind was pure suffering. In his miserable state, his conversations with Esaw, who had never been terribly sympathetic about his stints in jail, deteriorated significantly. She called him a crybaby and refused to visit.

"You don't visit me, I'm going to kill myself," he told her by phone.

"Don't kill yourself because of me," she said sharply. "Kill yourself because you want to be dead."

Garner had no reply to that.

"I refused to send him my money. I refused to send him any packages. I just refused," Esaw explains. "I used to tell him, 'If you needed all this stuff, you should have stayed your ass out of jail!'"

When Eric came home a year later, he was severely depressed.

"Money was his main focus," says Esaw. "Eric would look like he lost his best friend if he was broke. And the only time I can remember him being broke is whenever he got out of jail."

Garner tried, once again, to get a square job.

"I'm poking him every morning, saying, 'Get up, go find a job. Get up, do something, because you can't be laying up in the bed with me watching TV,'" Esaw says. "And he would walk up and down the street and ask the guys if they needed somebody to sweep the store, if they needed somebody to shovel snow, if they needed anything. Whatever he could do to make money, he would do."

But there wasn't much of a job market for an ex-convict who had been charged with selling crack during his last attempt at gainful employment.

He tried to put it off, but pretty soon he started to drift back toward old habits. Finally, in a state of desperation, he started asking around on the streets of Staten Island's North Shore who might put him back in business as a drug dealer. And people started giving him names. One of those names was John McCrae.

Tall, lean, and broad shouldered, John McCrae had been nicknamed Douse as a teenager, because when he hit someone, the lights went out. He was a fancy dresser and a flamboyant personality, a jokester who always had something to say to a pretty girl who passed by. You could hear his cackling from around the corner. Behind the laugh was a quick mind, long trained in the art of the hustle.

McCrae was the sixteenth of eighteen children in his family. His parents were too poor to provide beds for all those kids, just sheets filled with clothes on the floor. His father, an upright southerner from Bennettsville, South Carolina, had worked every day of his life—he'd even been on one of the work teams that helped build the original World Trade Center. But for all that backbreaking labor, he never made much money, certainly not for a family as large as his.

The old man would sit in a lounge chair after work, dead tired, chain-smoking Pall Malls, exhausted and stretched to the limit. John had pants with holes in them and would ask for new things, but his father usually couldn't help. So John had to get the money himself.

When he was nine or ten years old in Jamaica, Queens, he and his friends developed a scheme for robbing grocery stores. Kids would roam up and down the aisles of the store, pretending to shoplift, distracting the storekeeper. Meanwhile, the smallest of the group would crawl in the back room and snatch the strongbox. They called that scam the "creep deef." For the rest of McCrae's life, no hustle ever worked as well.

When he got older and moved to Flatbush, he fell in with a new crew that specialized in home burglaries. "Hitting cribs," he says. "Did that for a while." When crack came around, he started off running a con he cooked up with a girl named Nefertiti, who was as beautiful as her name. He'd run all over Flatbush selling vials of bread crumbs designed to look like crack, moving every few hours to stay alive.

"Actual drug dealers catch you at that, they'd kill your ass," he says. "Throw you off a roof. Worse."

Then he moved on to selling actual crack himself, which turned out to be his worst idea yet because he got caught. In prison, he quickly schemed up more hustles to survive.

At Downstate Correctional Facility, he traded on the sewing skills his father had taught him as a boy, stitching prison clothes with a little style. "Cons wanted to jazz up they greens," he says, chuckling. He also got so good at writing letters to prisoners' girlfriends that at times he found himself falling in love with the women on the other end. "I was good at that shit, too," he says, laughing.

McCrae went to prison for crack dealing in the early nineties, just like Eric Garner. A hustler his whole life, McCrae knew a con when he saw one and felt pretty sure the prison boom was one of them.

In jail, he spent a lot of time reading. He read that states in the Cuomo years earned matching funds and other incentives from the federal government if they committed enough resources to catching crack dealers. That explained why cops spent so much of their time and resources watching black people trade a few dollars of this for that. "Otherwise, nobody gives a fuck what goes on in our neighborhoods," he says.

After his stint in prison, McCrae eventually moved to Staten Island. He'd met a woman named Diana and tried to start a family and a quieter life, but they split up. She stayed in their apartment in the middle of the 200 block on Bay Street, where he spent a lot of his afternoons.

Over the years he'd tried parking cars, working HVAC jobs, construction. He looked into getting a commercial driver's license, but he could never stay excited for long about any of those options. He still hustled sometimes to make money, but the most he ever did now was deal a little weed.

But there was no future in hustling, either. Even in Tompkinsville

Park, where 98 percent of everyone you met had less than a dollar or two, the police were everywhere. They came by in patrols and kept plainclothes detectives staked out around the edges. Sometimes he'd watch them and shake his head in amazement. Did they think nobody noticed when a Ford Fiesta or a Dodge Neon with tinted windows parked and no one got out for two or three hours? And later, when they planted cameras and even hidden microphones in the park, he was blown away by how much effort they put into patrolling this tiny little trash-strewn triangle.

It wasn't always this way. "When I first came to Staten Island, I didn't see a cop for six whole months," he says nostalgically.

This was more than a repeat of the strange Cuomo-era policing incentives. Now that there were fancy condo complexes across the street, the park full of dead-broke drunks and addicts was monitored like it was an al Qaeda safe house.

He was in the middle of such reflections one afternoon in 2008 when a big, tall, burly-looking man in sweatpants and huge sneakers came lumbering toward him.

McCrae listened as the big man explained that the word on the street was that John was a man who could get him a job selling drugs.

This didn't go over well.

"I about lost my mind," says McCrae. "I thought I was being set up. I told him he had the wrong guy. And a few other things."

Eric Garner walked away with his head down. Even crack dealing was starting to seem impossibly beyond his grasp.

It wasn't long after that that Esaw made an offhand comment that would change her husband's life. While Eric was away in jail the last time, she'd picked up her own little side hustle—one she didn't realize was illegal.

"I'm selling cigarettes," she said.

Eric immediately raised an eyebrow.

"Selling cigarettes?" Eric said. "And how's that working out?"

"I make a lot of money in a day with these loosies," she explained.

He paused.

"How much money?"

. . .

Drug dealing was the wrong fit for Garner. As with the Ferris wheel at Coney Island, he preferred a ride with a little less bounce to it. In a stroke of good luck, he found one.

New York under its famed previous mayor, Rudy Giuliani, had dropped income taxes to their lowest levels in thirty years, to an average of about 8 percent. This was well below the 10 percent average seen under Mayors Ed Koch and David Dinkins. But the destruction of 9/11 created a massive hole in the budget, and the city needed money.

Term limits forced Giuliani to leave office after 9/11, and the incoming mayor, the billionaire media plutocrat Michael Bloomberg, had promised not to raise taxes. "We cannot raise taxes. We will find another way," he said.

It took less than a month for Bloomberg to go back on his word. The city's upper-crust financial sector had required huge amounts of state and federal aid to get back on its feet. The cleanup cost about $1 billion. But Bloomberg picked the most regressive conceivable tax as his first move to plug the hole in the budget, raising the city's cigarette tax from 8 cents to $1.50.

The Wall Street cleanup, in other words, was going to be paid for in part at least by a surcharge on cartons of Kools and Newports. Bloomberg hoped to raise $250 million a year with the new tax.

From the very first tax increase, people all over the city began selling bootleg cigarettes that came either from Internet sales or from trips to Native American reservations. Selling cartons became a way to make quick cash in a lot of poor neighborhoods.

Eric Garner saw the possibilities in the cigarette hustle from the start. Pinky was talking about selling loosies from packs, but before his wife could finish her story, Eric had gone out to find out where to buy a carton.

"Then he went to three, then five, then ten, then thirty, then sixty, then ninety," she says. "Then up to three hundred cartons a week."

What others did as a hobby, Eric quickly made into a full-blown business. Some entrepreneurial urge in him—the same urge, perhaps, that made it impossible for him to keep a straight job that shackled him to a desk or straitjacketed him into a uniform—kicked into overdrive. He built up a little crew of four or five to handle the volume and kept his "store" at Tompkinsville Park open almost all day.

The spot he picked to do most of his business was near the corner of Bay and Victory, in front of a check-cashing storefront, a high-traffic area. People from all over the neighborhood used to meet at the "check cash," and they always came out with money in their pockets.

Before Garner came, that spot had been occupied by a man named Doug Brinson, a slim southerner with wraparound shades and a deep voice who hailed from Wilmington, North Carolina. Brinson had a deal with the owners of the check cash, who allowed him to set up a table in front of their doorway where he sold things like oils, T-shirts, and incense and talked to every man, woman, and child who passed. "Oils and Incense and a Little More, that was the name of my store," he says. He thought of that little stretch of sidewalk as his home.

"You see that tree over there?" he'd say, pointing to a sidewalk planting. "I remember when it was a little shrub."

If white Staten Islanders had come fleeing "city problems" on the other side of the Narrows, black men and women often came to Staten Island fleeing problems that had followed them from even farther away. Doug Brinson was born in the Deep South in the heat of the civil rights movement and first tried to get out of the Carolinas as a teenager in 1970. He was so desperate he took a bus to Philadelphia with basically nothing in his pockets. Once in the big city, he hooked up with some other men from Wilmington, who convinced him to join them in a robbery.

The men lived in North Philly, but the house they'd cased was in another part of town, a white neighborhood. "I don't know how we got into the house, but when the shit got started, somebody was coming or something, and they broke away," Doug recalls. Sixteen, inexperienced, and now separated from the group, Doug froze. "I didn't know where the hell to go," he says. "So I ran into the backyard."

Doug was tall and strong but also skinny as a beanpole. He remembers he was wearing a light blue shirt and light blue pants, a bad outfit for a daytime home invasion. He ran into the backyard of the house in his sky-blue outfit and made a beeline for an eight-foot wall in the very back. He jumped up and started to climb over the edge.

"So I'm coming up that wall, and a police car is coming up the damn hill," he says. "I tried to look cool, but they came over. My heart sank."

"What's going on, man?" the policeman said, smiling.

"Nothing," Doug said, unconvincingly.

"Where you from?"

"North Philly."

"Well, then," the police asked, "what are you doing around here?"

"Uh, I was hanging around here with my boys," Doug said, trying to sound calm. He looked around. "But I don't know what happened to them."

"Yeah, okay," the cop said, chuckling. "Come walk around the corner with me, I got somebody that wants to take a look at you."

The police walked him around the corner. Apparently someone had seen Doug going into the house. When Doug saw this witness standing next to the squad car, he couldn't believe it. The guy had on glasses so thick, his eyes looked like ping-pong balls behind them.

"Them bifocals was so damn thick, they were like magnifying glasses," Doug says, laughing. "I said, 'Damn, how can you see anything?' And they put me in jail for that shit."

Doug says he ended up in Philadelphia's notorious Holmesburg Prison, one of the lesser-known monuments to America's lunatic past. He remembers arriving at the facility and being puzzled to see young men, mostly young black men, walking around with bizarre symmetrical patches of gauze on their arms and backs.

"I was walking around and people had tape and bandages on," he says. "They were having skin grafts and shit."

While the federal government in the infamous Tuskegee Study in rural Alabama was leaving black men with syphilis untreated, researchers at Holmesburg were paying inmates to allow them to perform tests and biopsies on patches of their skin. The studies were for developing skin creams, deodorants, moisturizers, suntan products, and other substances. This was the 1970s.

Doug was released from Holmesburg just before it erupted in a massive riot, part of a prison-revolt movement that engulfed penitentiaries from San Quentin to Attica. He ended up heading north, following relatives to Staten Island, and made himself a living as the colorful street character who sold stuff outside the check cash. Like Garner, Brinson would increasingly clash with police, who hassled him over his business, constantly asking him to move. He wasn't selling anything illegal but it still wasn't everyone's idea of a legitimate business.

"I was Eric Garner before Garner," he remembers. "Until he came along, I was the one they focused on."

For a time, the two men worked the same stretch of the block, and they came to be friends. Ultimately, however, the check-cash storefront closed up and was bought by a beauty supply store, whose owners didn't want Doug and his oils, incense, and "little bit more" around. So he moved, and Garner stayed.

It took a little while, but Bay Street and Tompkinsville Park became a central part of Garner's identity. He learned everything about this place. It didn't look like much driving through, but Tompkinsville was a refuge and a bazaar for people from all over the island who lived off the books. It had its own particular schedule, and Eric made sure his store kept the light on during business hours.

Diana, who goes by DiDi, is the queen of the block. She's a native Staten Islander, just like her mother, and had lived in a second-floor apartment overlooking Tompkinsville Park since 2000. The junkies came and went, the drunks came and went, the hustlers came and went, but over the years, DiDi was always there.

She was once John McCrae's common-law wife, and he was the one who brought her to live on this block. He had long since moved out, but even he'd come back to the block to hang out from time to time in the afternoons.

DiDi on the other hand was here every single day, a fixture. She was a handsome woman now in her early forties, always dressed cool in well-matched outfits of camouflage or leather. Her day's outfit would set the mood for the neighborhood.

You'd find her sitting on a bench on the outside of the park, or sitting on the stairwell inside her building, or leaning in her doorway. DiDi knows the schedule and the score of the neighborhood, who's arguing with whom, who's up to what, who's trying to play at being king of this particular hill. The block would teem with activity, but DiDi was its anchor.

"I could tell you something right now. You can look down here and look around all of these people out there, I'm the only one that lives here," she says.

When DiDi turns in at night, she takes to her bed in her second-floor apartment on Bay Street, with the window overlooking the park. She can hear everything on the street, but it's mostly quiet there. The place is different from some of the more notorious blocks in the city, DiDi thinks, because the hustlers keep to the block's business hours. It isn't a gangland battlefield. The drugs and booze go home every night.

That wasn't always the case. Some of the homeless and the addicts used to try to sleep in the park until, sometime in the 2000s, the city installed a sprinkler system that would go off like clockwork at about 4:00 A.M. There'd be people lying out on the park's benches and walkways, knocked out drunk, who'd suddenly wake up soaked and freezing.

Now, people didn't start showing up at the park until around five thirty in the morning.

"That's when I hear the first voice. When I hear the first person," she says.

Often those first voices are raised. "You'll hear people arguing early in the morning, which don't make no sense to me. You're just getting up! I put my TV on mute. Then I can just hear the bullshit."

Around 2011, she started hearing a different sound: people selling cigarettes early in the morning. Eric Garner had put an older man out there to sell for him, a foreigner with immigration problems whom Eric trusted. He was respectful and did his business quietly. And he made a lot of money, because the traffic came quickly, as soon as the sun came up.

In the very early morning the Bay Street crowd is multiracial. Just down the street from the park is the Bay Street Health Center, a methadone clinic that hands out doses in the morning. People from all walks of life come from all over the island, get their doses, then walk to the park and smoke and hang out. Addicts are the most diverse community in the world.

"Puerto Rican, black, white," Diana says. "It's more white people, though, on that heroin and shit than the black people." The traffic had gotten progressively heavier over the years as police cracked down on an exploding opiate craze on the South Shore.

The South Shore was below what Staten Islanders called the "Mason-Dixon Line," the ominous local name for Interstate 278, which bisected the island into north and south halves. Almost all the black people lived north of the interstate. They didn't much venture south of it, where the white people lived.

When white people came over the line to neighborhoods like this, it was usually for one reason. "The dope and the pills must have dried up over there on the South Shore, where the white people is at. That's why they come over here," Diana says. "That's what it is. They can't buy that in they neighborhood, in they mother's neighborhood, or where they go back to at night."

She'd hear these people making deals in the morning. "It's Oxy. It's Percocet, that Suboxone, all of that. They get scripts, they sell them."

Eric Garner would come a little later in the day, around 8:00 or 9:00 A.M., to catch the tail end of that morning wave. Diana got along with him right away. "He had that Fat Albert look, but he was a good guy, he really was. Everybody loved him," she says. "And he was out here, rain or shine, grinding, seven days a week."

Diana learned early on that if she cooked anything and word got out, Garner would tweak her about it. "Oh, you out here giving everybody something," he'd say. "But you didn't make me no sandwich." She learned that he would eat absolutely anything, with three exceptions. "Anything that had red peppers, green peppers, or onions," she says, laughing.

She got a good feeling about him, although she could tell he wasn't well. "His eyes was always running, his nose was always running, always big ashy hands. He was a croupy little thing at times. Shit, when he drank anything, it would go down his shirt," she says.

Garner positioned his shop perfectly. In addition to the early morning junkies, there were drunks and shoplifters who came to Tompkinsville because several of the neighborhood shops doubled as fences. You could swipe something off a shelf in a Stapleton store a mile or two away and bring it down to Tompkinsville to sell right back to another storefront for a few bucks.

Then you'd take your cash and buy one-dollar mini-bottles of booze at Shaolin Liquor on the corner of the park, a little place with a green-and-white awning that read WINES & LIQUOR TOMPKINSVILLE PARK out front. And once that crowd started drinking, they started digging in their pockets to find change for smokes.

There was also the working crowd. People on their way to the Staten Island Ferry, ready for a day's work in Manhattan, would stop on the way and load up on cheap smokes. People in suits bought from Garner just like addicts and drunks.

He mostly stood at a stoop near 220 Bay Street. Whether selling himself or watching others sell, he kept his eyes peeled for potential problems.

By then Garner and Diana's ex, McCrae, had become friends. The two used to stand together on Bay Street for hours each day. In the afternoons, they would often be joined by a third man, James Knight, who, like them, was an ex-con from Brooklyn. Knight had made his way to Staten Island at the end of a long road battling heroin addiction.

Knight was tall and physically imposing like Garner and McCrae. He'd found religion and gotten clean and now spent most of his mornings volunteering at a local shelter and food pantry called Project Hospitality. If Garner's talent was for numbers, Knight was a born politician, with the gift of gab. He kept current on everyone's business and had a word for every person he passed.

"Hey, girl, how you doing?"

"Your uncle out of the hospital yet?"

"I'll text you, baby, I'll text you!"

Like the other two, Knight had done time for drug dealing in the early nineties, but he was more of a user than a dealer. He'd been a heroin addict since his teens.

His mother had also struggled with dope. After school he used to find her wandering the projects of East New York in a nod, many blocks from home. James would take her by the elbow and guide her back to their apartment. "Sometimes we'd have to go through two or three projects," he said. "And people would be staring and laughing at me. But I didn't care. She was my mother and I loved her."

All the same, James would quietly glance at his mother as he towed her home and make a promise to himself: "That is never going to happen to me."

Not many years later, when he was a hard-partying teenager, he sent a friend to buy some coke and the friend came back with dope instead. James thought, "I bought it, I might as well try it." He leaned over, took a line, and any heroin addict knows the rest of the story. He spent the next thirty-three years getting high.

In 1991 James met some Puerto Rican drug dealers in Spanish Harlem who liked his gregarious personality and his gift for languages (he'd learned Spanish working in a bodega as a kid). He started dealing with them, but it turned out that avoiding police was not among his gifts. He was arrested after about five minutes.

He bailed out of jail and made a fateful decision. Afraid of prison, he decided to flee rather than stand trial. He spent five long years as a fugitive, carefully obeying every conceivable law so as not to get swept up in the zero-tolerance Stop-and-Frisk police dragnet he'd heard about, one that was ostensibly designed to catch people just like him.

"I read the news," Knight says now. "I didn't jaywalk or even think about jumping a turnstile. I was aware."

In a comical indictment of the ineffectiveness of Stop-and-Frisk, Knight eluded the net for five years and ended up getting caught not by street cops but by a stray bullet. He walked into a grocery store on New Year's Eve in 1996 and was in the process of leaning forward to give a female friend in the store a holiday hug when a tipsy store owner accidentally discharged a pistol he kept under his counter.

The bullet passed through the counter, through James's thigh and testicles, and rested in the other leg. James stumbled around in a daze and woke up in a hospital, where police became suspicious when he didn't want to press charges. They ran his name and found his old dealing warrant. He ended up doing a bid in Rikers Island. Although Knight had been terrified of prison, he thrived inside. He says his language skills got him elected dorm rep in Rikers and the store owner who shot him felt so bad he kept his commissary account full, allowing James to have his fill of cigarettes, cookies, chips, and whatever else they sold on the inside.

"I know how this sounds, but I had a great time," he says. "It wasn't like it was for other people. I was in four months, and I didn't have any trouble."

James got out of Rikers in late 1996. He was thirty-four years old. He went right back on drugs.

Thirteen years later, at the age of forty-seven, he finally got clean. He was living in Staten Island by then, and for a time he tried selling cigarettes to make a little extra cash. That's how he met Eric Garner. Knight says he was only briefly in the bootleg smokes business, but he remained friends with Eric and spent most afternoons hanging with him on Bay Street.

Knight, Garner, and McCrae became fixtures of the hood, the

Three Wise Men of Needle Park, talking to girls who passed by, joking with one another, and passing the time. DiDi was never very far.
Sometimes when it was cold, they would all duck inside her hallway
in the middle of the 200 block on Bay Street, a narrow smoke-filled
space Knight jokingly called the "Boom-Boom Room."

They also kept close watch on the crowd in the park. Garner broke
up a lot of fights. Arguments, violence of any kind, vandalism, all of
that stuff brought police, and police were bad for business. "He spent
a lot of time worrying about who was making the block hot," is how
one of his friends put it, years later.

It was a good setup. Garner had a prime location, a stone's throw
from the ferry docks. Soon he was doing a booming trade. At its
height he was clearing hundreds of dollars a day or more in profit.

He enjoyed selling smokes. He'd wholesale cartons to other men
on the street and then compete with them for customers. A drunk
would head toward one of the other men selling smokes at the park,
and Eric would step forward with a rap.

"Nah, nah, don't fuck with him! Bring that money here. Bring that
money!" he'd say.

At first, he used nearby Native American reservations to supply. He
wasn't alone. By early 2011, the Poospatuck Reservation, located just
south of the Montauk Highway in the middle of Long Island, was
taking delivery of about 6.6 million cartons per year, which worked
out to be about two-thirds as much as the 10 million legally sold cartons in New York State.

The Poospatucks only had a tax exemption to sell to other tribe
members, of which there were about three hundred. That meant millions of people a year were thumbing their nose at Bloomberg's reve-
nue plan.

Furious at the widespread revolt against the taxes, the state in mid-
2011 began to effect mass seizures of cigarettes destined for Native
reservations. The heat forced Garner to move farther south. He tried
a number of states, including Delaware, before settling eventually on
Virginia. He bought cartons of cigarettes there cheaply enough that
he could make very nearly a 100 percent profit back in Staten Island,
even after expenses.

The beauty of the scheme from Garner's point of view was the risk-
to-profit ratio. Once you got the cigarettes near the street, the risk of

punishment was very small. For mere possession of untaxed cigarettes, the state couldn't even hit you with a misdemeanor. Possession
alone was just a violation, and the state could at most fine you $150
for each carton above five you had on your person. The same law said
selling untaxed cigarettes in most any street-ready quantity was just a
misdemeanor.

It was the reverse of the crack situation, where the state created
disproportionately draconian penalties for selling the kind of cocaine
that black people in the projects bought. This time, for once, the loophole ran in the other direction.

It was the perfect setup, and Garner himself from time to time mar-
veled at the opportunity the mayor had created for him.

"He had a term for it," McCrae says. "He called it 'felony money,
misdemeanor time.'"

Eric Garner may have created a lot of his own problems, but he was
also the victim of bad luck and atrocious timing.

In the eighties and early nineties, when he was beginning to deal
drugs, the crack dealer had become public enemy number one. Garner also happened to ply his trade in the worst possible place: New
York State, ground zero for the mass incarceration movement. New
York's then governor Mario Cuomo spent the eighties and early nineties funding more than thirty new prisons using a loophole in an
urban development law that, perversely, had been intended to create
jobs in inner cities.

It was also the era of the infamous 100:1 laws, when long manda-
tory sentences kicked in for selling crack in weights 100 times smaller
than the weights required to send a powder-cocaine dealer away. And
Garner went to jail for crack dealing at a time when 72 percent of the
illegal drug users in New York City were white, but 90 percent of the
people who went to jail for selling drugs were black or Hispanic.

By the time Garner stopped dealing hard drugs, police had shifted
tactics, and in moving to cigarettes, Garner was swimming right into
the riptide. Now the number one enforcement target on the streets
was the minor criminal. The new watchword was "order." Police had
a mandate to shake down anyone who made the streets look disorganized and unruly.

Garner was harmless, but he was also a massive, conspicuous, slovenly dressed black man standing on a city block during work hours. People like him would become the focus of a law enforcement revolution that by the late 2000s had become intellectual chic across America with a powerfully evocative name: Broken Windows.

FIVE GEORGE

In rural Minnesota in the fall of 1963, a young white midwesterner named George Kelling was offered a new job.

Kelling was game for new experiences. He would be afflicted his whole life by a kind of intellectual wanderlust, drifting back and forth between the seemingly disparate poles of law enforcement and academics. Both realms fascinated him.

When he completed his studies as an undergraduate seminarian and philosophy student, he immediately took a job in the thick of real life, working as a parole officer in Minneapolis.

After doing that for a few years, he left the streets to go back to the University of Wisconsin–Milwaukee, where he got a master's in social work. After that, he once again pivoted to a tough city job, serving as the assistant superintendent of juvenile detention in Hennepin County, Minnesota, in the Minneapolis area. He worked primarily with a ninety-bed holding facility for troubled young people.

He was still working the Hennepin County job when he was offered a gig in Lino Lakes, Minnesota, about twenty miles northeast of the Twin Cities. The sixty-four-bed facility was looking for a fresh face to run the place.

"The previous administration believed in a philosophy of allowing children to act out almost regardless of the consequences," recalls Kelling now. "Children were attacking staff, each other, were acting out sexually, were destroying the facility."

A new and firmer hand was needed. Kelling had the academic chops for the treatment side but also had enough experience with the justice system and adult parolees to handle the hard stuff. And he was intrigued by the chance to try out some ideas he'd been pondering.

Kelling believed that kids could not get the help they needed while they were surrounded by chaos—they needed to experience at least a minimal level of violence-free order before they could benefit from any treatment. To achieve this, institutions would have to lay down simple and consistent rules and exercise a firm hand in enforcing them. Order was essential to creating a safe—and temporary— institutional experience.

"Keep their institutionalization as short as possible," Kelling says now, describing his thought process. "It doesn't matter how good an institution is, they can be and are dangerous places."

Another idea Kelling had was to discourage programs that accentuated a feeling of separateness and segregation.

"Don't build a chapel. Take those children who want to go to church to local churches," he says. "Don't build a swimming pool. Use local pools. Don't start a scout program; join the local scout program. And so on."

Kelling, like a lot of young people in the sixties, was moved by a spirit of idealism. This was the age of space exploration, the Peace Corps, of sweeping changes in law and race relations. The Supreme Court had struck down school segregation in 1954's *Brown v. Board of Education* and in 1961 had taken on police corruption in *Mapp v. Ohio,* which made it impossible to prosecute people on the basis of illegally seized evidence.

Two years later, Martin Luther King Jr. had delivered his "I Have a Dream" speech, the ultimate articulation of the better world this generation hoped to create.

Nobody back then was into half measures. The craze in the Kennedy years was for magic bullets, total cures, conquests. Through ingenuity or just brute industrial force and determination, Americans would end problems, not ameliorate them. Kelling wanted to change the world, too, and decided to take the reform school offer and use it as a laboratory for his radical ideas.

Over the course of his tenure at the Lino Lakes facility, Kelling would develop ideas that would have a revolutionary impact on American society. Germinating in the mind of this young white academic were the first inklings of a concept called Broken Windows, an idea that would have a profound impact on cities all over America— and on the life and death of Eric Garner.

From a sociological perspective, George Kelling occupies a place in American history similar to someone like an Oppenheimer or a Leo Szilard. He would invent a powerful tool. We would argue ferociously over its application. Lives would be lost. And Kelling was destined to become the reluctant symbol of a generational controversy.

...

In the small-town Minnesota setting of the Lino Lakes home, "disorder" didn't have anything to do with race. It wasn't a code word. Disorder was literally disorder: stuff on the floor.

Kelling's early observations of Lino Lakes, at least in his telling, read like a caricature of nut-bar liberal do-gooderism gone awry. The counselors and the psychiatric teams had taken their Freudian methods to the extreme. They refused to intervene in most any clinical situation, lest they interfere with a patient organically acting out his neuroses.

"You might have a situation where one of the kids would break a glass or a lightbulb in the bathroom, and there would be glass all over the floor," he says now.

"And I'd ask, 'Are we going to clean up the glass?' And they would look at me strangely, as if to say, 'What? No.' Like they were just there to observe."

He sighs. "They would literally leave broken glass on the floor."

Kelling's first great discovery was really just a commonsense reaction. He picked up the glass.

He recalls vividly another incident, where a group of female residents at the facility gathered in a common area, stood on chairs and tables, and began pulling tiles out of the ceiling.

Kelling arrived on the scene to see a parade of disturbed young women carrying ceiling tiles back and forth, with the therapeutic staff watching, taking notes, and conspicuously not intervening.

"They were pulling tiles down all over the place, and the staff was just sitting there, observing them like they were zoo animals," Kelling recalls.

Not being completely sure of his authority yet, Kelling hesitated at first to intervene, even with tiles flying all around them. Maybe he was missing something? Maybe he needed to be briefed on some background here? He gently asked a nearby staffer if anyone was planning on stopping the young women from, you know, ripping the ceiling open.

His incredulous staff told him no. Kelling frowned, waited a beat, and ordered the girls removed to their rooms. Then he set about fixing the ceiling.

Soon after the tile incident, he remembers, a pair of sturdy young male inmates burst into his office. They demanded to see the records of another one of the residents. The two boys, one white and one Native American, both well over two hundred pounds, explained that it was no big deal. They said they had routinely been allowed free access to records under the previous administration.

Kelling heard the boys out, then answered.

"First of all," he said, "go back outside, knock on the door, and wait for me to tell you that you can come in. Then, if I say you can, come in and ask me that question again."

The two boys went back outside and knocked. Kelling told them they could come in.

The boys entered, then once again asked if they could see the records.

"No," Kelling said.

Kelling in Lino Lakes ended up doing exactly what he'd imagined doing. He made order a priority and worked to normalize the experience of the children, trying to integrate them into the community as quickly as possible rather than keeping them stuck in the institution. They cut down on violence, assaults on staff, and soon had kids going to school, Boy Scouts, and other activities. It seemed a success.

In the years that followed, there was a drug revolution, campus unrest, a military quagmire in Vietnam, a cascade of antiwar demonstrations, and a series of emerging political divisions that felled President Lyndon Johnson.

By 1968, white Middle America was profoundly afraid of a collapse in the social order. Young people were angry. Blacks were angry. Cities were being burned, campuses overrun. There was a longing for order, almost at any cost.

In the midst of all this, a case called *Terry v. Ohio* reached the Supreme Court. There is no way to understand what took place in Staten Island in the summer of 2014 without understanding this case.

It was about a Cleveland police officer named Martin McFadden who saw two black men, John Terry and Richard Chilton, standing on the street corner outside of a city department store. The two later met up with a white man named Carl Katz. McFadden thought they looked suspicious and approached. The short version of the story is that he questioned the men and ultimately searched and found weapons on two of them.

The question before the court was whether or not McFadden had had the right to stop, question, and physically pat down the three men based on little more than a detective's hunch that something was up.

The Supreme Court of Earl Warren had become known for expanding civil liberties and curtailing police power, for instance by ending the "third degree"—a euphemism for torture as an interrogation tactic—and forbidding the use of illegally seized evidence, in the 1961 case *Mapp v. Ohio*. But now, as some Americans were beginning to panic over a perception of massive urban unrest, the court reversed course and gave the police a new weapon. They ruled McFadden's arrest had been a good one and thereby created a new legal framework for police interactions with people on the street.

The *Terry* decision essentially said that the legal standard for a whole generation of field searches would henceforth rest in the minds of police officers. Now police could stop—and physically touch—anyone, if they had a "reason." Police could now stop and question anyone if they had a "reasonable" suspicion that a crime was about to be committed. Moreover, in such field interrogations, a police officer could now pat down a suspect if he had reason to believe him or her armed and dangerous.

In his majority opinion, Earl Warren, who at the time was under increasing criticism for having created an atmosphere that "coddled" criminals, wrote something very strange:

> The wholesale harassment by certain elements of the police community, of which minority groups, particularly Negroes, frequently complain, will not be stopped by the exclusion of any evidence from any criminal trial. Yet a rigid and unthinking application of the exclusionary rule, in futile protest against practices which it can never be used effectively to control, may exact a high toll in human injury and frustration of efforts to prevent crime.

Translated loosely, what Warren was saying was that even if all of those complaining black people are right about police abuse, my Supreme Court lacks the power to do anything about it. It's going to happen no matter what.

However, he wrote, while helpless to stop police abuse, we do have the power to make fighting crime easier.

Therefore, Warren suggested, we will worry about one and not the other.

We can't do anything about racism or police brutality. But we can do something about crime.

Through the seventies there were two beliefs about policing that, at the time, went unchallenged in mainstream American thought.

The first defined the fundamental role of the police: to combat serious crime in an essentially reactive role, by patrolling and investigating.

Thanks in part to the ideas of former Chicago police superintendent Orlando "O. W." Wilson, most urban police forces were organized around the idea that with the aid of technology like the patrol car and the two-way radio, advanced professional policing would not just contain crime but eventually eliminate it.

The other largely unquestioned belief was a sociological theory about the origins of crime.

"The conventional wisdom at the time was that crime was caused by poverty, racism, and social injustice," says Kelling. "And since the police couldn't do anything about that, they couldn't do anything about the causes of crime."

Kelling says even he believed that second notion through his early adulthood.

"It was the dominant theme of sociology, which was that in order to prevent crime, you had to go through macro social change," he says now. "In the early 1970s, I had no quarrel with that. It seemed to me entirely reasonable that you had to deal with problems like unemployment in order to prevent crime."

Still, he was interested in investigating alternatives. After leaving Lino Lakes, he returned to academic work and was eventually hired by groups like the Police Foundation, a privately funded think tank, to study new ideas in policing, a hot topic in the post-sixties hangover years.

Kelling's first major project, in 1972, was a grant to study the effectiveness of random automobile patrols in Kansas City. Later, he did a major study of the efficacy of police foot patrols in Newark, New Jersey.

He devised experiments to explore each case and came to two major conclusions.

The first is that varying the frequency and prevalence of radio car patrols had no real impact on either crime or the fear of crime. Cars apparently weren't the panacea policing wizards had believed them to be since the days of Jimmy Cagney movies.

The second is that while increasing foot patrols had little objective impact on actual crime rates, it had a profound impact on the fear of crime.

Having officers on the street reassured people. This was in part because police themselves were more visible and in part because officers on the street spent a lot of time attacking what one might call the outward symbols of disorder, like panhandling and public drinking.

Riding around in cars with cops in Kansas City, Kelling saw how police in vehicles were physically cut off from their neighborhoods. He remembers being struck by the image of a police officer rolling down his car window and having to wave his arms to get a pedestrian to come closer to the car, so that they could talk.

Meanwhile the cop on a Newark foot patrol was in regular intimate contact with his environment, constantly gathering intelligence and enforcing the rules of the neighborhood. Some of the rules followed the laws on the books; others were more intuitive.

"You could panhandle from people who were moving, but not from people who were standing still," he explains. "You could have a bottle of booze, but only out of a paper bag. You could drink, but not on the main drag. Basically, they were doing order maintenance."

The enforcing of these invisible laws created a sense of safety and reassurance for citizens, which to Kelling was a major step forward. If neighborhood fear was real enough to keep elderly people indoors at night, that was a kind of crime, even if it wasn't easy to quantify.

Eliminating that fear was therefore an end in itself. Understanding this led Kelling to a simple but groundbreaking conclusion:

Policing is not just about enforcing the law.

Policing is about maintaining order.

Sometime later, a Harvard professor named James Wilson called Kelling and told him he wanted to write an article with him for the *Atlan-*

tic magazine. Wilson was already known as an original—if sometimes controversial—thinker on criminal justice issues. Kelling accepted.

For their *Atlantic* article, Wilson wanted to incorporate the ideas of famed Stanford professor Philip Zimbardo. Zimbardo had performed an experiment involving disabled vehicles in two locations, a rough section of the Bronx and an upscale section of Palo Alto. In both places the car had its license plate removed and was left with its hood up.

In the Bronx the car was skeletonized by locals almost immediately, with the radio and battery ripped out right away. Before long the car had become an impromptu playground for neighborhood kids.

The Palo Alto neighborhood of upscale white people left the car alone completely until Professor Zimbardo came by a week later and smashed part of it with a sledgehammer. As soon as what Wilson and Kelling later described as "respectable whites" saw that damage, they acted as if they had been given implicit permission to destroy the car and quickly began vandalizing it.

Zimbardo was testing a theory that many social scientists had long held, that went something like this: "If a window in a building is broken and is left unrepaired all the rest of the windows will soon be broken."

This gave Wilson and Kelling the title for their *Atlantic* article.

The power of "Broken Windows," published in March 1982, turned on the simple insight that had animated much of Kelling's work: that order as an affirmative concept changed the behavior of the surrounding society in beneficial ways.

This insight had helped Kelling transform that small Minnesota home for troubled youths, where cleaning glass off bathroom floors turned the volume down on the psychoses and neuroses of a handful of adolescents. The same idea was now about to be hypothesized as at least a partial solution to a problem of immense political and historical complexity: crime and unrest in America's cities.

What Kelling and Wilson argued for was a more activist police force whose mission was something that could not easily be put into words. In fact, they said, the idea that the sole job of police was to enforce clearly written laws was part of what was holding police back.

"For centuries, the role of the police as watchmen was judged pri-

marily not in terms of its compliance with appropriate procedures but
rather in terms of its attaining a desired objective," they wrote. "The
objective was order, an inherently ambiguous term but a condition
that people in a given community recognized when they saw it."

This definition of "order" was an echo of Supreme Court justice
Potter Stewart's famous formulation about obscenity: "I know it
when I see it." To enforce these ambiguous codes of conduct in a bigger community like a city neighborhood, Kelling and Wilson theo-
rized that it may be necessary to allow a certain amount of, well,
ambiguous behavior on the part of police:

> Until quite recently in many states, and even today in some places,
> the police made arrests on such charges as "suspicious person" or
> "vagrancy" or "public drunkenness"—charges with scarcely any
> legal meaning. These charges exist not because society wants judges
> to punish vagrants or drunks but because it wants an officer to have
> the legal tools to remove undesirable persons from a neighborhood
> when informal efforts to preserve order in the streets have failed.

Translation: just as everyone understands what we mean when we
talk about order, so too do we understand that laws against things
like vagrancy or suspicious behavior are really just tools police can
use to maintain that indefinable standard.

Kelling and Wilson went on to explain that sometimes even giving
police these essentially limitless powers to arrest people is insufficient
to get the job done. The authors talked, for instance, about how Chicago police in a tough neighborhood in the early sixties dealt with
gang violence.

"What the police in fact do is to chase known gang members out of
the project," they wrote. "In the words of one officer, 'We kick ass.'"

The essence of the "Broken Windows" article therefore was that to
make the theory work, police might have to be given expanded lee-
way to enforce the nebulous and unwritten concept of order. And
though it doesn't say so explicitly, the article seemed to imply that in
order to do that, cities should find ways to approximate those old,
blurrily defined vagrancy laws and maybe turn a blind eye to the oc-
casional ass kicking.

Kelling in particular was keenly aware of the potential for misuse
of his ideas.

"I'd already been exposed, in South Boston for instance, to people whose idea of 'maintaining order' was keeping the black people out of their neighborhoods," Kelling says now. "So I knew that was a potential problem."

He and Wilson addressed the issue in their famous article.

"How do we ensure . . . that the police do not become the agents of neighborhood bigotry?" they wrote.

In the end, Kelling and Wilson weren't sure. Their conclusion was that they just had to hope it wouldn't turn out that way.

"We can offer no wholly satisfactory answer to this important question," they wrote. "We are not confident that there *is* a satisfactory answer except to hope that by their selection, training, and supervision, the police will be inculcated with a clear sense of the outer limit of their discretionary authority."

This conclusion was remarkably similar to the conclusion Earl Warren came to in the *Terry* case. Kelling and Wilson, like Justice Warren, were saying that they didn't have a solution to the problem of how to prevent systematic discrimination and police abuse, except to hope it wouldn't happen.

What they did have, they thought, was a tool that would help reduce crime. They weren't sure if it would be abused or not. But they were pretty sure it would work.

While Kelling was working on "Broken Windows," America's great cities appeared to be crumbling. New York, America's greatest city, was the worst symbol of this decline.

Crime soared, common areas were decrepit, and the "scariness" of the city—typically represented in the media and by politicians as an angry or desperate black or brown thief or panhandler—became a signature part of its identity. The fearfulness of upper-class white New York soon became a major theme in popular culture. The media depicted the city as a place under virtual siege by an unconquerable, zombie-like army of homeless people, squeegee men, drug dealers, graffiti artists, roving gangs, pimps, and prostitutes.

Movies like *After Hours, Quick Change,* and *The Warriors* told the story of New York as a place where just getting home could at any time turn into an epic survival tale.

The subway was where those fears were felt most keenly. In truth, actual crime rates were higher aboveground than they were below-ground. But people were afraid of the subway. They feared its chaotic appearance and its "unpredictable and obstreperous people," as Kelling would describe them in a *City Journal* article in 1991.

Kelling had by then become a key consultant to an effort to transform New York's subways. His ideas emphasized what in his mind was a crucial point, one that he'd learned in his earliest studies.

"People frightened of crime," he said, "are already victims."

Kelling believed strongly that the best way to reduce fear was to conquer the external symbols of disorder. He wrote approvingly of the city's Clean Car Program, an ambitious effort to wipe out perhaps the most visible symbol of disorder in the city: graffiti on subway cars.

The program was started by Ed Koch at the depths of New York's chaotic post-bankruptcy years and involved taking cars with graffiti out of service until they'd been scrubbed. This removed the primary motivation of graffiti artists, the chance to see their work traveling the city's four subway-connected boroughs. Most New Yorkers were unaware that this process involved an intense, almost guerrilla-like war with taggers, who shifted their focus to painting the interiors of tunnels, so that those could be seen. But even those areas were eventually scrubbed, and by 1989, the last "dirty" car was pulled out of service. To people like Kelling, a big part of the war against visual disorder had been won.

The shift was palpable for city commuters—a trip that had once been a daily reminder of the wild lawlessness of the city slowly became something more blissfully uneventful.

This emboldened the city to move to the next step: ridding the subways of "obstreperous" people.

The city's first plan was an ill-fated Commando Cleaning program. This used the preposterously aggressive technique of blasting certain areas of subway stations at odd hours with water from high-powered hoses. Ostensibly designed to clean the subway stations, the hoses' actual objective was to blast away the people who were using those stations at odd hours—which meant the homeless.

George Kelling opposed the tone-deaf Commando program. This was a real chance to try out his Broken Windows theory in the biggest city in America, and he didn't want it going sideways. He insisted that any program that stereotyped people instead of focusing on behavior was wrong and in any event would be opposed by the police asked to do those jobs.

Kelling was anxious to keep Broken Windows from turning into a symbol of thuggery and state-sanctioned racism. He wanted it to be perceived as fair. And he wanted the police enforcing his ideas to feel like they weren't doing something to outrage their consciences. Kelling's constant concern that his theory could be put to bigoted uses is evidence of his awareness of just how racially coded the fear of civic disorder had become.

He predicted the Commando Cleaning program would fail, and it did. It was panned in the media and quickly discontinued. Soon after, he was invited by Transit Authority president David Gunn to participate in a new panel, designed to come up with better ideas for how to restore order to the subway.

After a few fits and starts, the reform of the subway really took off when the Transit Police Department got a new chief, a brash, macho Bostonian named William Bratton. Bratton had been chief of the Massachusetts Bay Transit Authority (MBTA) Police and was a staunch proponent of Kelling's ideas.

In fact, Bratton was himself a sort of pioneer of Broken Windows, having used similar techniques while working as a police commander in the Fenway Park area in Boston in the late 1970s.

Bratton learned surprising lessons working the Fenway. Bostonians at community meetings proved more concerned about things like dirt, uncleaned streets, and illegally parked cars than they were about serious crime. When police attacked the small stuff, people felt safer.

So Bratton retrained his officers to focus on these minor offenses. "It wasn't the easiest lesson," he said. "We wanted to make the good pinch . . . We didn't want to be wrestling with drunks."

Once named chief of the Transit Police in New York, Bratton instituted a campaign that employed the Trumpian theme of "taking back the subway."

Almost overnight, the subway became a symbol of how policing was destined to work all over New York City. Police would later insist that the crime rate underground dropped precipitously after the Clean Car Program. In a report written well after the fact, Bratton himself would say that between 1990 and 1993, underground crime rates fell by more than 35 percent, compared to a 17.9 percent drop aboveground. This became a key part of the rationale for using quality-of-life policing aboveground.

It's difficult to look back now at the public comments made by officials at the time and not see some ominous signs of where Broken Windows might be headed. Kelling himself began his 1991 *City Journal* article about subway policing with an anecdote about a helpful, civic-minded citizen who is accosted by a panhandler:

> At midday in a New York City subway train, a man carrying a paper cup approaches a woman and thrusts the cup in front of her. She ignores him. He thrusts the cup nearly under her nose. She glances about, checking her situation—the train is approaching the terminal. If he's hungry, she says, there's a church nearby where he can get some food—she is specific about its location. He glowers at her, and pushing the cup even closer says, "Mind your own f——in' business, b——ch." The train stops. The woman gets off the train.

The passage is race neutral, in Kelling's careful way, but it's not hard to image the racial composition some in his audience, primed by politicians, the media, and the anecdotal evidence around them, would have projected onto the fictional scene. For those readers, anecdotes like Kelling's were stories about how their city and even their personal space were being violated by menacing black and brown bodies. That white people are inherently afraid of black people, and particularly black men, has been established by countless scientific studies, ranging from the prosaic (police officers shoot black suspects more quickly than whites in video simulations) to the bizarre (white people are more likely to ascribe superhuman or paranormal powers to black people than to other white people). This fear lurks under the surface of a wide spectrum of controversies past and present. The "subway shooter" Bernhard Goetz became a hero to white New Yorkers not because he was an introverted nut with a quick trigger finger but because so many white New Yorkers could identify with the experience of being afraid of black people on the subway. There was no other way to explain it: New York's reputation as a "scary" city was inextricably linked to the perception that it was a black city, or at least a place where white people couldn't safely avoid having to deal with black people.

Kelling didn't necessarily look at things that way. He believed sincerely that people who were afraid of crime were already victims of crime. If one could somehow decouple that concept from irrational fears of other races, his would be an absolutely true observation. His tale of the panhandler in the subway was, for him, a parable about how disorder makes victims of people even if they aren't robbed, beaten, or raped. It was also a story about why the city was failing.

"Disorder undermines not only the subway but the quality of life and the economic vitality of New York City," he wrote.

Kelling wanted Broken Windows to be a tool that would be remembered for restoring the quaint, almost Victorian quality of civility and decency to a city that had become legendary for the opposite. But his vision would become almost impossible to decouple from another, less lofty idea.

Kelling, unwittingly perhaps, had set in motion a massive government program that would be warped from the beginning by a chilling syllogistic construct:

New Yorkers who are afraid of crime are already victims.
Many New Yorkers are scared of black people.
Therefore, being black is a crime.

In 1994, the newly elected Rudy Giuliani empowered Bill Bratton to run America's largest police force. Bratton not only committed his army to George Kelling's Broken Windows theory but to a separate mania that belonged much more to him personally: statistics.

The academic in George Kelling spent a lot of time thinking about more amorphous issues, like how safe people did or didn't feel under certain kinds of police strategies.

The hard-charging, macho Bratton was more intensely interested in counting the progress of cops. The idea of the friendly street patrolman idly policing a block that had one or two muggings a month had no appeal to him. He wasn't interested in counting things that didn't happen. He wanted action.

Bratton was disdainful of the old model that focused on simply solving crimes one at a time. From an organizational perspective, having cops simply work cases as they popped up was a managerial sinkhole. How can you measure the progress of a detective sitting at his desk, coffee in one hand, telephone in another?

"Work on crime is usually done on a case-by-case basis without any real strategic oversight," Bratton complained. "As a result, police organizations can be particularly subject to drift."

So Bratton began to implement what he liked to describe as a "goal-setting" culture, which was heavily based on laying out numerical targets and making sure everyone hit them, or else.

Captain Joseph Concannon liked the new changes. He'd been a cop for decades and thought the police had been on the defensive for too long. By the mid-nineties, the barrel-chested six-footer had worked in virtually every part of the city.

He'd served the 114th Precinct in Queens as a beat cop, been a sergeant in Forest Hills, worked as a lieutenant in Brooklyn's Seventieth Precinct. He'd operated in Staten Island and the Bronx, and he would end his career with tours captaining two Manhattan precincts, the Seventeenth in Midtown and the Twenty-fourth on the Upper West Side.

He would be one of the first to see the CompStat system in action. And he was impressed. The cops were finally taking the fight to the criminals.

Concannon's memories of police work were all stored in what he calls the "library" of impressions that traveled with him everywhere on the job. The stuff in the library, a catalog of vivid experiences, was the raw material of any cop's muscle memory.

There was the time he got caught in a no-man's-land between the projects in Astoria and Queensbridge, a place all grown over with weeds. It was a spot where thieves dumped the hulks of stolen cars. Cops cruised the place sometimes, looking to catch people in the act.

One night he and his partner get a call: "Man with a gun." They're sent to the lot with the weeds. They drive up and eventually stop a young black guy driving a small black car. He's got a gun on him, a little Raven automatic, but they can't restrain him or get the gun. All three men end up in the backseat of a tiny car, wrestling for their lives.

"We're beating the piss out of ourselves, because we can't get ourselves on this motherfucking kid with a gun in his hand," Concannon remembers. "And we're trying to control the gun, we're trying to control his hands, we're in the backseat of this car, you know?

"So those are all of the things that are in the back of your head."

That episode ended without serious injury, but there were other memories. Concannon recalls the riots and the protests across the years, but what he mostly remembers is being shouted at and having stuff thrown at him and being told not to fight back.

He came up during an era in the seventies and eighties when New York police had a different mandate. The old, O. W. Wilson school of policing—based on cars, radios, and quick patrol response—turned out to have the effect of distancing cops from neighborhoods. Police were guys in cars who passed through like tourists, but they were told not to violate the *Star Trek*–ian prime directive—*Don't interfere*—even when provoked.

Inwardly, police like Concannon stowed those insults in the "library."

"I've been up in Washington Heights when Molotov cocktails were being thrown at the cops," he remembers. He describes showing up at the scene of a riot in a tough neighborhood and being told, when a store was set on fire: " 'Watch it. Don't do anything. Let them burn it down to the ground.' "

So he liked Bratton's new ideas. At least, they had potential. They were tough on captains like himself, but he didn't mind.

A huge part of Bratton's new push was the CompStat system, which will be familiar to fans of the HBO drama *The Wire*. On a daily basis, high-ranking police commanders started meeting in a corporate-style conference room to discuss current crime statistics and plot strategies.

The giant room full of sweating commanders that put high-ranking police officials on the spot was designed to be intimidating and ritualistic. The corporate imagery was very deliberate. Bratton, the exacting CEO in his own emerging corporate metaphor, talked about watching departmental progress "with the same hawk-like attention private corporations pay to profit and loss."

In these miserable, stress-filled ass-whipping sessions, local chiefs like Concannon were regularly asked to stand in front of the ranks and describe the progress of their sectors in painstaking detail.

"I'd be at a little podium here by myself, and behind me was a twenty-foot-by-twenty-foot electronic map," says Concannon. "And then [in front of] that map, I would have to defend . . . what I was doing to address the crime patterns in my area."

Concannon soon realized that commanders who weren't on top of the numbers in their sectors were screwed.

"All of this different data gets brought up," he says.

Recalling a typical scene, he plays both parts, the bosses and the commanders.

"They say, *'Inspector Charlie, in your command, we're getting a lot of radio runs for assaults,'*" Concannon says. "*'Can you tell us what's going on in that area?'* And he says, 'Yeah, we've gone down there, we've taken about sixteen different reports for assaults in the area.'"

Concannon turns to play the role of the bosses interrogating the commander and waves his hand to indicate the great twenty-by-twenty screen.

"*'Captain. This is a picture of your domestic violence officer. We understand she only has sixty ARs.'*"

An AR was a domestic violence activity report.

"Then they'll start eating away into why he's got so many assaults," Concannon explains. "They'll say, *'Captain, we're making you see that your assaults and your domestic violence are very much related, and that you better get on top of your domestic violence, Officer. Otherwise, we're going to get on it for you.'* You follow me?"

Now, even without having explicit numerical targets set for him, the captain had still been told in no uncertain terms that his domestic violence officer needed to start making more arrests. Otherwise, he wasn't going to be captain anymore.

Concannon believed CompStat was a great thing for the department. He believed it instilled accountability and organization in a police department where morale had sagged. "It's a very, very deliberate management process that's in place, and it's very much professionalized," he says. "But it's got to be managed and supervised."

Concannon remembers hearing direction about Stop-and-Frisk in CompStat meetings. The bosses would gripe if there weren't enough 250s written (again, the UF-250 was a form police filled out after they completed a stop). It was presented as the solution to every problem.

"[They'd say,] 'Hey, listen. You've got robberies here, you've got car break-ins there, you've got this going on all over the place,'" he recalls. "'How many two-fifties do you have in that area?'"

Like all the captains, he got the message. The brass wanted more 250s.

. . .

The Bratton programs were an immediate hit in the media, particularly after stats began to show a sharp drop in the crime rate in New York.

Time put Bratton on its cover, dressed in a trench coat and standing at night on a New York street conspicuously empty of anything but a squad car. The headline: "Finally, We're Winning the War Against Crime." In the blink of an eye, police departments in cities big and small began adopting similar programs. Kelling watched in amazement as versions of his ideas spread around the country. In each place, the concept was more or less the same one he'd advocated: ditching the old reactive policing model for this new, highly interventionist, proactive strategy that focused on the visible symbols of disorder.

But the idea that spread around the country was not exactly what Kelling envisioned. In some places, they called it "community" or "quality-of-life" policing. But in others, it was called "zero-tolerance" policing, a term that troubled Kelling to the point where he would ultimately find himself reluctant ever to say it out loud.

"Zero tolerance implies the police have no discretion," he says. "But the program really depends upon the police exercising good discretion."

Kelling believed a key to good policing depended upon police knowing when to throw the book at people and when to negotiate problems away quietly. Moreover, "zero tolerance" implied police were arresting everyone everywhere by the book, without making their own judgment calls, which was certainly not the case. Cops were not throwing zero tolerance at stockbrokers in high-rent neighborhoods. It was discretion here, no discretion there.

Moreover, the sheer number of stops and searches was growing at an ominous rate. At the policy's height in New York, police were stopping more than 680,000 people a year and issuing upward of half a million summonses a year. And throughout the life of the program, black and Hispanic residents made up 80 to 90 percent of all stops (usually closer to 90 percent), in a city where they made up roughly half of the population.

This disparity echoed an earlier bizarre statistic showing that 90 to 95 percent of all people imprisoned for drug offenses in New York in the nineties were black and Hispanic, despite studies showing that 72 percent of all illegal drug users in the city were white. Clearly a certain form of discretion was being exercised.

Bratton moved to Los Angeles in 2002 and launched a similar program there. Before long, L.A. was making more than 870,000 stops a year, a rate significantly higher than was ever seen in New York. Chicago, too, was still stopping people at a rate four times higher than New York as late as 2016.

In Baltimore, a little-known city councilman named Martin O'Malley won a surprise victory in the 1999 mayoral race on a platform of zero-tolerance policing. Within a few years, O'Malley's police force was arresting 108,447 people in a single year, or about one-sixth of the city's entire population.

In its first years, Broken Windows wasn't just popular among law enforcement. It became intellectual chic. In 2000, America's leading fast-food philosopher, Malcolm Gladwell, helped establish his place in the intelligentsia on the back of a half-baked analysis of Broken Windows in a book called *The Tipping Point*.

Gladwell sold Middle America on the idea that making little changes in an environment can bring about big results, and you can fight crime the same way you start a fashion trend. So just as you can sell lots of Hush Puppies shoes by getting a bunch of kids in a chic neighborhood like the East Village to wear them, so too can you stop felonies and murders by busting graffiti artists. Or something. It sounded convincing enough to the millions of people who read the book.

The only people who had a problem with Broken Windows seemed to be the ones living in the target neighborhoods.

People in black and Hispanic neighborhoods of New York and other cities began showing up in lawyers' offices with horror stories of being knocked down, strip-searched on the street, and busted repeatedly for nonsense charges like obstructing government administration, loitering, or obstructing pedestrian traffic.

The theory behind the program had evolved—by making people in certain neighborhoods aware that they could be stopped and/or searched at any time, for any reason, it would discourage them from bringing guns or drugs out on the street. A black state senator named Eric Adams would later testify that Ray Kelly, the city's commissioner throughout the Bloomberg years, had told him openly that the goal was to change the psyche of young black and Latino men by "instill[ing] fear in them that every time that they left their homes they could be targeted by police."

"How else would we get rid of guns?" Kelly asked Adams.

But the program had the effect of making a city full of nonwhite people of infinitely varied backgrounds experience a nearly identical sense of dread and uncertainty about when the next stop might come. College students, working professionals, and bloodthirsty gang killers all felt the same thing.

Eric Garner thought he had the system beat once he found the cigarette scheme, but soon he was feeling that same dread. Right or wrong, the threat of being stopped went from an annoyance to a thing that took over his life.

SIX JEWEL

Jewel Miller didn't like government offices. The dislike dated back to when she was twelve years old, when she put herself into foster care after her parents died.

"I needed a minute," she explains.

Growing up, she'd never known any serious problems.

"I lived in a nice house. I knew nothing about welfare and projects. I had parents that went to work," she says. "My mother was a secretary. I had it good."

But her mother and stepfather had been heroin addicts when Jewel was born and didn't get clean until she was three years old. When they got sick with AIDS nearly a decade later, she didn't understand. "AIDS was for people who did drugs," she says.

When they died, her biological father was in prison, so she ended up in the foster care system. For the rest of her life state offices and state aid gave her an uneasy feeling.

By the time she reached her thirties, though, she had four children of her own to take care of. She had split from their father, a college basketball player who had NBA dreams but never made it to the big time, and was raising the kids alone. She had a good job with benefits at a temp agency in the city, but when the 2008 financial crisis hit, she was laid off, and her kids needed health insurance, which meant Jewel had to return to the system.

So one day in late 2010, she went to the Medicaid office in Staten Island, which is located at 215 Bay Street, directly across from Tompkinsville Park. She was trying to sort things out for her four kids, but the woman behind the counter wasn't making sense to her. Only the big man with the deep voice behind her seemed interested in helping.

"I was fussing and cussing, and he was trying to help," she says. "He was telling me which numbers to call, how to do this, how to do that."

By amazing coincidence, cigarettes were the first thing Jewel Miller asked Eric Garner about. "I asked him, 'Who sells bootleg smokes around here?'"

Garner smiled and puffed out his chest. "I got packs," he said.

They exchanged numbers. "We was friends for like a year," she says.

Jewel was outgoing, quick-witted, and proud. She wasn't afraid to tell you who she was or what she thought about things. She was bisexual and open about it. She knew Eric was after her, but she didn't want a relationship at first.

"I was playing girls at the time," she says. "I'm like, 'I'm free, I'm single, I have no time for no man.'"

Also, Eric wasn't exactly her type.

"I like them six two, two hundred ten pounds, drink of water, you know what I'm saying?" she says. "And Eric wasn't that. But he had a good heart. He was a good person. That's what won me over."

It was six months before Eric told Jewel he was married. Jewel didn't like it. She wanted Eric to get a divorce. If he liked her so much, why was he going home to a wife?

"No, I want you," Eric said.

"I was going, 'What? A divorce needs to be done,'" Jewel recalls. "I said, 'I don't date married men.' That was my biggest thing. 'I don't date married men.'"

Then Jewel found out that Eric's two young sons, Eric Jr. and Emery, were in foster care. "I started finding out about the children, and at the time the children weren't at home, they were actually in foster care," she says. "I was like, 'Oh, hell no! You're out rolling with us while your kids are in care?'"

Eric started to listen to her. "I was like, 'Well, we definitely can't date until Emery and Eric come home,'" Jewel recalls. She told him, "I don't know how you live, but in the world that I live in, we just don't do that. We take care of our kids, you know?"

Eric had come to treat the status of his children with resignation, but now he resolved for the first time to do something about it.

Shortly afterward, Eric moved out and began to live with Jewel. Eric even took Jewel to meet his mother and stepfather. He hadn't gotten a divorce and he hadn't succeeded in getting his kids out of care, but Jewel was satisfied that he was making an effort to go down that road, and finally, they were together.

This didn't go over too well with Esaw.

"I was very jealous," she says. "There was no way in hell I was going to let him go." When he started disappearing for long stretches, she called more and more.

"[Jewel] used to get mad because I would call his phone. I called his phone every day," Esaw says. "And if he didn't call me, I would be texting his phone, like, 'What's going on? Why aren't you answering your phone, why aren't you calling me?'"

For a while, Garner continued to insist nothing was going on between himself and Jewel, even after he'd moved out.

Esaw drops her voice and does her own polished Eric Garner impersonation as she recounts the scene of her husband explaining his nights away with Jewel.

"He'd say, 'Baby, that's just my friend. She's not my girlfriend. She just gave me a place to stay.'"

"And I'd say, 'Eric, you expect me to believe that shit? I don't believe that shit.'"

Eric Garner would just shrug. He put about as much effort into finding a good cover story as he did into buying clothes for himself, which is to say not very much. Jewel Miller was about to discover what Esaw had already long known, which is that Eric Garner pushed the act of not taking care of himself almost to an art form.

In many ways, Garner acted as if his own life and health were permanently damaged and disposable, not worth keeping in repair. All he really cared about was the money he kept flowing to his family. His life was ruined the day he got picked up for selling crack when he was eighteen. Maybe before that. But his kids had an unblemished future, so that's what mattered. And the only way he knew how to show that concern was with money.

Even in his interactions with police, the self-annihilating instinct came through. He was more than willing to go to jail, to sleep in the unventilated, urine-soaked air of the 120th Precinct house, so long as they left his money alone.

It was the same with his health, which had worsened considerably since his first prison stint. As recently as the mid-2000s, Garner had been in good shape. An excellent athlete in his youth, he passed on his genes to his son Eric Jr., who was on his way to becoming a scholarship college basketball player.

Garner had suffered from asthma since childhood. He didn't know it, but this was a common problem among black people of his generation. Black kids born in the seventies and beyond, like Garner, were far more susceptible to disease than the national average—roughly two and a half times more likely to suffer from asthma, and more than five times more likely to die from it. No one is exactly sure why; even the CDC has said it doesn't know for sure. In any case, Garner's illness was such an ever-present part of his life that after his passing, his mother, Gwen, would line a living-room memorial to her son with asthma inhalers.

In prison, the family says, officials treated his asthma with steroids, which made his weight balloon. After his last stretch behind bars, he gained nearly a hundred pounds. It wasn't all steroids, though; he also ate in heroic amounts. John McCrae tells a story of Eric going to the new Domino's on the corner of Bay and Victory, ordering a whole pie, and eating it standing up.

"He would take a whole pizza, fold that motherfucker in half, and eat it like you and me eating a slice," he says.

Esaw says that when he got out of jail the last time, eating became Garner's main recreation. "We didn't go dancing, we didn't go swimming, we went to eat," she says, laughing. "And don't let him get hold of a location where a good buffet is. Forget it! He'd have about eight plates!" She chuckles. "His favorite meal was spaghetti. Spaghetti and pork chops."

But it caught up to him. Now pushing 350 pounds, he very quickly developed other complications.

By the 2000s sleep apnea made his nights miserable. His snoring was a thing of legend. His wife, Esaw, recalls that when Eric went away to stay with Jewel, it took her family a long time to get used to the absence of his snoring.

"When he was with her, we missed his snoring in the house," she says. "Then we got used to not hearing it, so that when he came home, we were like, 'Oh, shit, here we go with the snoring.'"

Both wife and mistress speak with awe about Garner's messiness, like it was a mystical thing.

"He'd make himself a sandwich at night, and you'd go down, there'd be enough mayonnaise on the spoon to make you and me both a sandwich," Jewel says. "Then he'd come to bed and put his clothes in a pile next to the bed. 'Babe, are you gonna get those?' you'd say. And most he would do is sort of scoot 'em over."

Just as his own children loved watching scary movies with their father, Jewel's four kids loved playing with the mountainous Garner and often pigpiled on top of him in bed. Jewel recalls entering her bedroom and having to reprimand adults and kids alike for bringing food into the room.

"I'd say, 'All of y'all need to get out of my bed. Eric, you too! It's time!' And they're all covered in crumbs, Oreos and shit . . ."

She laughs and tells a story of confronting Garner in the morning. "One time, I said, 'Listen, babe, don't eat in here.'" She looked down. "Eric, you've got sandwich wrappers here. What time did you eat that sandwich? This morning?"

And he'd say, "Oh, I forgot. I'm gonna get that right now."

Jewel tells the same story about Eric refusing to buy himself shoes that his wife tells. This was despite the fact that his feet ached so much. "You could argue until you were blue in the face, he didn't want to buy stuff for himself."

His wife, Esaw, concurs. "The only time he would buy something for himself is if it was something he needed, like a coat," she explains.

Garner buying himself fine things was so out of character that it sometimes backfired on him when he tried. One time, he showed up at the park in Tompkinsville wearing a big, shiny, puffy black North Face jacket. He bragged to everyone about his purchase.

"Yo, E, man, that shit is fake," McCrae told him.

"Nah," he said. "I paid four hundred dollars for this."

Another one of the men on the block shook his head. "Eric, look at the logo. It's too big and on the wrong side," he said.

Garner cursed out loud. The whole block burst out laughing.

Almost everyone who knew Eric Garner reports that the man liked to argue. Not aggressively, mind you, but recreationally. In a half-serious way, he absolutely refused to lose any debate. As a maker of jokes and wisecracks, he was corny, no stand-up comic. But the manner of his relentless arguing was funny. On the streets and at home, people would start rolling their eyes and chuckling as soon as he got going.

"Eric was never wrong," says Jewel. She points at a box. "You'd say something silly like, 'This is just a box.' And just to argue, he'd start telling you where the box was built, what it was made of, that it was some special super kind of box and not just a box like you said. You couldn't win."

He didn't let anything go, not even a cigarette. Although Garner was known to hand out dollar bills to kids when the ice cream truck drove down Bay Street, he wasn't big on handing freebies to grownups. Over the years, a few people tried buying smokes on credit and not paying back. "Eric didn't go for that shit," says McCrae. "He'd show up at your house."

With any subject that mattered to him, you could count on Garner to know what he was talking about. Football stats were one area of expertise. Another was closer to home.

"He knew the law," says his mother, Gwen Carr. "He knew what was legal and what wasn't. Knew it inside and out."

Garner knew the laws surrounding cigarette sales. He knew how many packs he could carry on him at a given time, knew what constituted a sale, knew what actions would trigger an arrest. He knew he could be charged with serious offenses with longer potential sentences if he was caught crossing state lines with a trunk full of cartons but that he wasn't risking as much time standing on a street corner. Street corner time was time he could live with.

As careful as he was, once Garner built up his operation he began having trouble with the police. He had roughly a half-dozen misdemeanor arrests and convictions in his first few years selling cigarettes, but those didn't bother him so much. He was more upset that police kept stopping him or pulling him over when he was driving, searching him, and then vouchering his smokes and his money.

The legal word for this is "forfeiture," but Garner just called it "taking my shit." Police take anything they turn up in a search that they think is contraband, i.e., the proceeds of an illegal activity, like for instance gambling or drug dealing or selling untaxed cigarettes.

Police might stop your car or stop you on the street, and it didn't matter what you said, they'd find a way to go through your stuff. You waited while they went through your pockets.

If they found a wad of cash or a carton of smokes, they might just take it and dare you to come to the station and prove where it came from. Even when they're wrong, the tactic never really backs up on the police.

"Sometimes the cops will take something that they believe is contraband but actually isn't," explains Staten Island defense lawyer Joe Doyle, who later represented Garner. "Pills are a good example of this. The cops seize some Oxy from your client, but then the case gets dismissed because your guy has a prescription for it."

The lawyer adds: "Clients will ask if they can get the pills back. My advice is normally, 'I get it, you should get them back, but I just don't see it happening.'"

Garner had no illusions about what he did for a living or whether the police had a right, legally, to take his money. The issue was more about how they took his money.

Were there rules? Could they reach into his pockets anytime they wanted? Not according to the law. Police did not, in fact, have the right to reach into his pocket anytime they wanted, just because they knew he was Eric Garner, the guy who sold cigarettes. Police had to have a "reasonable suspicion" that he was armed and dangerous in order to effect even a pat-down search.

Jewel estimates that Eric was stopped and searched in excess of a hundred times during the few years they were together. It got to the point where she would carry her pay stubs with her in her pocketbook, so they wouldn't take her money, too.

"This one time, I was like, 'You better give me back my money, because this is my money!'" she says. "And they'd say, 'Release the money. She's got pay stubs.'

"But they took seven hundred, eight hundred dollars from Eric."

Sometimes Garner would try to argue that the money in his pocket was actually Jewel's, and he would frantically point to her pay stubs. Police usually didn't buy it. They'd take his money away and his eyes would follow it.

Whole days spent standing in the snow on his swollen feet handing fifty-cent cigarettes to drunks would disappear in an instant, thanks to chance meetings with snickering cops who always had a little extra word for him, too.

"They'd be like, 'You want to go to jail?'" Jewel remembers.

Bloomberg's cigarette taxes had made a street cottage industry not just for people like Garner but for the police who patrolled them. All over the city, the neighborhood loosie dealer became an easy mark for police looking to make a quick bust.

Garner was the perfect person to help cops make their arrest quotas. Unlike drug dealers, who used runners and other middlemen to make the ultimate criminal transaction harder to trace, the loosie dealer usually did the whole exchange by himself, money for a smoke, hand to hand in the street. Eric and the other dealers in his small crew were sitting ducks.

The typical loosie dealer in New York was also an older man, sometimes homeless or close to it. He was an easier takedown for cops compared to some young hotheaded drug dealer who might be armed or want to make a name for himself going down swinging in an arrest.

In 2011, for instance, *The New York Times* profiled a Manhattan version of Eric Garner who called himself Lonnie Loosie. Lonnie, like Garner, was an ex-con without much in the way of real job prospects. He took advantage of Bloomberg's tax laws to make a living but lamented that he was an easy bust.

"They call me a fish," he said, "because I'm easy to catch."

Slow moving, often sick, and easy to spot, Garner was an even easier catch. He got stopped over and over again. It got to the point that Garner was running into Staten Island police everywhere he went, even when they were off duty.

"We were in Pathmark once," says Jewel. "And these cops in street clothes, guys he knew from Bay Street, they came up to us and started giving it to Eric.

"They were like, 'Yo, man, you got any New-pawts? You got Kools? You got menthols?' Real cute like that, and laughing. That sort of thing."

The pressure from the law, on top of the physically exhausting nature of the work, started to take its toll. There was also the matter of the growing feud between Esaw and Jewel. Even though Garner had all but moved out, Esaw did not let her husband go. She went into combat mode to get him back.

She presented her husband with a very simple choice. He either had to come home, or at least support her, or she would go after Jewel physically.

She recalls, "He would tell [Jewel], 'That's my wife, those are my children. I have to give her whatever she wants, because if I don't, she's going to come over and cause a scene.'"

Esaw claims things got so bad that the two women came to blows. There are, to put it mildly, differing accounts of how these confrontations played out.

"My threat to him was, 'Anytime that I ask you for something, if you don't give it to me, I'm going to beat up your girlfriend,'" Esaw explains. "I beat her up three times."

Jewel, who calls Esaw "Satana," says that the venom came from the fact that Eric was changing and was happy. "He was a new guy, trying something new," she says. "And she didn't take it well."

SEVEN NUMBERS

In early August 2013, unbeknownst to Eric, a decades-long effort to force a judge to rule on the constitutionality of the Stop-and-Frisk policing Garner faced on a regular basis finally reached a head.

The tale of how Stop-and-Frisk finally made it into court was a long and twisting one. As in all things related to law enforcement reform, the road was littered with obstacles and legal leprechaun tricks.

Way back in 1971, the NYPD started a specialized squad called the SCU, or Street Crime Unit. The SCU was a roving gang of plain-clothes ass-kickers who roamed all over the city and targeted pimps, rapists, stickup kids, muggers. Frequently undercover, they employed decoy squads and considered themselves the cream of the crop.

The squad was also heavily white. According to some reports, the group was less than 10 percent minority, compared to 30 percent across the NYPD generally.

In the early nineties, when Bratton first took the commissioner job, the SCU took off. The expanded use of *Terry* stops meant the self-appointed commandos didn't have to pussyfoot around anymore. Now they could jump out of cars anywhere and everywhere and jack up people in search of things like guns.

And they took the job seriously. At one point, despite being less than 2 percent of the whole NYPD numerically, they seized 40 percent of the guns.

In 1996, the group had T-shirts printed up that quoted Ernest Hemingway:

THERE IS NO HUNTING LIKE THE HUNTING OF MAN, AND THOSE WHO HAVE HUNTED ARMED MEN LONG ENOUGH AND LIKED IT, NEVER CARE FOR ANYTHING ELSE THEREAFTER.

Howard Safir, the squirrelly, oddly nondescript man who took over the commissioner's job from the swashbuckling Bratton in 1996, took the SCU and tripled it in size. In 1997, it went from 138 members to 380. The mandate of the SCU was like the mandate for the police department generally: make numbers. It came out in a *New York Times* story as far back as 1999 that the group was operating on an unofficial quota, which demanded that each officer turn up one illegal gun a month.

"There are guys who are willing to toss anyone who's walking with his hands in his pockets," one officer told the *Times*. "We frisk 20, maybe 30 people a day. Are they all by the book? Of course not; it's safer and easier to just toss people. And if it's the 25th of the month and you haven't got your gun yet? Things can get a little desperate."

On February 4, 1999, four white SCU officers—Edward McMellon, Sean Carroll, Kenneth Boss, and Richard Murphy—thought they had spotted someone matching the description of the suspected serial rapist of twenty-nine victims.

Dressed in plain clothes and driving an unmarked Taurus, they jumped out at 1157 Wheeler Avenue in the Bronx with the intention of doing a stop-question-frisk of a black man standing in a doorway.

What the Guinean immigrant Amadou Diallo did next is a matter of some dispute. But everyone agrees that he was not armed, that when asked to "show his hands" he reached not for a gun but for a wallet, and that, in an instant, the four officers responded by shooting at him a preposterous forty-one times.

The SCU's unofficial motto was "We Own the Night," but in February 1999, they owned not the night but the headlines. The incident became the latest touchstone for complaints by the city's nonwhite population about police behavior.

When community groups and lawyers got together to figure out what to do, they decided to focus on the signature part of Bill Bratton's revolution, the Stop-and-Frisk campaign.

They did this for a number of reasons. First, the SCU that shot and killed Diallo was responsible for a massive number of stops: 18,023 in 1997 and 27,061 in 1998. A few hundred mostly white men responsible for tens of thousands of stops a year was definitely something to raise an eyebrow at, especially when one factored in the racial breakdown of the people being stopped.

When the attorney general's office did a study of Stop-and-Frisk in response to the Diallo incident, for example, it found that while blacks constituted 25.6 percent of the city's population, 50.6 percent of all people stopped were black.

The uproar over Diallo and Stop-and-Frisk produced a lawsuit in 1999. *Daniels v. City of New York* was brought by the Center for Constitutional Rights, led by attorney Darius Charney, along with an attorney named Jonathan Moore from the firm Beldock, Levine and Hoffman. Ironically, Moore would later represent Eric Garner's family in their lawsuit against the city.

Daniels targeted Stop-and-Frisk generally and the Street Crime Unit specifically. The story of how the city defended it provides a clear view of the intellectual toxin buried deep underneath seemingly banal statistical imperatives like Stop-and-Frisk.

Four years into the case, a new mayor was elected in New York named Mike Bloomberg. He in turn brought in a new commissioner, another mouthy Bostonian named Ray Kelly.

"So Kelly and Bloomberg come in, and they immediately do two things," recalls Charney, the lawyer on the *Daniels* case. "First, they offer to disband the SCU, which was great. Then they say, 'We want to settle this case.'"

Charney and his cohorts were at first surprised but assumed this was good news. They entered into settlement negotiations.

In the end, the settlement turned into a classic Manhattan story. What the city offered, and what the plaintiffs unwittingly took, was a handful of wampum.

First of all, the agreement ended up including the following language: "Municipal Defendants deny that they had or currently have a policy . . . that deprived persons of rights, privileges, or immunities secured or protected by the Constitution and laws of the United States."

This was a "neither admit nor deny" deal. The city agreed to make changes but formally denied that changes had ever been necessary.

Next, the city eagerly promised to make up a new set of written guidelines expressly forbidding racial discrimination in the city's police department. The new NYPD operations order, issued on March 13, 2002, issued a strict instruction:

All police-initiated enforcement actions, including but not limited to arrest, stop and question, and motor vehicle stop, will be based on the standards required by the Fourth Amendment of the U.S. Constitution or other applicable law.

It went on:

Officers must be able to articulate the factors which led them to take enforcement action, in particular those factors leading to reasonable suspicion for a stop and question.

The new written policy was simply a promise to follow the existing law governing street stops. It even used the same language as the *Terry* case, talking about articulable, reasonable suspicion.

Since the city was already obligated to follow these laws and had been since 1968, the offer of a new written operations order on that theme was a bit odd, to say the least. Even Charney shrugged at the new policy. "I think everybody understood that this was already illegal," he says.

Beyond that, though, the city offered to maintain regular audits of the department's policies to make sure there were no more shenanigans. They also promised to turn over their data about Stop-and-Frisk and start a public education program.

The plaintiffs' lawyers assumed that what was essentially a four-part settlement (new written policy, regular audits, data turnover, public education program) amounted to a legally enforceable promise to stop racially profiling people. Since this was the goal of the suit, they agreed to the deal. Judge Shira Scheindlin approved the settlement on December 12, 2003. It seemed like a major victory.

But very soon after, when Charney examined the first set of numbers the NYPD delivered, he was dizzy with disbelief. Not only had the city not stopped its discriminatory practices, they'd significantly ramped them up, massively expanding the number of stops.

In 2002, before the deal, the NYPD had stopped 97,296 people. In 2003, that number jumped to 160,851. By 2004, it was 313,523. Then, by 2007, the city was stopping almost half a million people every year. In each of these years blacks and Latinos made up well over 80 percent of the stops, despite being less than 50 percent of the population.

The CCR lawyers were flabbergasted. In year one of their settlement the city doubled the number of stops, and their own data showed the same clear evidence of racial profiling. Within four years, the city had quintupled the number, and all evidence suggested that a Bloomberg-led city would continue to order more and more stops in nonwhite neighborhoods. The new administration might as well have used the *Daniels* settlement as toilet paper.

"We were going crazy," Charney says. "So we went to the judge and we were like, 'Your Honor, they're not in compliance. They're still doing it.' "

But Judge Scheindlin had bad news for Charney and his colleagues. The NYPD had fulfilled all of their promises in the settlement. They did the education program. They did the audits. They turned over the data. And they wrote the new policy.

That they didn't stop mass violating the constitutional rights of 50 percent of the city's population was, sadly enough, immaterial. The city hadn't actually promised to change, as far as Judge Scheindlin saw it. They'd merely promised to write a new policy prohibiting the wrong behavior and turn over some numbers.

"She said, 'If you want to change this, you need a new lawsuit,' " Charney recalls.

So in 2008, they sued again.

The new case was called *Floyd v. City of New York.* Charney wasn't sure what to expect, but certainly the city's defense this time around was a surprise.

In *Floyd,* the city suddenly stopped denying that enormous numbers of people were being stopped for no good reason.

Instead, the city introduced two lines of defense. First, they said, Stop-and-Frisk had reduced crime. This was a curious nonanswer to a charge of mass civil rights violations.

More important, the city argued that it was not stopping people because they were black or brown. Instead, they were stopping them because black and brown people were statistically more likely to be criminals.

When asked to justify the fact that in 2011 and 2012, blacks and Hispanics represented 87 percent of all the people stopped, the city's answer was that "approximately 83 percent of all known crime suspects and approximately 90 percent of all violent crime suspects were Black and Hispanic."

Therefore, they contended, it was reasonable to be suspicious of the entire group.

This reasonableness also made it legal, by the city's logic, to stop anyone who belonged to those groups. In other words, in a court, before a judge, the city essentially now argued that they had falsified millions of Stop-and-Frisk forms. All of those reasons justifying the searches that the city's cops had cited on official forms countless times—"furtive movements," "bulges," "inappropriate attire," etc.—were just convenient euphemisms. In truth, there was a single, blanket justification that covered "reasonable suspicion" for at least 80 percent of those searches: they were black or Hispanic residents of high-crime neighborhoods.

The city's defense against accusations of profiling was to argue that profiling works.

Pedro Serrano testified in that suit, and his tapes were played for Judge Scheindlin. She heard the critical exchange between the whistleblower cop and his boss, Christopher "Red Rage" McCormack. McCormack not only told Serrano that "male blacks, fourteen to twenty, twenty-one" were "the right people" to stop, but that people who didn't fit this description, even if they might technically be breaking the law, were the *wrong* people. He told Serrano, for instance, that he didn't encourage stopping "a lady [who] was walking through St. Mary's Park when it was closed."

Scheindlin was struck by this and other testimony and concluded that the police had a two-faced policy designed to hide a program of mass profiling. She struck down the program in a lengthy ruling, which contained the following key passage:

> The NYPD maintains two different policies related to racial profiling in the practice of stop and frisk: a written policy that prohibits racial profiling and requires reasonable suspicion for a stop—and another, unwritten policy that encourages officers to focus their reasonable-suspicion-based stops on "the right people, the right time, the right location."

As Scheindlin put it, "Rather than being a defense *against* the charge of racial profiling, however, this reasoning is a defense *of* racial profiling."

City leaders were furious with the woman Donald Trump would later infamously call a "very against-police judge." Bloomberg, still the mayor, was perhaps angriest of all. On August 12, 2013, he stood on the steps of City Hall with his commissioner, Ray Kelly, and issued a lengthy statement.

Bloomberg directed his ire at the "one small group of advocates—and one judge" who overturned what he implied was otherwise an overwhelmingly popular program.

"Throughout the case, we didn't believe that we were getting a fair trial," he said. He lamented the fact that Judge Shira Scheindlin had not wanted to hear any of the city's arguments about the effectiveness of Stop-and-Frisk.

His statement buzzed with loaded language. Judge Scheindlin, Bloomberg said, had "ignored the real-world realities of crime" in striking down Stop-and-Frisk. He angrily denied that his administration had been engaged in racial profiling and cited the fact that he had passed a law banning the practice.

He neglected to mention that the practice was already illegal.

As to what the mayor meant by "real-world realities," his commissioner, Kelly, shed some light when he issued his own statement.

Kelly's defense of Stop-and-Frisk was a parody of the city's legal argument. It came out as a tautology: we stop more people in neighborhoods with higher crime rates because those neighborhoods have higher crime rates. "That's where the crime is," he said.

"That's where the crime is" became the go-to explanation for anyone defending the statistically lopsided policing tactics of the zero-tolerance era.

There was an irony in this.

The neighborhoods at which Ray Kelly and Michael Bloomberg pointed were not just a statistical location for criminal acts. They were crimes themselves.

Most of the crime-ridden minority neighborhoods in New York City, especially areas like East New York, where many of the characters in Eric Garner's story grew up, had been artificially created by a series of criminal real estate scams.

One of the most infamous had involved a company called the Eastern Service Corporation, which in the sixties ran a huge predatory lending operation all over the city, but particularly in Brooklyn.

Scam artists like ESC would first clear white residents out of certain neighborhoods with scare campaigns. They'd slip leaflets through mail slots warning of an incoming black plague, with messages like, "Don't wait until it's too late!" Investors would then come in and buy their houses at depressed rates.

Once this "blockbusting" technique cleared the properties, a company like ESC would bring in a new set of homeowners, often minorities, and often with bad credit and shaky job profiles. They bribed officials in the FHA to approve mortgages for anyone and everyone. Appraisals would be inflated. Loans would be approved for repairs, but repairs would never be done.

The typical target homeowner in the con was a black family moving to New York to escape racism in the South. The family would be shown a house in a place like East New York that in reality was only worth about $15,000. But the appraisal would be faked and a loan would be approved for $17,000.

The family would move in and instantly find themselves in a house worth $2,000 less than its purchase price, and maybe with faulty toilets, lighting, heat, and (ironically) broken windows besides. Meanwhile, the government-backed loan created by a lender like Eastern Service by then had been sold off to some sucker on the secondary market: a savings bank, a pension fund, or perhaps to Fannie Mae, the government-sponsored mortgage corporation.

Before long, the family would default and be foreclosed upon. Investors would swoop in and buy the property at a distressed price one more time. Next, the one-family home would be converted into a three- or four-family rental property, which would of course quickly fall into even greater disrepair.

This process created ghettos almost instantly. Racial blockbusting is how East New York went from 90 percent white in 1960 to 80 percent black and Hispanic in 1966. The inflated mortgages sold to refugees from southern racism and underqualified buyers—which then led to one-family houses being foreclosed on and converted into poorly maintained multifamily rentals—is what turned this black and Hispanic neighborhood into a ghetto. And companies like ESC got rich for their role.

The scale of these scams was, for the times, massive. Federal prosecutors estimated that in 1968 alone, companies like the Eastern Service operation created $100 million in defaults and more than five thousand empty houses in New York City alone.

Decades later, when the 2008 crash happened, it turned out that

one of the major factors in the crisis was a mortgage fraud rip-off almost exactly similar to the Eastern Service scam, only executed on a
much grander scale.

There was no direct bribery element in 2008, but everything else
was more or less exactly the same: wholesale falsification of financial
records, the aggressive effort to get people with poor credit histories
into homes, falsified employment data, inflated appraisals, etc.

At the heat of the subprime craze, white real estate agents spilled
into black neighborhoods in huge numbers, offering free mortgages
and no-lose investments. They explained that a surging home market
and fancy new loan instruments would once again deliver the promise
of home ownership. They said that times were so good and the financial conditions so strong that even the most modest home owners
would now get to ride the gravy train with the rest of the country.

But the people who signed on the dotted line ended up upside-
down on giant albatross loans almost from the jump. They would
have been better off never listening to the pitch at all. From forty
acres and a mule to the Great Society to subprime, it was the same
swindle, over and over and over again: promises that turned into brutal obligations that turned into life-ruining debt and neighborhood-
destroying foreclosures for some and massive windfall profits for
others.

On August 13, 2013, the day after Ray Kelly and Bloomberg held a
press conference to denounce the end of Stop-and-Frisk, Jewel Miller's house burned down.

At the time, Jewel and her four children were living in a multifamily home on 30 Norwood Avenue in Staten Island. She was living on
a Section 8 state-subsidized voucher in a building that was a typical
low-income housing nightmare. As of that morning, the home had
thirty-nine open violations, ranging from bedbugs to mice and roach
infestations to mold to broken electrical outlets, violations that had
never led to real punishments.

Things like this are part of what drive the resentment toward police
in nonwhite neighborhoods. For the most part, people living in low-
income housing and in project towers don't see the more egregious
double standard in the justice system enjoyed by, say, Wall Street CEOs
committing massive real estate scams that decimated neighborhoods.

But you do notice that your landlord is getting away with decades of violations without consequence. In the case of Jewel's place in Staten Island, the landlord, the aptly named Mad Realty Holdings LLC, had done nothing to fix most of her building's many problems. A lone $280 fine for emergency repairs was the only government sanction in the public record.

The only reason Jewel wasn't in the house at the time of the fire was that she was out trying to deal with the vermin problem. "I had just left my home," she says. "I found bedbugs in my carpet. So I threw everything in my living room out. I woke up at, like, eight thirty that morning, my living room was bare. Couches, pillows, curtains, I threw away everything.

"So I went to Home Depot to get a steam cleaner. As soon as I signed my name on the [rental agreement], my son called me and said, 'Mom, the house is on fire.' I'm like, 'Our house is on fire?' He said, 'Our house.' I said, 'Oh, my God.'"

It turns out a tenant in the apartment below Jewel had left an electrical appliance on too long. It was the second time in a week this had happened. Nobody was hurt, but the fire completely destroyed Jewel's apartment. The blaze was so big it made the local newspapers. One of the other tenants complained in print that even before the fire, her ceiling had caved in and the pipes didn't work.

"It's typical low-income housing," said the tenant, Susan Antonelli. "It happens."

The hits kept coming. In the first days after the fire, Eric and Jewel moved to a hotel. On August 22, they drove from there to Bay Street to do some laundry, a little shopping, and to wire his daughter Erica fifty dollars via a check-cashing shop there.

After they were done, as they pulled out, a police car followed. Police ended up pulling them over outside the Western Beef supermarket on Forest Avenue.

Jewel, who was driving, looked over at Eric.

"Did I forget to signal?" she said. "What did I do?"

"Nothing, babe," Garner said. "Just pull over."

A police officer walked up to Jewel. "License and registration," he said.

Jewel was driving without a license. The officer sighed.

"Step out of the vehicle," he said.

As Jewel tells it, the police tossed the car, throwing all of the clothes

on the ground, as well as the shopping bags from a trip she and Eric
had taken to one of those Family Dollar stores. Police ended up arresting them both, and Eric and Jewel spent the night in jail.

The next day, Jewel went to court expecting to be charged with
driving without a license. Instead, she found out the police were
claiming she had a joint in the car, and she was being hit with a possession charge. "I had no idea," she says. She insists there was no
joint in the car. "I didn't even know the charge until I was standing
before the judge."

Garner was hit with possession charges, as well as charges for some
cigarettes in the car. They released him on a thousand dollars bail,
which was high in his experience. His business was getting more and
more expensive.

Garner thought he'd found a nice little legal loophole through
which he could quietly make money without much interference. Instead, he was becoming regular sport for a group of Staten Island
police who, he was starting to believe, probably didn't have quite
enough real work to do.

According to friends and relatives both, after this arrest Eric Garner got fed up and actually called One Police Plaza in Manhattan.
They say he spoke to the Internal Affairs Bureau and tried to file a
complaint for harassment.

This decision might seem strange on the surface, calling the police
to complain about the seizure of money that Garner was, after all,
making illegally. But it fit absolutely with Garner's temperament. He
was fixated on the idea that there had to be rules. And somewhat
naïvely perhaps, he expected the police who chased after him to follow the rules. The rules were, if they caught him in the act of selling,
so be it. Charge it to the game. But to stop his girlfriend for no reason
and then bust her for driving without a license or drugs or whatever
and use that as a pretext to take more of his money when all he was
doing was sitting in the passenger seat? That was wrong.

"His thing was, 'If you catch me, you catch me, I'm not gonna
argue,'" recalls Jewel. "'But if you don't catch me, don't go making
up a case.'"

Rules were all he wanted. Everyone knew that the government
didn't care about the law; if it did, Jewel's landlord wouldn't be free
to run his business in open violation of dozens of building codes. If
the law mattered, cops wouldn't be stopping and frisking hundreds of

thousands of people every year in violation of the law. Eric knew that the city didn't run according to the law but according to the unwritten rules. But those rules needed to be followed or there was no way for a person to live. If the cops could stop him from doing his business—the only business left to him—whenever they wanted, on whatever pretext they could find, according to nothing more than their own whims, then there were no rules, just chaos. Friends and relatives say his complaint led to a visit and interview by Internal Affairs officers. To this day, many members of Garner's family believe that this IAB episode led to trouble for officers of the 120th Precinct, which increased the level of hostility between Garner and the local cops.

Garner's stepfather, Ben Carr, a taciturn, serious man who after Eric's death could be found most every day sweeping a sidewalk memorial at the site of Garner's homicide, insists that the police had it in for Eric from the moment he called Internal Affairs.

"They weren't going to let that go," he says.

The NYPD has declined to comment on whether or not Eric Garner ever initiated an Internal Affairs investigation. Freedom of Information requests on the subject were rejected. But one thing is certain: by late 2013, the police had become a serious problem for Eric Garner.

Meanwhile, after the fire, Jewel was in a panic. The school year was about to start and she didn't know where to keep her kids.

Eric was not a solution. He couldn't have his own place and had moved back in with his mother. New York is one of many states where a person with a drug conviction can't get public housing. In fact, in many places in America, a convicted murderer can get public housing but not a former drug dealer.

That left renting privately, and even though he could certainly have gotten together a first and last month's rent, getting a lease with no credit, no on-the-books income, and a criminal record was a different story. It was a nonstarter, just like getting his name on a car loan or a mortgage or a credit card or anything else.

Eric Garner's name, like his wardrobe and his health, was shot. By that time in his life, he'd actually gone through two names. Eric Garner was the name on his birth certificate, Garner being the name of his father, Elliott Garner. But when he started hustling in his teens, he switched and began using his mother's maiden name, Flagg. His first arrests were under the name Eric Flagg, and eventually, after he'd run up enough of a record on that name, he decided to switch back to Garner.

But by 2013, the Garner name had its own problems. To find a place to sleep, drive, or do a hundred other things most people take for granted, he had to depend on a circle of friends and relatives, mostly women, whose names were still good. As someone who had defined himself even as a child as the man of the house, it was humiliating. And now he was about to endure one more humiliation.

With four kids and nowhere to go, Jewel ended up in a temporary housing facility called Help 1, on Blake Avenue in Brooklyn. The setup wasn't bad: two bedrooms, a kitchen area, and a bathroom. But the rules were strict. Even as a grown woman, Jewel couldn't have company in the room at night. There was a seven thirty curfew. And she definitely couldn't have a man who was not her husband sharing her bed.

Eric, who turned forty-three that September, was being kept from spending a night with his girlfriend. It was like having a slow dance refereed by a high school chaperone.

Jewel and the kids, meanwhile, began a new, grueling routine, with the children still commuting to school in Staten Island every day.

By November, Jewel had another thing to worry about. One night in the shelter, she sat in the bathroom, staring down at some surprising news. "I was in the bathroom, pregnancy test in one hand, cigarette in another," she says. The test was positive. "I was like, 'You can't be serious.' Like, 'Fuck, fuck, fuck.'"

She called Eric, still holding the test and the Newport. "We're about to be parents," she said.

"Oh, my God," he answered.

Jewel wanted the baby. "I wasn't trying to go to the chop shop," she says. "That wasn't going to work."

They talked and tried to make plans, but what Jewel didn't know was that Eric had made plans of his own. Eric had decided to give Esaw another chance.

On Bay Street, on the rare occasions when he brought it up, Garner told his friends that he was only moving back in with his wife because he had nowhere else to go. He talked a big game about being a ladies' man and told his friends not to think anything of the fact that he was going back to his wife of so many years. He also said he couldn't keep living with his mother, who wouldn't abide him keeping illegal cigarettes in the home.

But there was more to it than needing a stash spot. Some part of Garner still loved his wife, despite all the wicked episodes between them, and the profound personal problems they'd both had over the years. For a man who was open about so many things, this was one of his most closely held secrets.

"Love is a powerful thing," his daughter Erica remembers. "To be in love with someone who has [issues] and not give up, or degrade them . . . he was a strong man. He took a lot. And he loved her."

EIGHT ERIC

By the spring of 2014, Eric Garner was back living with Esaw and still working his cigarette business. It had been a long, cold winter. He was having a harder and harder time on Bay Street. His margins were getting smaller.

It wasn't only a matter of not being caught in the act of selling untaxed cigarettes. It was also a question of not keeping all of his money and/or his smokes in one place, where they could all be confiscated.

One way to diversify his risk was to disperse it to others. You give packs and cartons to other people on the street, and they do the selling and the holding. He had one man doing his early early morning business. Another, also named Eric, a younger Latino man who was the son of a navy cook, handled some of his inventory, particularly during the rush-hour traffic.

Young Eric today says he got packs for eight dollars and would sell them for nine. He sold loosies for fifty cents apiece, which came out to ten dollars if you sold a whole pack that way. "So I made a dollar selling packs and two dollars selling loosies," he says now. "But those packs went fast. Like in minutes usually, especially when it was busy in the mornings."

That was great for Eric's workers, but every pack that someone else sold was money lost for Garner. He was going through an extraordinary amount of effort just to make a few dollars—arranging for the drives to Virginia, stashing the inventory, dealing out cartons to his crew, and, finally, handling the bulk of the street sales himself. The effort seemed magnified in the winters. He would stand on the corner, sniffling and wheezing, stomping his feet to keep the circulation going, eyes peeled all the time for someone with fifty cents to spare.

Despite the fact that he went to great pains not to be caught with either a lot of money or cigarettes on his person, it didn't always work out.

On the afternoon of March 28, 2014, he was walking out of the check-cashing storefront on the corner of Bay and Victory when police stopped him. They asked him where he was going and asked for ID. Garner protested that he didn't have any ID on him. They asked where his ID was.

"It's in my car," he said.

"Let's go to your car," they told him.

He went with the police to his car, which was parked around the corner. While he looked for his wallet, police took the opportunity to search inside the car. They found a carton of untaxed cigarettes and arrested him on the spot.

He was brought to jail and charged with selling untaxed cigarettes and slapped with a thousand dollars bail, again, an extremely high amount for such a small offense. He was already out on thousand-dollar bail as a result of charges from the previous August's car stop. Even that bail had seemed high, but that at least had involved a drug charge.

Now he was having to pay a thousand dollars over cigarette charges alone. When he went back out on the street, he couldn't stop talking about it. Now even when he didn't have cigarettes on him on the streets, he wasn't safe.

The stakes kept getting higher and higher, the odds worse and worse.

His wife, Esaw, says he had a large amount of cash vouchered after that March arrest and also had his cellphone taken. She claims that Garner was hoping to do a stint in jail in exchange for the return of his money.

"His idea was, 'Before I step in anybody's cell, you put the money in my wife's hand,'" she explains.

His mother, Gwen Carr, remembers Eric talking about the same thing. She says that after one of his arrests that spring, he'd been told by a police officer that he had to do ten days in jail.

"He said they told him, 'You're gonna do ten days,'" she says. "And he said, 'I'll do the ten days. Just give me my money. I'll come in and I'll do the ten days.'"

. . .

The police weren't Garner's only problem.

Tompkinsville Park wasn't the South Bronx or even Staten Island's notorious Park Hill projects, also known as Killa Hill. But it wasn't completely safe, either. Where you had drugs, you had danger. The police were always picking people up and springing them, and you never knew who was informing and who wasn't.

DiDi, from a park bench, would cast a hand across the daytime crowd. "These people are always getting locked up," she says. "They get caught with some shit on them. Then the next thing you know, they're getting their snitch checks. There are people who will deal with you and then go right around the corner and call the police."

For that reason, Diana didn't deal with new people. "There's a lot of informants running around. I don't want you near me or in my building. I'm not doing anything illegal, but get away from me, you know what I'm saying?"

At least twice Eric was attacked on the street by young kids trying to rob him. The first time, back in 2011 or so, he fought off three young men in the park. Years later, Doug Brinson and a local black Muslim named Frank, often seen on the block dressed in a suit and tie, recalled the spectacle of three not quite men bouncing off the massive Garner, who stayed on his feet and never once went down.

"He whipped their asses," Frank says, whistling.

"That man didn't play," agrees Doug.

In that incident, the kids eventually got tired and ran off with nothing.

But in 2014, shortly after his March arrest, Garner was robbed again, and this time it hurt.

A young man in his late twenties, someone Garner not only knew but knew was part of a Staten Island chapter of the Bloods, offered to buy a carton. He told Garner he didn't want to buy it on the street and asked if they could do it inside.

Garner shrugged and said that was fine.

The two then ducked into the Boom-Boom Room.

There were two other young men inside, and Garner quickly found himself surrounded. One of the men was armed. Garner didn't resist and handed over his smokes and his money, north of eight hundred dollars.

Later, when Garner told McCrae what had happened, McCrae

stared back at him, wondering if something was wrong with his friend. Was he slipping?

"Man, how did you let that happen to you? You didn't see that coming?"

Garner just shrugged.

The two incidents—the arrest and bail and the street robbery—happening in such quick succession put Garner in a hole. He'd been beat for large sums of money twice within days, and he needed to keep his business going. To keep his head above water, he had to borrow money from a local storekeeper. He would have been fine soon enough had the police not stopped him again, just as he was getting back on his feet.

The next arrest was on May 7. This time, he wasn't carrying very much on him, just about six packs or so, when he spotted police cars circling the park. He pointed them out to McCrae. "I'd better go," he said, then slowly walked down Bay Street to a nearby bodega, where he hid in the bathroom.

He waited for about twenty minutes, popped his head out, and saw the police were now parked outside. He went back into the bathroom and waited some more, hoping they'd leave.

No luck. "He came out and they were still there," McCrae remembers. Garner walked out of the store and tried to go down the block, but it was no use. Police rushed him, cuffed him, and brought him to the 120th.

Even by Staten Island standards, the case stank. The police didn't even try to charge him with selling cigarettes, just possession, which of course raised the question: If police didn't see him selling anything, then why were they searching him and finding what was in his pockets in the first place?

Even the judge in the case seemed skeptical. He released him without bail, which in the context of the borough's ongoing squabble with Garner was a bit of a middle finger to the police and their dubious arrest. After all, Garner had been hit with thousand-dollar bail decisions in his previous two cases.

But the judge didn't go so far as to throw the case out, which is characteristic of how the system often operates. Even when the police get sloppy, the convictions conveyor belt still keeps moving forward. It may slow just a little, but everything keeps moving in the same direction.

Garner was gloomy after the bust. "He was getting locked up more and more," Jewel says.

The news wasn't all bad that spring.

Garner's sons were out of care, back home, and doing well. The now six-foot-eight Eric Jr. was getting attention as a budding basketball star. On the streets, Garner talked about his son constantly. He bragged up and down Tompkinsville about his exploits, said he was a better athlete than his favorite football player from the Giants, Plaxico Burress.

The dream started to become a reality in the second week of April 2014. Eric and his son went to Newark for a few days to visit Essex County College, which was considering offering a scholarship to Eric Jr. He left for that trip in an excellent mood.

Then on April 12, 2014, Jewel woke up feeling unwell. She had moved back to Staten Island by then, having gotten out of the Help 1 shelter in Brooklyn. She brought her four children into a small, single-family, Section 8–subsidized home not far from Tompkinsville. It had plain pine floors and there were a few cracks in the walls, but it was her own space, finally, and her mood was lifting again. But then on that April morning, everything changed.

All of Jewel's other children had been born at term. "They were all eight pounds," she says. It never occurred to her, when she awoke that morning and found herself in discomfort, that she might be in labor.

"I was at twenty-seven weeks," she says. "'Scared' is not even the right word. I was traumatized." At about eight thirty in the morning, she got into an ambulance with her son Cassius and her sister Tanisha, aka Pebbles.

She was calling Eric's cellphone frantically, but it kept going to voice mail. By the time they reached the hospital, Jewel was obviously in labor. Finally Eric called back and Jewel explained that she was in the hospital.

"For what?" he asked. The due date for the baby was July 12, three whole months from then.

Garner wasn't ready for this news. "Oh, God," he said. He told Jewel to call his mother and explained that he would get to her when he could.

At the hospital, the news was bad. Doctors huddled up and explained that they would have to do an emergency C-section. "We don't want to risk you straining or her turning; she's too little," they told Jewel. "We have to go get her."

Nearly a full day after admission, Jewel had the C-section. Legacy Garner was born on April 13. She weighed two pounds, one ounce. Pictures of her show an almost impossibly small child who had to be intubated and given regular transfusions to stay alive. She had her father's face, but she also had his asthma.

When she was born, her father wasn't there. He was still away with Eric Jr. and didn't get back until well after the birth.

When Eric finally did arrive, the mood in the hospital wasn't exactly celebratory. "It was just no words. Neither one of us really had words as we stood there," Jewel recalls. Still in recovery, she was angry. "I was like, 'You missed the birth,'" she says. She was also in a state about Legacy's health. Eric kept talking to the doctors for her, but she wasn't hearing it.

"I was just like, 'I'm over all of these people,'" she says. "These doctors, they keep saying she's fine, and I'm not seeing anything fine about any of this."

Jewel was under no illusions. She knew things were probably beyond repair between her and Eric. "The trust was gone," she says. So the scene at the hospital was melancholy.

Legacy Garner was destined to stay in the hospital for nearly two months before coming home. She was so tiny that touching her was dangerous. Jewel's father remembers that even months after her birth, he was afraid of breaking her bones just by holding her.

As Jewel now sees it, there was a benefit to her premature birth. Eric Garner got to meet his daughter. Legacy's due date was July 12, which turned out to be the last week of Eric Garner's life.

"I could have had her the nineteenth, I could have had her the twenty-fifth, you know?" Jewel says. "I'm just thankful that she had those three months with him."

. . .

Eric and his oldest daughter, Erica, stayed close throughout the years, but it was a complicated relationship. This was particularly true in the last year of his life, when Eric went back to Esaw.

"He was with her and I was fighting with her," she remembers. "So it was awkward."

Erica saw Staten Island as a kind of sanctuary. By 2014, she was a young single mother who was struggling with money and trying to make some kind of living working at a Dunkin' Donuts in Long Island City. At the time, she was living in Far Rockaway, a good distance from Staten Island.

Still, every now and then, she would take a bus to Staten Island to go see her father. "Even if it was just for twenty dollars and a cigarette, it was a break," she remembers. "And he used to talk to me."

She remembers particularly one meeting they had in early spring 2014. "It had to be April or May, because it was still a little cold," she remembers. She came to Staten Island and sat in the front seat of his SUV, talking. Erica was despondent. She was stressed about money, angry that her opportunities seemed so limited. She was glad for the job at Dunkin' Donuts, but was that all there was? How was she expected to live, and with a daughter?

"I don't know," she said. "Maybe I should just go out and sell drugs. It's easy money, isn't it? You did it, right?"

Garner stared at her.

"Listen," he said. "What I did, back then, I did because I had to stand up as a man and take care of my family. I didn't have choices. But you do. You have people who will love you and help you. Don't go down that road."

Erica asked her father how he was. She could see that he wasn't well, that he had gained an enormous amount of weight, and that his diabetes had worsened.

"Me? I'm fine," he said.

But she could see it wasn't true. She thinks back on that moment now. "The thing about that last year is that he really was in pain." She pauses. "My father suffered," she says.

But for all the problems he was having with police and with his health, and with getting stuck up on the streets, it wasn't all bad for Eric. The pride over his son's possible entrance into college had him beaming. His children were all out of care. There were disruptions, but some semblance of normalcy, too, was returning to his life. It wasn't perfect, but at least his relationships with his kids were getting better.

On Father's Day, June 15, Eric met all of his older children out at Sternberg Park in Brooklyn. While the other family members hung out and ate barbecue, Garner pushed his two granddaughters—Erica's daughter, Alyssa, and Emerald's daughter, Kaylee—on a swing inside the park.

At one point, Erica noticed that her father had been gone so long, he hadn't spent any time with anyone else. She looked and saw him pushing the two girls, one after the other, lost in thought.

She walked over to the swing set.

"Dad, do you want a break?" she asked.

He shook his head. "What? No, I'm good," he said, and kept pushing, and pushing.

Thursday, July 10, 2014, was a day of mixed emotions.

Garner had just found out that his son had been accepted for a scholarship. He had a picture on his phone of his son signing papers for Essex County College and was showing it around Bay Street. "He couldn't stop talking about Eric Junior," says McCrae, whose own son was a budding football star. "Went on and on about that shit. I must have seen that picture a hundred times."

Because of this, maybe, Garner was particularly impatient when police stopped him later that day.

The NYPD has not confirmed that this incident took place. Still, the city's police union would later say that Garner had been "warned" to stop selling cigarettes a week before his death, a likely reference to this incident.

In any case, many on Bay Street say Garner was in that same check-cashing storefront on the corner of Bay and Victory when police tried, again, to arrest him for selling untaxed cigarettes.

This time he didn't even have six packs in his pockets. He had maybe a pack or two at the time he was stopped.

"What, I can't have a pack of cigarettes?" he snapped.

Police argued with him. Garner recoiled, stood up to his full height, and said flatly that he wasn't going to jail that day. Not on this particular day, not when the news was so good.

"Fuck this shit, it's too hot," he said to the police. "I ain't going."

James remembers that day. "He told them, 'You're not taking me nowhere,'" he says.

There was a brief standoff, but ultimately police let it go.

Ramsey Orta was like Eric Garner in the sense that he didn't come to Tompkinsville Park to hang out but to make money. Lean, wiry, and light skinned, the twenty-two-year-old sold pills and dope. Despite his slight frame, some in the park found him intimidating and unpredictable. He'd even tried to take Eric Garner for a pack of cigarettes once, which didn't go over well, although they later became friends of a sort, despite the fact that Garner was much older.

On the street, Ramsey was known to have a temper, and there was one thing he wasn't shy about: he hated cops.

He had his reasons. When Orta was still in his preteens, he pulled a knife in a fight at school and ended up getting sent away to a youth reform facility in the Bronx called Spofford.

This notorious dungeon-like youth prison would eventually be closed down in 2011 amid complaints of guard abuse and unsanitary conditions. Ramsey had the bad luck to be there in its last days. He says the guards were too lazy to do their jobs and used to get the kids to do the dirty work.

"[The guards] used to pay other inmates to try to keep the house in check," he says. "I was actually one of the kids that was offered food from the outside to beat up other kids."

The way Orta tells it, the guards gave special privileges to their junior goon squads. "I used to get food from the street. I used to get longer phone calls. More visits. I used to get to do whatever I wanted in the house that I was in," he says.

"It was more like the cops would rather sit there and babysit than do they jobs, so they let us do their jobs.

"And us doing their jobs was violent. Beating each other up."

At Spofford, Ramsey says he was asked to target any kid who'd done anything to incur the wrath of authorities.

"It was like, 'He makes the house hot, he's gotta go.' Or, 'He's always breaking things, he's gotta go.' Or, 'He's a thief, he's gotta go,'" he says.

After Spofford, he started getting in trouble almost right away. "It was a string of . . . getting high, getting trouble, little bullshit robberies here and there," he says. From there it escalated. He had cases for menacing with a gun, assault, and drug dealing. There was a sex-assault case that was dismissed. Each time, Orta kept getting out with relatively thin penalties, a fact he now points to as more evidence of how crazy the system is.

"I have over twenty-seven arrests, and fucking violent arrests and felonies and all that, why haven't I done real jail time?" he says. "Why is that, if I'm such a criminal?"

In May 2014, Orta got busted again, this time with a fifty-one-year-old man named Michael Price. In this bizarre case, Ramsey seemingly got arrested for ripping off a customer. The indictment describes how he received ten dollars from a man in return for an "undisclosed item," and that instead of delivering, he told the man, "Fuck you, you're beat."

That case was still open when Orta's problems really began a few months later. This also happened to be the day that started Ramsey Orta down the road to being famous.

The date was July 12, 2014. It was a Saturday afternoon. Orta watched as a figure named Jeff Thomas, who went by the nickname Blacko, was approached by police.

Thomas had some things in common with men like Garner, John McCrae, and James Knight. He was past forty, African American, originally hailed from Brooklyn, had a record for drug dealing, had done time, and now called the quieter Staten Island his home. By all accounts he was long since out of the drug game, but he liked to come to the park, drink, and hang out.

"Blacko liked to get his drink on, but he's a good dude," is how McCrae puts it.

Two other facts about Thomas: he liked chess, and he had false teeth.

"We was playing chess, listening to music, shit like that," Orta recalls. "He was playing with the false teeth in his mouth. And the cops supposedly thought it was crack."

Thomas was pondering a chess move and playing with his dentures when suddenly he looked up and saw that he was surrounded by police.

"Open your mouth," they said.

Police questioned him about what was in his mouth, apparently thinking he had drugs stashed in there and was trying to swallow contraband.

Thomas explained: I just have false teeth.

Police knocked him off his chair and tossed him to the ground. In an instant the usual arrest ritual was under way. He had two cops, a Hispanic man named Geovani Sanchez and a female officer described in court papers as a Jane Doe, on top of him. They were pushing Thomas face downward into the sidewalk.

A third officer, tall and red faced with a close-cropped head, stood behind Thomas and pulled out his nightstick.

Orta took out his cellphone and started filming.

The police version of the story is that an officer on the scene spotted an open container of alcohol near Thomas and that Thomas refused to produce ID at police insistence. But he was never charged with an open container violation.

However it got started, the way it finished is that Thomas took a beating in broad daylight. The red-faced John Doe officer behind Thomas started whacking his shins with the stick, while the other two police restrained and cuffed him.

If this was over an open container of alcohol, why the hell was this necessary?

Orta by then was filming, and the rest of the incident was captured.

"Stop it!" a woman shouted. "Leave him alone!"

But the police repeatedly slammed his legs. Orta started shouting at the policeman swinging the stick.

"You fuckin' big pussy!" he shouted. "Yo, he's beating him up! Why y'all doing that?"

When Orta got too close, the officer turned and raised his club in Orta's direction. The idea of whacking the kid with the camera seemed to flash through his head, then he seemed to think better of it.

"I wish you would swing that shit at me!" Orta yelled. "Yeah, swing that shit at me, g'head! G'head, tough guy!"

The officer turned around.

There is a strange phenomenon in some of these police videos. It's clear that in some cases, police are not only aware they're being filmed, they also start acting, to affect the interpretation of the scene.

In this case, someone among the officers began shouting at Thomas, who was already on the ground: "Stop resisting!"

But Thomas didn't look like he was in much shape to resist. He was already facedown and handcuffed. They kept hitting him on the legs anyway.

"Look at his legs," Orta shouted. "You got a lawsuit, Blacko!"

Police started telling Orta to back up.

"Step back," said one.

"You can tell me as many times as you want, I know my rights," Orta snapped.

"Back the fuck up. Record that shit over here."

"Y'all tough as hell beating on niggers," Orta yelled. "Y'all tough as hell with them sticks!"

Police hauled Thomas away.

Thomas reportedly tested negative when they checked his system for drugs. He couldn't have swallowed anything. And if he never had an open container, then basically it was just one more stop gone wrong, a beating in broad daylight over nothing.

But the police didn't fold their hand. They followed the usual play-book and charged Thomas with obstructing government administration and resisting arrest.

"The police are like a gang," Thomas said at the time.

Later on, the city quietly ended up dropping all charges against Thomas, all but admitting there was no real reason for the original arrest. Thomas himself vanished from Staten Island a few weeks later, not wanting to be in police crosshairs. The word on Bay Street was that he went to Brooklyn somewhere. He would later hire a lawyer and file a federal lawsuit against the Staten Island police.

It was a textbook case of what police and lawyers both call "test-a-lying." A police officer will come into court at a probable cause hearing, for instance, and a judge will ask him why he pulled over so-and-so's car.

The officer will respond in a deadpan: "I saw drugs lying on the center console of his vehicle." Defense lawyers laugh about the omni-present "center console" detail in arrest warrants.

The drugs in reality will turn out to have been found in a jacket pocket, or under the seat, after an illegal fishing expedition. But the police will tell it in court another way. Particularly in misdemeanors and drug cases, cases without profile, judges routinely buy these dubious bits of testimony and let dirty cases move through the system.

Judges rarely throw out police testimony, and even when they do, actual charges of perjury against a police officer are rare. That doesn't mean that all or even most police are dirty. It just means that in places like Staten Island there's little downside for police to cutting corners on arrest warrants and searches. If instead of waiting to see an actual crime committed, you want to just grab a guy off the street and shake him to see what comes out of his pockets, there's a very good chance that it won't stop your case from moving forward.

Eric Garner's court-appointed attorney that summer was Legal Aid's Joe Doyle. At around the same time that Jeff Thomas was getting busted, Doyle had a client who came in facing weed charges. He'd been arrested after police claimed they smelled weed from inside their cruiser, one hundred feet away from the suspect. And they told that story in court. And it flew.

"The judge was like, 'Okay,'" Doyle says, shaking his head. "What can you do?"

Sometimes these half-legal or even plainly illegal arrests and searches turn up bags of weed or knives or other contraband. But sometimes the busts come up snake eyes, and all you end up with is a guy with false teeth and bruises all over his body. Or worse.

Eric Garner spent all summer telling those close to him that he was exhausted being out on the street. "He was really tired of it, he really was," says Esaw.

He was only forty-three, but he felt much older. He would talk sometimes about somehow getting away from the streets and spending his later years watching his grandchildren. Garner had good memories of visiting his grandmother's apartment in the Coney Island Houses as a child and wanted to re-create that experience.

He told Esaw, "I'm ready to sit on the porch and sip mint julep and watch the kids run around in the front yard."

"That was his dream," his wife says. "His dream was for us to get a house and to have the grandkids running around and him just sitting there sipping his mint julep, as he called it." She laughs. "He was ready to settle down and stop hustling and just be at home."

His daughter Erica also remembers her father talking about just wanting a little space to himself.

"All he really wanted was a house," she says.

Throughout that summer, Garner remained in contact with Jewel, who brought Legacy home in June. Garner would come by to see the little girl. He would talk with Jewel, too, about getting off the streets. She also noticed that his health seemed to be worsening. Sometimes, when he came over after a day out on Bay Street, his feet would be so swollen he would have difficulty getting his sneakers off. But he refused to go to a doctor.

When Garner talked to Jewel, his fantasies were even more modest. He didn't even need a house. He just wanted to get off his feet.

Jewel had long talked of a plan to get out of Staten Island and move south, to someplace like Georgia. Her idea was that he could get a little smoke shop there.

Eric for the most part didn't go for the plan. He didn't like the idea of being away from his kids and grandkids.

But one detail about the Georgia idea appealed to him. The fantasy smoke shop would have a stool.

"That was the idea," says Jewel. "To sit down."

On the night of July 16, 2014, Garner was walking through Tompkinsville with a friend when he saw a commotion on the street. It was a young relative of Diana's and McCrae's, whom we'll call Chuckie. He had a rep for always being high on something and not being able to get his life in order. Garner later said he saw the boy robbing a man of his wallet.

Still stinging from being robbed a few months before, Garner watched as the young man snatched the cash and then ran right past Garner toward Victory Boulevard.

Garner walked up to the man who'd been robbed and advised him to call the police. Word quickly circulated on the street that Garner had given information to the cops about the robbery. It was bad. Police were the enemy: historically, practically, in every way. Garner, whose rep on the streets was impeccable, was being talked about in the wrong way—as a possible snitch, no less—for the first time.

That night, Garner did not sleep well. "He was really sick," Esaw says. "He wasn't sleeping."

She and Eric had also been fighting all week. She had been telling him to get off the street. "The cops know who you are," she said. "They're going to keep picking on you."

Garner answered, "I can't make money staying at the house."

On the morning of July 17, they rehashed the same argument. Garner suggested he could get his work in early, before the police showed up. "I'll go in earlier," he said. "And if I see the police, I'll go home."

Esaw protested, but Garner didn't want to hear it. "The rent was due, the cable was due," she says now.

On the way out, he asked her what she was making for dinner.

"Pork chops, fat boy," she said.

"You ain't so slim yourself," he answered, and left.

When Garner arrived at Bay Street that morning, the park crowd wanted to know what had happened the night before with Chuckie. Diana was the first to approach him. She remembers being struck by how bad he looked physically, worse than usual. He looked haggard and tired and agitated. "This is awful to say, but I remember thinking, 'Damn, this man ain't gonna live a long time,'" she remembers. She wondered if maybe the agitation came in part because he knew people on the street were "bad-talking" him about the incident the night before.

"He was hearing it from people," she says. "And I stopped him right on the corner and asked him about it. He said it wasn't true, that he hadn't been snitching. And that's okay, I wasn't on [Chuckie's] bandwagon anyway, I knew what he was like. So I let it go. I talked to him about it a few more times throughout the day, but I let it go."

It was different with McCrae, with whom Garner had a loud argument on the street that morning, at about ten. McCrae angrily confronted him. Garner shouted right back, recounting the story of McCrae's young relative zooming past him with a handful of cash.

"I didn't know [Chuckie] was no track star," snapped Garner.

"I didn't know you was no snitch," shouted McCrae.

The two men almost came to blows. Then they separated, the argument unresolved. McCrae left the park and would never see Garner alive again. He would spend a lot of time thinking about that moment. Years later, when asked why he thought Garner told the cops about the boy, McCrae would shake his head.

"I don't know, man," he'd say. "Fucking Eric, he probably thought he was helping him. I don't know."

Shortly after the exchange with McCrae, Eric's mother, Gwen, called. They hadn't spoken for a few days, which was unusual; Eric talked to his mother most every day. She was calling to remind him, among other things, that she had a family reunion planned for that weekend.

"I said, 'Don't forget,'" she recalls.

"I didn't forget," he said. "What do you want me to bring?"

"Bring water and soda," she said. "We got the rest."

"Okay."

"Okay, I'll see you Saturday, Eric."

"Okay, Ma."

"Love you, Eric."

"Love you too, Mom."

James Knight's normal routine was to volunteer at Project Hospitality in the morning, then come up to Bay Street in the afternoons to hang out. There was a small group of people with whom he passed the time, Eric Garner being one of them. He and Garner frequently passed whole afternoons sitting or standing next to each other.

When he arrived at Bay Street on the afternoon of July 17, Knight was worried about his friend. He'd heard the rumors about the cops the night before and didn't believe them. He also knew the talk alone could do damage enough. Up close, he noticed that Garner didn't look well.

"Man, are you okay?" he asked.

Garner shook his head and stood up.

"I have to go to the bathroom," he said.

Garner walked down the street. He tried the Spanish restaurant on the corner of Bay and Victory, but there was no toilet in there. He ducked into the bodega across Victory: same thing. So he ended up crossing the street and going to the Medicare office.

James remembers noticing how long Garner was gone. Finally, at a little after two, Garner came back, looking distressed.

"Man," he said, "my stomach is in bad shape. I've been diarrheaing and constipating at the same time."

"You don't look so good," James said.

"I'll be all right," Garner insisted.

A few minutes passed. Garner at one point looked down at his phone and texted his wife.

I'm okay, babe. I'll be in soon.

Shortly after that, James noticed a commotion starting on the street. A park regular, a black man nicknamed Twin, and an older Puerto Rican man were squaring off to fight.

Twin's name came from the fact that he has an identical twin. No one knows why Twin has the nickname and not his brother, but that's the way it goes. Twin is easy to spot around Bay Street. He often carries a boom box around, like the Radio Raheem character from *Do the Right Thing*. He drinks a bit and has something to say to almost everyone. On this day, he apparently said something to a young woman, and the girl ran and told her father, who came to the park to confront him.

The crowd inside the park rushed over to watch the action. A man named Twan Scarlett, aka Pure, a well-known character in the park who'd caught his own beating from police six months earlier, was one of the first to sound the alarm. He was so excited to see some action he tore his shirt off and ran toward the commotion.

"It's a fight!" he shouted.

Hearing the commotion, Garner sighed, stood up, and went to break it up.

James remembers the moment when Garner stood up, because he looked down the street and saw, parked at the corner, a black unmarked police vehicle with a pair of detectives sitting in it.

"They were already here," he says. "I remember that for sure."

Though the two officers got out of the car, they didn't bother to break up the fight. There are multiple explanations for why the detectives were there that afternoon, but the one that comes closest to being the official version was relayed by the head of the police lieutenants' union, Lou Turco. Turco later told reporters that a lieutenant from the 120th Precinct had passed by Bay Street that morning. The lieutenant had seen some questionable street characters he'd gotten calls about in the past and arranged to have two detectives sent there to clear the street.

This was later confirmed by Bill Bratton himself, who would say a day later that "police officers assigned to the 120th Precinct in Staten Island and assigned to the Plainclothes Anti-Crime Unit were directed by a superior officer to address specific conditions in the vicinity of Tompkinsville Park."

Eric Garner must have been the "specific conditions" the lieutenant had been upset about.

A police officer explains that this situation is far from unusual. "You'll have a precinct where a senior officer sees a homeless guy on a highway on the way to work, or a panhandler on some spot where he's not supposed to be," the officer says. "And when he gets to the precinct, he orders a sergeant or someone to remove the guy. A few hours later, they'll send someone to pick him up."

The officer explains a key detail here. "They're going to want an arrest number, to show you did something. It's not enough just to ask the guy to move. They need a case. It's all about the numbers. But if the guy you're talking about is not breaking the law, you have to get creative."

The difference between an arrest and a simple request to move was, in the case of Garner, the whole difference.

The two detectives got out of the car and moved toward the crowd.

A wizened older gentleman named Fred Winship, another Tompkinsville regular who at the time was living in the Richmond hotel/flophouse up the street, was in the park that day.

He also picked himself up and ambled over toward the fight. He could see that Twin was mixing it up with a Puerto Rican man, but the fight never turned into a serious melee. Right from the start, Garner got between them and settled them down. "He let the Puerto Rican guy go first," Winship says.

During the fight, Winship remembers standing next to a white man wearing a green T-shirt that read "99" on the back. He had no idea the man was a policeman. "I thought he was an observer just like me," he remembers.

Word started to filter through the crowd that the cops were there. The fighters, now separated, seemed puzzled as to why the police weren't coming for them. Twin stood for a moment, not sure of whether or not to run.

"He was like a deer in the headlights," Knight explains.

Convinced finally that the police were not interested in him, Twin crossed the street quickly and got the hell out of there, following in the same direction as the other man, toward Victory Boulevard.

Once the fight was over, Winship watched as the two men ran down the street. When he saw police cars arriving, he was sure it was about the fight. "I was kind of baffled," he says. "The guys ran right past the police."

The two officers in the crowd instead made a beeline for Eric Garner, who by then had made his way back to his spot along the wall on Bay Street.

Winship was standing close enough that he heard Garner talking to the two cops. He was patting his pockets. "I got nothing," he said. "I got nothing."

Knight was standing off to the side.

Ramsey Orta, on a low-slung blue bicycle, lazily rode back and forth along the block, keeping a close eye on the situation.

All the witnesses there agree that Garner was approached more or less immediately after the fight ended. There was no possibility that he could have sold a cigarette in that time. Knight remembers absolutely that Garner did not sell anything in those frenzied seconds. Garner was still catching his breath after the excitement.

In fact, Knight says, he was certain Garner had not sold a cigarette that whole afternoon, at least not since he'd returned from the bathroom.

Even the official police explanation later on hinted at this. Bill Bratton, when he talked about it, hedged his language, saying only that two officers "approached a forty-three-year old male, later identified as Eric Garner . . . *concerning* the sale of illegal cigarettes."* Bratton hinted that what more likely took place is that a "superior officer" may have seen him selling while driving by earlier that day, then sent two detectives to scoop Garner up.

* Emphasis mine.

Selling loose cigarettes, Bratton told reporters later, was "apparently the action that the officers were asked to address at this location."

Again, this would explain why the police ignored the fight. They were likely more worried about following the orders of a lieutenant than they were about anything else that may have been going on in or around the park. Being "addressed" by a superior to deal with the situation probably also prevented the plainclothes cops from just letting the situation slide.

In any case, no official has ever said that Garner was actually selling cigarettes at that moment, except for the two police in the video, who at one point try lamely to argue that they saw Garner selling a cigarette—to Twin, who was in the middle of a fight the entire time.

In the end, none of it mattered.

The two officers who swooped in were a matched set of buffed-up little white dudes in plain clothes. Though he didn't know his name, Knight thought he recognized Daniel Pantaleo, who wore a green T-shirt with the number "99" on the back, khaki shorts, and a baseball hat.

This same officer, he believed, had stopped him and his son on the street earlier in the year. Knight and his son, James Jr., had walked into a grocery store in a different Staten Island neighborhood, passing a group of kids selling weed out front. As they walked in the store, a police car passed, and the weed dealers yelled out to the cops, "Go fuck yourself!"

The car doubled back, and by the time they reached the spot again, James and his son were back on the street. A short Italian-looking cop demanded to see IDs.

James Knight Jr. is the spitting image of his father, tall and barrel-chested. He took offense to being stopped without reason.

"What the fuck are you stopping me for?" he'd shouted.

The elder Knight apologized for his son and urged him to comply. He didn't want trouble. And the young cop looked a little off to him, like he wasn't all there. Knight had developed a sense for these things over the years and he could feel this was not a police officer worth riling up.

That incident passed without further problems.

Months later, Knight now felt sure he recognized this same officer approaching Garner.

Pantaleo's partner, Justin Damico, was in a blue shirt, a blue baseball hat, glasses, and gray shorts. Damico's forearms were covered in a swirly tribal tattoo.

They looked like two guys you might see chatting up girls in an Applebee's. They did not look like hard-core investigators.

Nonetheless, they immediately got tough with Garner, telling him it was time to go. He was being arrested.

James backed up, as did everyone else on the street.

Orta took out his phone and started filming what became an internationally infamous exchange.

"Let's go," Damico said.

"For what?" Garner snapped. "I didn't do anything."

"For selling cigarettes."

"I didn't do shit," Garner snapped.

He began to plead his case.

"I was minding my business," he said. "There was a fight, and I stopped it, and you come after me? You leave those fighters to walk away? Are you serious?"

One of the two officers turned to Orta.

"Take a ride down the block," he said.

"I live here," snapped a defiant Orta.

"You can't stand here," the officer replied, incorrectly.

Orta didn't budge and kept filming.

Meanwhile, Garner's anger and confusion were building. He seemed not to be able to process the idea that even when he *didn't* sell cigarettes, he could be arrested.

He asked Pantaleo and Damico, again, what he was being arrested for. They said selling cigarettes.

"To who?" Garner shouted.

Damico pointed down the street in the direction of Victory Boulevard, where Twin had run away.

"That's who was in the fight!" shouted Orta.

"Are you serious?" Garner asked.

"Yo, boss, that's who had the fight!" Orta repeated.

The two police hovered in and out, alternately approaching and retreating from Garner. Knight remembers Pantaleo calling for backup. "He was getting on the radio, calling for more," he says.

Garner meanwhile was making it clear that he wasn't budging from the spot. At some point in the confrontation it seemed to dawn on Garner that these two officers had come for him specifically, that they'd ignored a fight to get him, and that there was nothing he could have done, or more to the point nothing he could have avoided doing, to have headed this situation off.

His arrest may have been inevitable from the moment he woke up that morning.

Even worse was the fact that this harassment was coming from two undersized weightlifters, parodies of cops who, despite looking to be in their twenties, were talking to a grandfather like he was a child.

"If it had been anyone else, Eric might have gone," McCrae said later.

Garner looked at the two men and shook his head. His face seemed to express equal parts despair and hopeless determination.

"Every time you see me, you mess with me," he said. "It stops today!"

They argued some more. Garner pleaded: "I'm minding my business, Officer! Please just leave me alone!"

Damico approached as if to grab Garner, then retreated quickly. He stood for a while, staring forward, audibly chewing gum. From time to time Pantaleo spoke into his walkie-talkie.

Garner kept repeating, over and over, "I did nothing. I did nothing. I did nothing, y'all."

Finally the two police began moving toward him. Pantaleo swung his arm over a time or two, like a baseball pitcher loosening up. Backup had arrived. They were going in.

"Hands," Pantaleo said to Garner, approaching quickly.

Garner recoiled.

"Don't touch me, please," he said.

Pantaleo reached out to grab him.

Sometime later, after he'd had more than a year to ruminate on what happened on Bay Street that day, James Knight would recall another story from his younger days.

He remembered being in Brownsville in the early nineties, watching police checking people outside an old folks' home for open container violations. The sight of young white police smugly manhandling
and questioning gray-haired black folks about their beverages left
James openmouthed.

"You're talking to an eighty-five-year-old lady for carrying a can
of something, not even beer. This is an older person, who's lived
through things, someone you should have respect for," he says.
"Would you ever see that go on at an elderly home in a white neighborhood?"

This was during a time when James himself was a fugitive from a
drug charge. While he avoided detection, James watched police arrest
others for things like jaywalking and continued to be bothered by the
same thought: Are they arresting people for jaywalking in white
neighborhoods?

"It's ridiculous. Give a nigger a ticket and walk away," he thought.
"Why arrest him?"

Later, Knight would reflect on all of this and shake his head at how
similar the new policing tactics were to the excesses of America's past,
in particular the Black Codes and the Jim Crow laws.

"It's not like it's new," he said. "They just repackaged it under a
new name."

Ultimately, the fatal flaw of Broken Windows was its ignorance of
history. Even if you put the best possible spin on it and stipulated that
it was conceived by well-meaning people as a race-neutral tool for an
ostensibly race-neutral problem, in its implementation it drifted in-
exorably in another direction. To the black people who were its most
frequent targets, the real-life, nontheoretical version of the program
instantly evoked overtly racist policing programs from the past. For
them, Broken Windows and Stop-and-Frisk never had a chance of
being taken seriously as anything but the latest excuse to harass minorities.

George Kelling had the foresight to understand that the optics of
blasting homeless people with fire hoses in the Commando subway
cleanup program would be bad. But somehow nobody worried that
ticketing hundreds of thousands of people a year for obstructing pedestrian traffic or loitering might strike a particular chord with a population of people once targeted en masse for crimes like vagrancy and
"impudence" for nearly a century after the Civil War.

The Black Codes that arose in the years after the end of slavery placed criminal law at the center of almost every part of a black person's life. They barred the ownership of weapons, restricted property rights, outlawed assembling in groups, and imposed severe penalties for extremely minor crimes.

The practical impetus for these laws was often a labor shortage. A black vagrant could be taken off the streets and conscripted to work as free labor for white landowners, who of course had been stripped of a huge pool of cheap workers by the emancipation.

But even after the economic reasons for the Codes passed, the same legal concepts survived almost everywhere in America. No matter what the time period, police from the Civil War through the later Jim Crow period always had series of highly flexible laws ready if they felt the need to arrest any black person uncooperative enough not to have committed an actual crime.

Vagrancy, like a furtive movement or obstructing government administration or refusal to obey a lawful order, was so loosely defined as to be legally meaningless. Even after fighting a major battle to end slavery, white America remained fearful about integrating in any real sense. The Black Codes were transparently designed as a ready-made legal excuse to act in any situation when black people started to get too comfortable exercising their basic rights in the presence of white people.

Just as the Codes appeared after the end of slavery and the fall of Reconstruction, Broken Windows grew out of a brief but powerful moment of racial reconciliation in the sixties: the end of segregation, the passing of civil rights laws, and the launching of Lyndon Johnson's War on Poverty. The Great Society programs that came out of that War on Poverty set into motion a series of unintended consequences. The assistance programs always had a strong bureaucratic and even punitive element. The government created armies of inspectors and social workers who, in the process of administering public assistance, got involved in regulating every aspect of life in poor black neighborhoods. This regulation became even more intrusive when the Supreme Court in the seventies gave the state a permanent right to enter any home of anyone on public assistance. Even sexual freedom wasn't absolute. Housing inspectors asked single mothers who their boyfriends were, and how many nights a week they slept over, to ensure that the women were eligible for the aid they received. No other

form of government aid—from corporate welfare to agricultural sub-
sidies to the mortgage interest deduction—required this level of intimate intrusion.

With the nineties and the welfare reform movement that was
pushed by Republicans and by Bill "the end of welfare as we know it"
Clinton alike, parolees and welfare recipients all had to show proof of
employment, or else.

And thanks to the drug war, huge numbers of young men came
home from prison sentences unable to vote, live in public housing, or
obtain licenses to be barbers, pet shop owners, even sanitation workers. They were kept under constant surveillance, watched even when
they urinated for parole officers. New programs like "predictive policing" told residents of high-crime neighborhoods and people with
criminal records that even their future selves had already been judged
threats to society.

On top of all of this came Broken Windows and Stop-and-Frisk,
which had made going from anywhere to anywhere problematic,
though standing in place was just as bad.

All of this came into play in the life of Eric Garner, whose world
got smaller and smaller every single day, and who felt so much pressure from all sides in his last days, until finally he was literally crushed
under the weight of it all.

Pantaleo made the first physical contact. He grabbed Garner's right
arm with both hands. As Garner turned back toward Pantaleo in protest, Damico reached out and grabbed Garner's other arm.

Garner now turned, glanced at Damico, and recoiled, pulling his
left arm away.

The act of turning around to face Damico proved disastrous. Garner's hands were raised, and with his attention on Damico, his back
was now turned to Pantaleo, who on film disappears behind Garner's
giant upper body. This afforded Pantaleo the opportunity to snake his
right arm under Garner's right arm, reaching upward and grabbing
him by the shoulder. With his other arm, he reached up and over Garner's left side.

Pantaleo was so small in comparison to Garner that he nearly
needed to jump up to get his arm up over the man's shoulder. Because

ERIC 119

of this, he was unable to get his arm fully around Garner's neck at first, and his hand came to rest under Garner's chin.

But Pantaleo then gathered himself and pulled, seemingly with all his might, knocking Garner backward.

The two men rolled sideways together, crashing up against the plate glass of the beauty supply shop at 202 Bay. By then two more uniformed police had arrived on scene, men named Mark Ramos and Craig Furlani. They rushed in to assist. But for many crucial seconds this melee was pointedly a two-man affair, with the mute Garner struggling and Pantaleo doggedly straddling him from behind, determined to bring his man down.

Garner was caught in the crossfire of a thousand narratives that had little or nothing to do with him personally. Everything from a police commissioner's mania for statistics to the opportunistic avarice of real estate developers had brought him in contact with police that day. So he was fighting one man who rode his back, but also history.

Experienced police would later second-guess Daniel Pantaleo on a number of fronts, beginning with the question of whether or not an arrest was even necessary, given that Garner may not actually have been selling cigarettes at that moment. Also, he'd just been in the middle of a fight and was likely to be wound up, a "bad time to jack a guy up for nothing," as one currently serving New York officer puts it.

Pedro Serrano would later look at the tape and shake his head. "It's exactly what happens when a two-fifty goes wrong," Serrano says. He talked about times in his career when cops opted to get aggressive from the jump rather than just talk to a guy man-to-man. Now, he says, it's a takedown situation and you've got to call backup and brace for war. "You turned it into something else," he says.

The irony of the stats regime is that an increase in the overall volume of stops makes it an inevitability that more brutality cases will happen. Garner was the victim of that crooked dice roll. Wrong day, wrong time, wrong moment in his life, and as it turned out, the wrong arresting officer.

. . .

For a moment after the two men slammed against the window, it appeared that Garner might fall on Pantaleo. But the detective shifted sideways, and in an instant Garner was on his hands and knees, with the detective still behind him, clasping him in a chokehold.

Garner then fell to the ground and rolled slightly onto his right side, but still Pantaleo did not shake loose. If anything, he appeared to readjust and tighten his hold around Garner's neck.

As he lay sideways on the ground, surrounded by four police, Garner for one brief moment thrust his right hand out. His fingers were all extended, his palm facing upward toward the sky. He appeared to be indicating surrender and reaching for open space at the same time.

Then the outstretched hand twitched, as if in a spasm. Garner now coughed and for the first time gasped, "I can't breathe."

One of the uniform cops saw his outstretched hand and grabbed it, hoping to throw cuffs around it.

"I can't breathe," Garner repeated. "I can't breathe."

The four officers bent and twisted Garner's great body around so that his arms were now behind his back, his face pressed into the sidewalk entrance to the beauty supply shop. A hundred people a day stepped on this spot. Crucially one of the uniforms now lay atop Garner's back, increasing the pressure on his chest. Pantaleo by then had released his chokehold and repositioned himself near Garner's head.

With his right hand, Pantaleo pressed downward onto Garner's face, pushing him into the sidewalk. Pantaleo then pushed down with such force that he lifted his own body, a kind of kneeling push-up.

Garner now called out again, in obvious distress, "I can't breathe. I can't breathe."

More police arrived on the scene, and Orta was asked once again to back off. He kept filming, but it was no longer possible to really see what was going on under the pile.

Inside the beauty shop store, Kwan Lee, the store owner, heard a loud banging noise. From his usual spot near the register he couldn't see very well out onto the street, so he had no idea there was a commotion outside. But he heard one now and rushed up to the door to see what was happening.

Lee, like most of the store owners in the area, was friends with Eric Garner. He talked to him almost every day and liked the man. "I even bought a loosie from him a few times," he remembers. One of his main recollections about Garner is that right up to the day of his death, he'd never heard the man curse, which was unusual for the crowd outside the store.

"If we had old ladies, or people who used walkers coming in, he always opened the door for them," he remembers.

So he was shocked when he ran to the front of his store and saw police on top of Garner. He arrived at a critical moment, just as Garner was losing consciousness. Pantaleo, he recalls, seemed unaware of how far gone Garner was. He was still pressing down on Garner's face with all his might when Kizzy Adonis, the sergeant and ranking officer at the scene, rushed up. Adonis, a black woman, tried to get Pantaleo to release Garner.

"Let up," she said. "You got him."

It would later come out that in an internal police report on the incident prepared later that night, Adonis would tell investigators she didn't think Garner was really in trouble. "The perpetrator's condition did not seem serious" and "he did not appear to get worse," she reportedly said. But she was concerned enough at the scene to tell Pantaleo to let up.

Lee recalls at that moment, Pantaleo looked up, saw Adonis's face, and for a moment appeared confused as to who she was. He reached his hands toward his weapon at the sight of her.

"He didn't put his hand on his gun, but he put it around his gun," recalls Lee. "It was like, 'Don't fuck with me.'"

Soon after, the officers got off of Garner, who by then was unconscious, handcuffed, and facedown in the doorway of the store. Nobody was even considering the need to administer aid. Lee was mortified. He turned to one of the officers, a uniformed white man, and asked him what was going on.

"How come you're not giving him CPR?" he asked.

The cop looked down at Garner and shrugged.

"He's fine," the cop said. "He's breathing."

Minutes passed. Garner lay unattended, facedown on the sidewalk, alone.

. . .

The entire confrontation with police had taken about twenty minutes, sixteen of which were on Orta's tape.

At approximately 3:32 P.M., after Garner had lain on the ground unattended for a period of minutes, police radioed for an ambulance. A similar request was made a minute or so later. Officially, paramedics arrived at 3:36 P.M. Their behavior was filmed by another bystander, a woman named Taisha Allen who had come down to Bay Street to shop for clothes.

The medical professional who arrives on the scene either late or on time and uninterested is a consistent character in police brutality controversies. In this case, Allen captured an eight-minute scene in which Garner lay on the ground like a piece of meat, essentially ignored by officers. She would later claim that when paramedics first approached Garner, they blithely asked him to wake up, as if he was "faking it."

An EMT worker named Nicole Palmieri finally leaned over to Garner, took his pulse, and felt his neck. Another EMT named Stephanie Greenberg went to get a stretcher. In all, there were five medical professionals there, and none seemed in a great hurry to get Garner squared away.

It took some time for Garner to get into an ambulance, which incidentally was parked up the street from the actual scene. Ludicrously, Officer Damico was told to ride in the ambulance with Garner.

Eric Garner's pulse gave out at 4:15. EMTs administered CPR in the ambulance, but it was no use. He was pronounced dead at 4:34.

Gwen Carr, born Gwen Flagg, had raised six children.

Three were her own. Eric was her first, born in 1970, and her daughter Ellisha the baby, born in 1975; son Emery had come in 1972. The children's father, Elliott Garner, died in the mid-seventies. This was a primary reason Eric Garner grew up feeling like he needed to be the man in the family, even though his mother had remarried, to a North Carolinian named Ben Carr, when Eric was still young.

Of those three children, baby Ellisha was the hellion, always trying her mother. Gwen tells a story of coming home one day and hearing Eric and Emery jumping up and down on their beds. Gwen burst into the room and told them to cut it out, or else. Eric and Emery tried to blame it on little Ellisha, saying she had been the one doing the jumping, but Gwen wouldn't have it. "I heard y'all, and don't blame Ellisha, she's just a baby and she doesn't know any better." Ellisha wasn't even three at the time.

A week later, she came home and heard the same ruckus. This time, however, she heard Eric from behind the door, warning his little sister to stop jumping up and down, because their mother would hear and she would let them have it.

Gwen again threw the door open to see Ellisha jumping up and down. When she asked her daughter what she was doing, Ellisha snapped, "I'm a baby and I don't know any better."

She spent much of the seventies raising those three. Then, after she moved to an apartment in the Gowanus projects in Brooklyn, the children of her brother Joe unexpectedly came to live with her. Both Joe and his wife died young. "I knew Joe would have done it for my children," she says, about taking them in. Stevie, Kim, and little Joe came to Gwen. The neighboring kids in the Gowanus projects thought all six children were brothers and sisters.

Gwen was strong and strict and dragged herself to difficult jobs day after day, year after year to keep her family together. She worked for the New York Telephone Company in the early seventies, then had a long career working at the central post office in downtown Manhattan, and then finally became a subway operator for the MTA in the early nineties. As they would be for her son Eric, holidays were important for her. Stevie tells a story of a special Christmas tree she made one year, one that was covered all over with money as ornaments. A hundred-dollar bill was at the top.

"I think she was testing us, to see if we'd take them," says Stevie.

But they didn't. "They knew I would give them money if they asked," Gwen says.

Gwen Carr had already lived through tragedy. In 2013, her brother's son Joe, whom she'd raised and called Little Joe, was killed in a shootout in Newark, New Jersey. Joe was straitlaced and hardworking and had built up his own deli in New Jersey, as well as a contracting business called Flagg World that cleaned up vacant lots in and around Newark. Joe had made it a point to hire ex-convicts. Over the years, he'd hired hundreds of young men in an effort to get them back on their feet.

On October 27, 2013, Joe hadn't planned on going to work but wanted to help out with crowds coming to and from a local football game. Just after 1:00 P.M., three teenagers came in, robbed him, and shot him to death.

It was around that same time that Eric came home to live with his mother, after Jewel's house burned down. Gwen disapproved of Eric's cigarette business, but she also loved him and believed strongly that what he was doing wasn't a serious crime. Still, she was baffled by the amount of police attention he seemed to be attracting. She remembers having to bail him out many times, as she would frequently be his first phone call.

"He'd say, 'Ma, I got locked up,'" she recalls. "'Will you come bring me home?'" And just as he had with his wife, Eric would tell his mother to go find money he'd hidden away somewhere, to help with the bail.

"He'd say, 'Well, I got some money in my shoe, in my sneaker,'" she remembers. "I would go and I would get him, and I would tell him, 'Stop selling those cigarettes up there, because you keep getting locked up.'"

On the afternoon of July 17, 2014, Miss Gwen was doing her normal job, driving a subway car. "I operated trains from Coney Island to Astoria," she says. "I'd do two round trips a day. That was my job for that particular day, to do two round trips on the N train." Subway operators aren't allowed to have cellphones on while they drive, so she made the first leg of her trip, from Coney Island to Astoria, not knowing that terrible news awaited her.

"I have a thirty-five-minute break when I get up to Astoria. I usually sat on the bench, because it was summertime," she says. "I'd usually sit out there on the bench, and I would see who called me. That day, the phone started ringing soon as I turned the phone on. The two people who I answered first, nobody had firsthand information.

"They just told me they'd heard something. They'd heard Eric had a confrontation with the cops. Then the next person called me and said, 'Miss Gwen, I don't know, Eric, they told me that the cops made Eric have a heart attack.' Stuff just started racing in. I said, 'I got to get over there and see what's going on.'"

She wanted to leave work right away (for subway operators it's called "booking off"), but she realized she had a serious logistical problem. She was all the way in Astoria, far away from Staten Island. If she left work now, there was no way she could get home quickly, absent a helicopter ride. So she made the extraordinary decision to complete her first round trip.

She hopped back in the N train and drove a normal route back to Coney Island, her mind racing a thousand miles an hour the whole way.

When she got to Coney Island, her bosses wanted to know how she intended to classify her departure from work that day. Was it a sick day?

"They wanted to know what code," she says. "I said, 'I don't care what code you put me down for, I got to go!' And they says, 'All right, all right, call us back,' just like that."

Her husband, Ben, was waiting for her at Coney Island.

"We went. My husband already knew, but I didn't know yet. He already knew. I don't want to know the answer until I got to Staten Island, because I want to go and see what's going on. I kept on asking Ben, I said, 'Did you hear anything?'"

"No, no, we're going to go see what's going on right now," he said.

"But did you hear? People are calling me, I know they called you," she implored. "Finally he just broke down and started crying, and he told me," she remembers. "When I heard, I lost my mind. I said, 'This cannot be happening.'

"For the next forty-eight hours, I was in a daze. I don't remember a thing."

Esaw was on the phone with her daughter, Emerald, when it started blowing up.

"I got a message: 'Get down on Bay Street, your husband isn't breathing,'" she recalls.

She looked around the apartment in a panic. Her son Emery had just run outside to go to the store. "He asked me if he could hold twenty dollars," she said. "I'd said, 'Okay, get my bag.' But then he came running back in and said, 'Mom, I just heard outside that the cops choked Daddy!'"

Esaw's mind was everywhere at once. A surge of fear shot through her. "I remember I just threw on anything. Gray shirt, gray sweatpants. No bra, no underwear . . ."

Outside, she hailed a cab. "There were messages on my phone, 'Pinky, you need to go down to Bay Street.'"

Instead, she went to the Richmond University Medical Center, where Eric was due to be taken. "When I got to the hospital, I knew right away something was up," she says. "They led me all the way around the back way, away from the front where they meet people. And into a back room with just a phone and a chair."

Pinky waited in the bleak little room for just a few minutes.

"Finally the doctor came in and said, 'I'm sorry, we tried everything. But there was nothing we could do.'"

She pauses.

"They told me I could look at him one more time," she says, crying a little. "I looked in. It looked like he was sleeping."

Jewel had actually been at Tompkinsville Park earlier that day. Ironically, she had gone to the Medicaid office with Legacy, to clear up something involving her insurance. It was the place where she and Eric had met. She didn't stay long. Legacy was still tiny and frail.

"I didn't want to stay on Bay Street. It's dirty, you know?" she says. "I didn't want her outside."

She saw Eric from a distance that morning but didn't talk to him.

She got home at around twelve or twelve thirty. Legacy fell asleep, giving Jewel a little time. Her father had come over as well. "I said, 'I'm gonna fry me some chicken,'" she remembers.

When the food was ready, she sat down and ate quietly. No TV, she was just zoning out. And suddenly the phone rang. It was a friend of hers named Mink. "I didn't even know what she was saying at first. I'm like, 'What? Eric who? Not my Eric!'" She thought to herself, "Who would be crazy enough to choke Eric?"

She called Eric's sister, Ellisha, and the two women started crying on the phone. After several more calls, Jewel stepped outside and stared blankly out at the street.

"It was no more," she says. "I couldn't feel him. I couldn't feel him anymore."

A police union official would later tell a story about a form Staten Island authorities apparently filled out that night, around the time the family was learning of Garner's death. Called a UF-49 or just a 49, an "unusual occurrence report" is written up after events of particular significance. "Cases with profile," is how the official put it.

The UF-49 apparently makes no mention of any use of a choke-hold. As *The New York Times* would later report, it only cites the testimony of Taisha Allen, who is quoted as saying, "the two officers each took Mr. Garner by the arms and put him on the ground." Even this statement wasn't correct; Allen would later try to tell a grand jury that Pantaleo did in fact use a chokehold.

Absent the cellphone videos, in other words, nobody would likely have heard how Eric Garner really died. This would have been written up as an unhealthy man with asthma and diabetes who had a heart attack after a routine arrest on a minor charge.

A photographer for the *Daily News* named Ken Murray was driving through Staten Island on another assignment that day when he heard chatter over a police radio about a mobilization of police on the north side of the island. He called back to the paper's news desk and got the okay from his editor, Kevin McDonald, to check it out.

Once he reached Bay Street, he asked around and heard about a kid who'd captured the whole thing on film. Before long he was talking to Ramsey Orta, who gave him the video for nothing. "It was unusual," Murray said. "I guess he was just so outraged, he wanted it out there."

Within a few hours, the video was up and going viral around the world. Staten Island, the redheaded stepchild of New York boroughs, was suddenly at the center of the universe.

That night, Orta couldn't sleep.

"I was up at four o'clock in the morning," he says. "I was actually playing a video game, *Black Ops*. And I turned off the game, and I'm about to lay down. Suddenly this big spotlight lights up the room."

He ran to the window, looked outside, and saw a police cruiser drifting past his place. The little hand-guided spotlight near the driver's-side mirror was being aimed up and at his window.

Orta stood staring down at the street, light filling his bedroom for a moment.

The car drove away.

John McCrae had a nightmare that night. He would go on to have it on a regular basis.

He'd been at home when he got word that Eric had been attacked and rushed to the scene, but it was too late by then. Eric was gone.

In his dream, Eric would appear next to McCrae and urge him to come see something around the corner.

"He was telling me, 'Come on, come on, man, come on, man. I got a new Cadillac! Come on, man, just get in, John.'

"And I was like, 'No, fuck that, I'm not getting in your fucking car.'

"He just kept telling me to come on and get in. And I'm like, 'Fuck, man, I'm not getting in!'"

Months later, he would still have the dream.

"Bitch is always in my head," he'd say.

PART II
THE PERPETUAL
INJUSTICE MACHINE

NINE ERICA

Erica Garner was born with a striking physical resemblance to her father. She had the same deep, brooding, intense eyes, the same broad cheekbones, and, as she grew up, the same commanding voice and upright posture. Adults who knew Eric sometimes did a double take when they saw his little girl, so close was the resemblance.

Erica always wanted to be her father's favorite. As a child she worked at staying close to him. She remembers as a little girl going on family car rides and fighting with her sister Emerald to see who got to sit next to her father in the front seat of the family Cadillac.

"I always won. Always wanted to be next to Dad," she says.

She remembers the good things about him. He tried throughout his life to take care of all of the kids financially. They never went to school in September looking disheveled. "We were always in brand name," Erica says.

Erica's resemblance to her father was a big part of her identity throughout her life. At times, it was a negative, as other members of the family made her the proxy for complaints they might have had about Eric. Erica's older half sister, Esaw's oldest child, resented Eric from the time she found out he wasn't her real father. But she went after Erica because she looked like Eric, but unlike Eric, she was around.

As Erica herself grew older, she began to be more like her father in character. Some of this was natural—she was just born that way—but some of it was taught.

One day, when she was about nine or ten years old, Erica got into it with some girls at school. It was a nothing dispute, something that started in the cafeteria. "They were *Mean Girls* types, basically," she remembers. "They were giving me a hard time about where to sit. And I said something about fighting them after school."

When school ended, though, it was three girls against Erica.

"They wanted to jump me. So I ran home to my mother and father," she remembers.

This was back when the family was living on Mother Gaston Boulevard, in Brownsville.

Eric, furious, took his daughter by the hand and went back downstairs.

"Erica, come on," he said.

Erica thought Daddy was going to protect her. It went another way.

The imposing Eric Garner confronted the three little girls.

"I'm out here. Nobody is gonna jump my daughter. But if y'all wanna shoot the fair, then Erica, get down here."

In other words, if you want to fight one-on-one, my daughter will step up. Erica was mortified and chickened out. She ran back upstairs.

Eric was upset. And when he told Esaw what happened, she was upset with her daughter, too.

"You know, Erica," Esaw said, "you play Big Billy Badass with your brothers and sisters here at home, but when someone tries to fight you, you back down. It's not right."

From that point forward, Erica remembers, she never backed down from anyone. Her father added some advice.

"If a group of people want to fight you," he told her, "pick the biggest one out of them and fight that one. And the rest will run away."

As she grew up, Erica began, slowly, to take on her father's signature characteristic, the tendency toward never giving in in an argument. This wasn't about imposing physical dominance; it was about showing backbone. Father and daughter alike couldn't be argued off the spot in a dispute. On the street in Eric's last years as a cigarette salesman, it was something people joked about. But it was no joke: Eric and his first child's stubbornness were rooted deep inside them.

"We believe that we are right," Erica says. "And once we find out that we are right, you can't tell us that we're wrong. We'll research. We'll argue down to the core. We're not going to stop until you see our point of view."

Erica speaks in weirdly even, nonjudgmental tones about the troubled childhood years she spent as the daughter of an often absent father in a home environment fraught with drugs and violence. Some of the stories she tells are horrifying, but she doesn't describe them that way.

"I hear all these stories about people being on crack and the struggles that they go through, like being raped by their stepfather or something like that, or prostituted out or sold to a drug dealer," she says flatly. "I have no experience with anything like that."

But she did spend a lot of time and energy warring with her mother, with whom she had a turbulent relationship her whole life, particularly whenever her father was away in jail. Erica wrestled constantly with anger and mistrust. She reached her teens rebellious and spoiling for a fight.

Things came to a head when Erica was about fourteen. During one of her many arguments with her mother, Erica knocked over a TV stand not far from where her mother was. Esaw believed at that moment that she could no longer take care of Erica and started proceedings to put her daughter into voluntary foster care.

This is an arrangement where parents, without being forced to do so, essentially swear to the court that they are unable to take care of their child.

On the day Erica was meant to leave, city workers came and she was asked to pack up a bag and go. Her mother was sitting in the apartment weeping.

"I don't want to sign you away," Esaw said.

"If you want me to go, I'll go," Erica said.

For all of her tears, Esaw saw this as a necessity, a last-resort move to deal with an unruly daughter at a time when she was having trouble holding her own life together. For Erica it was devastating, an event that would haunt her for her whole life.

"I was like, 'Okay, I'm going to make it through this,'" Erica recalls. She moved in with a family in Far Rockaway, Queens. Her new caretakers were a deacon and his wife who had kids of their own, as well as other foster kids. This new family was a godsend for Erica, an angry and directionless child whose life began to turn around very quickly.

"I had my own room," she remembers. "They would ask me to come down and help cook and be part of things. They took me on family trips. Family vacations! There were fourteen of us, piling in a plane to go to Universal Studios. I had never known what this was like. I loved them like they were my own parents, still do."

In fact, Erica's new family offered to adopt her. Erica considered it. She went to her mother with the idea. That didn't go over well. The adoption never happened.

But she remained close her whole life with her new family, who helped usher her into adulthood. It was none too soon, as Erica became a single mother very early in life. Her daughter, Alyssa, was born in 2010, just around the time Eric Garner was coming back from jail and remaking himself as a cigarette dealer.

With her foster family's help, along with her father's counsel and support, she managed to stay out of trouble at that time and dedicate her life to her daughter. She was on the right path.

On the afternoon of July 17, 2014, just minutes before Daniel Pantaleo approached her father on the streets of Staten Island, Erica Garner called her mother for the first time in ages.

"It was hard, but I wanted to make up with her," Erica remembers.

Repairing long-broken family connections had also been a preoccupation of her father's in those months. Father and daughter were so close, they often moved and thought in sync.

In his later years, Eric had been deeply troubled by the rift between Esaw and Erica and had subtly lobbied both to patch things up. By late July 2014, Erica was only just summoning the determination to reach out. Dialing the phone was not easy that day, but she did it, extending an olive branch over her daughter's coming birthday. That she did so at this exact moment was one of the odder coincidences of this whole sad story.

"I asked if she wanted to help plan Alyssa's birthday party," Erica remembers.

The call came as a surprise to Esaw, who cried and told her daughter she was glad she'd called.

"Your father is gonna be happy," she told Erica. Eric, Esaw explained, had been asking about Erica every day when he came home. "Did she call yet?" he'd say.

The two women talked for a short while and made plans for the party. Erica hung up, pleased and full of warm emotions.

Just minutes later, her sister Emerald called in a panic.

Something had happened on Bay Street. All her sister could tell her was that their father had stopped breathing.

"I thought, 'It's hot, he has asthma, maybe he's sick,'" Erica remembers. She was working at the time at a Dunkin' Donuts in Long Island City. Immediately, she asked out of work and rushed toward Staten Island.

Before she even crossed the bay, she got a call from her aunt Elli-sha, Eric's sister.

"She told me he was gone, that the cops had killed him," she says.

She reached her grandmother's apartment in Staten Island and gathered with the rest of the family for a time. Then at about ten at night, she felt a strange urge to walk outside by herself. Without thinking about it, she drifted in a particular direction.

"I don't know why, but I went to the spot where he was killed," she says. "I remember I just stood there for a long time, almost in a daze."

Erica was not known on Bay Street, but she looked so much like Eric Garner, standing there on the spot he'd occupied for so many years, that some of the people from the neighborhood began to gather around her, drawn to her like moths to a lamp.

"They were like, 'You must be Erica,'" she remembers. "They said to me, 'Your father talked about you all the time.'"

"Like seeing a ghost," is how one of the Bay Street residents re-members it.

She stood on the spot for a long time, well into the night.

With her father gone, she was deprived of an important confidant. In place of him now rested a gnawing need for answers.

Why had this happened? Was there something wrong with the of-ficer who'd killed her father? Did he have a violent past, and if so, why had he been on the streets? Why had her father been stopped in the first place? Why didn't the other officers intervene?

These questions ate at her and wouldn't go away. The passage of time didn't quiet them down, either. Viewing everything through the prism of these questions threw the entire world into relief. There were only people who helped and people who didn't. She would see who was who. The dominant concern was to see that the officer who'd killed her father be brought to justice. She was unable to accept the idea that there might be no punishment for the offense.

Erica wasn't experienced in politics or government. She was from the streets and hadn't been able to see much of the outside world from behind the counter of a Dunkin' Donuts.

But after her father's death, when her family was suddenly thrust into a hurricane of international attention, she had to take a crash course in how the great forces of the world worked. She had to learn about the media, politics, civil law, and especially the criminal justice system.

Erica had no natural antipathy for police. They were just a fact of life growing up. In her early years she associated police with safety, but as she got older, things got more complicated. One night the police chased her and her brothers and sisters out of a park after hours, and she remembers feeling annoyed and a little frightened. But it wasn't like she spent a lot of time thinking about them.

Her father had dealt with police at the street level only. He was killed in the end by a small group of line officers, the police equivalent of infantry. It was those men, not the generals above them, who became the villains in the headlines about Eric Garner's death. In police brutality cases the bad guy is always the individual cop, never the system behind him.

Erica Garner was about to inherit her father's lifelong tangle with the authorities, but her battle would take a very different and more frustrating form—she'd be fighting the system that Eric never saw.

Police brutality cases always begin with unplanned spasms of rage or bad judgment, usually an individual police officer losing it on the streets. But before the bodies even cool, the crime moves up the chain.

From the first knock on the door, family members find themselves facing a series of intractable bureaucracies designed to make cases against police officers vanish in blizzards of political excuses and unintelligible legalese.

These bureaucracies are designed to frustrate and exhaust families bent on getting justice, grinding them down over time until finally they become dispirited and give up. The quest for answers becomes a war of attrition, and the state almost always wins. The families eventually give in and soon everything is forgotten, allowing the process to repeat itself.

The city of New York went to extraordinary lengths to disappear Eric Garner's death down this institutional memory hole, into the vast sewer of blood and unpunished murder that raged under its sidewalks. The main obstacle in the way of this process was the family, and within Eric Garner's family, the one most determined to fight back was his look-alike daughter.

Items on Loan

Library name: Warrenpoint
Library
User name: Fearon, Gerry
(Mr)

Author: Taibbi, Matt,
Title: I can't breathe
Item ID: C902235527
Date due: 24/10/2019,23:
59
Date charged: 3/10/2019,
11:52

LibrariesNI
+ +
Make your life easier
+ +

Email notifications are sent
two days before item due
dates
Ask staff to sign up for
email

In life, Eric Garner had driven everyone crazy, friends and foes alike, with his stubbornness and refusal to give in in even the smallest argument. He also had the longest of long memories. If you even once tried to beat him for fifty cents, he never forgot it.

These qualities were now reborn in his daughter's quest for answers and justice following his murder. Erica would need them for the harrowing and frustrating journey she was about to take through the city's tortuous criminal justice bureaucracy, which is designed to push her to do what she couldn't do: forget.

At first, the whole country was riveted by Eric Garner's death, as captured on Ramsey Orta's video. It seized headlines all over the world, sent people demonstrating on the streets, and had black and Latino officials howling for indictments.

"This was a murder," said State Senator Bill Perkins. "Without even being arrested, he was choked to death."

"He was left to lie on the ground for eight minutes like a piece of meat. And I say piece of meat because if he was a dog, they probably would have assisted him," said Councilman Jumaane Williams, a rising black politician loathed by police almost as much as the Reverend Al Sharpton, who was also destined to play a major role in the case.

Newly elected mayor Bill de Blasio played his part, acting the role of the abashed, mortified elected official who pleads for calm and promises action.

"Like so many New Yorkers, I was very troubled by the video," he said, promising a "full and thorough" investigation.

At the same presser, Commissioner Bill Bratton followed along, appearing subdued. The father of New York's Broken Windows strategy seemed to grasp that Garner's death might be viewed as a referendum on his enforcement strategies.

His first remarks inadvertently emphasized that the tragedy had taken place at what may have been the ground zero of Broken Windows arrests in Staten Island.

"The immediate area had been the subject of numerous community complaints by local residents and merchants," Bratton said. "Year to date at that location, there have been ninety-eight arrests for various offenses, and one hundred cease summonses issued mostly for quality of life offenses."

Under intense questioning by reporters who asked if Officer Pantaleo's aggressive response was necessary for such a minor offense, the
macho Bratton uncharacteristically demurred. He went on to concede
that a banned procedure had been used to take down Garner.

"Yes, as defined in the department's patrol guide, this would appear to have been a chokehold," Bratton sighed.

This seemed like a pretty important admission from the city's police commissioner. But he was careful to add, immediately afterward,
"As to whether in any way, shape, or form [it was] a violation of law,
that would be a determination of the District Attorney's criminal investigation."

Bratton tossed the hot potato to the next official in line, the district
attorney of the borough of Staten Island. It was there, in the office of
Dan Donovan, that the case began the time-honored process of disappearing down the rabbit hole.

What Erica remembers most about her family's first meeting with
Donovan, Staten Island's pale, balding district attorney, was the commotion.

"There were just a lot of people," she says. "It was disorganized. It
was weird."

Donovan would later boast to the press that he'd devoted more
resources to the Garner case than any he had handled since taking
over the DA's job in 2004. He said he'd put eight assistant DAs and as
many as ten detectives on the case.

During this meeting with the Garner family, which she recalls taking place eleven days after the killing, on July 28, 2014, many of these
attorneys and investigators were present. Donovan led an hour-long
meeting, during which time he promised mainly to conduct a thorough investigation. He continually stressed that whatever would happen would take a while.

In a thick Staten Island accent, he pleaded for the family's patience
and promised to leave no stone unturned in search of the truth.

Esaw began crying at one point during the meeting. Erica must
have been rolling her eyes, because Donovan kept looking her way,
perhaps sensing she wasn't buying what he was selling.

Jewel Miller was there, too, listening closely. It was no small thing
that she was being included in family matters like this, though she

got the strong sense that the family only reluctantly brought her along.

"They didn't want me nowhere," she remembers. "But the lawyers were like, 'If we don't have her, if we don't allow her some room, this could get ugly.' So they kind of spoon-fed me a little bit."

Jewel had a bad feeling about Donovan from the start. "He put it on thick," she remembers. "He said he was really going to make sure things got done. He was really going to be on top of it—turning over every stone to make sure that things got done, and so on. It was almost believable."

She pauses.

"But I'm born and raised here. I'm listening to him and I'm like, 'Fuck it, this is Staten Island. If this was Brooklyn or something, Queens, Manhattan, maybe it would be a little more believable. But I know.'"

The district attorney was born and raised in Staten Island, too. In fact, Dan Donovan grew up in the very neighborhood of Tompkinsville where all this drama took place. Only he lived there back in the seventies, back when it was more of a white neighborhood.

In a detail he didn't share with the family at the meeting, he went to the same Catholic all-boys school as the ostensible chief suspect in the case, Daniel Pantaleo, graduating in 1974.

The son of a longshoreman and a garment worker, Donovan then pursued the typical path of smart Catholic boys intent on a career in law enforcement in New York. First he went to St. John's undergrad, then Fordham law.

After passing the bar, he worked as an ADA in Manhattan under famed prosecutor Robert Morgenthau in the late eighties and early nineties. Then he returned to Staten Island in 1996 to get into politics, serving as the chief of staff to Guy Molinari, the legendary machine-pol borough president who was to Staten Island what Richard Daley was to Chicago or Billy Bulger was to Boston—a patron, fixer, and bare-knuckle fighter in the us-versus-them tribal wars that defined urban politics.

In 2003, longtime Democratic district attorney William Murphy stepped down, and Donovan was put forward as the Republican candidate. He won and quickly made his name on another case involving Tompkinsville: a death penalty verdict for a twenty-one-year-old named Ronell Wilson, who in 2003 had shot two undercover detectives who'd been trying to buy a TEC-9 semi-automatic pistol from him on St. Paul's Avenue and Hannah Street, just two blocks away from Tompkinsville Park. He later successfully prosecuted a famed member of the Wu-Tang Clan, rapper and actor Method Man, for tax evasion. Method Man was a celebrated son of Staten Island, but the wrong Staten Island.

These convictions made good headlines for winning votes south of the Mason-Dixon Line, where Donovan was very popular. But he was a virtual unknown to the rest of the island. It was hard to say what he was all about. Even his face was a mystery.

Apart from a few tufts of thinning hair and broad forehead, Donovan's features were curiously indistinct, like something drawn in sand. "I met him five times before I remembered him," says one Staten Island lawyer. "I wouldn't have been able to pick him out of a show-up."

Erica remembers listening to Donovan speaking and feeling alternately encouraged and uneasy. She also noticed something odd.

"A lot of Donovan's people were dressed wrong," she remembers. "They didn't look clean. Their shirts were ruffled. Like they hadn't prepared for the meeting or something.

"I had this weird feeling they weren't taking it seriously."

Erica went home that night feeling puzzled. She had no idea that she was about to start down a long and crooked path. During the course of a years-long effort to keep her father's case alive, Erica would find out what the families of people like Yusuf Hawkins, Amadou Diallo, Sean Bell, and so many others had already learned: in police violence cases, the law is a thousand miles high and filled with false peaks. Every time you think you've finally taken the hill, there's another ridge ahead.

In these cases, obscure exceptions and precedents are constantly unearthed to narrow the field of culpability to a vanishing point. Often, in the end, the law says that not only is no one responsible for the death of someone killed by a police officer, no one can be responsible.

Another recurring theme in these stories is that while the cases often begin as unplanned murders and assaults committed in heat-of-the-moment situations by working-class cops, they end as carefully orchestrated cover-ups committed in cold blood, through the more ethereal, polished, institutional racism of politicians, judges, and attorneys.

In other words, one murder might be the fault of a single bad cop. But many murders are almost always the fault of politicians, through the systems they construct to make those murders disappear. As Erica was about to find out, following the trail after the case leaves the streets is the hardest part of all.

TEN DAN

Erica didn't know much of anything about Mayor Bill de Blasio before her father was killed.

"All I knew was that he had a black son with a Afro," she says now, laughing.

De Blasio was a bit of a mystery to the rest of New York, too. To the extent that he had a reputation, he was thought of as one of the more openly liberal elected officials in the country. He was also deeply distrusted by the police force even before the Garner affair, in large part because of his relationship with the Reverend Al Sharpton, who was destined to play an important and controversial part in the case.

Sharpton remembers exactly where he was on July 17, 2014, the day of Eric Garner's death. "I was in Las Vegas, on my way back to the airport, when I got the call," he recalls. His National Action Network had been involved in a voting drive in Nevada when Cynthia Davis, the head of the Staten Island chapter of NAN, called and told him what had happened just hours before on Bay Street.

Sharpton spoke with Garner's mother, Gwen Carr, on the phone that evening. Before he got on a plane back east, he promised to put her son's case front and center in his weekly Saturday rally. According to the family, he also arranged to pay for Garner's funeral.

Two days later, Sharpton gave a speech at his Harlem office, making demands for justice while flanked by Garner's family members, Erica included.

It was a strange and somewhat subdued address. Erica didn't know it, but Sharpton was in a curious spot politically. For years now, and especially since the election of President Obama, Sharpton had become more of an inside player, in contrast to the firebrand activist who'd once shut down the city's trains and roadways with his remarkable "Days of Outrage" in 1988. In fact, Mayor de Blasio was a personal friend of Sharpton's. Sharpton had campaigned openly for de Blasio dating back to at least 2009, when he ran for the city's public advocate job. "I even campaigned for him over a black candidate," he says now, referring to the later mayoral race of 2013, when Sharpton supported de Blasio over city comptroller Bill Thompson.

But a key reason Sharpton had supported de Blasio was de Blasio's rhetoric on issues like Stop-and-Frisk. Like many activists, Sharpton had taken some time to understand Stop-and-Frisk as a racial issue. "When I first started hearing about it in the early nineties, under Giuliani, I remember thinking, 'What is this?'" he says. "And when I looked into it, my first thought was that this was going to be a civil liberties issue, not a race issue."

But over time, and especially following the Amadou Diallo case, Sharpton changed his thinking. When he saw data suggesting that these practices were being used disproportionately in certain neighborhoods and against certain people, he made challenging Stop-and-Frisk a priority.

Ultimately, he supported de Blasio's political runs precisely because de Blasio used such strong language on the subject. When de Blasio ran for mayor in 2013, he promised to be "the only candidate to end the Stop-and-Frisk era that targets minorities."

So Sharpton was, to say the least, mystified when de Blasio, after being elected, made an alliance with Bill Bratton, the godfather of Stop-and-Frisk. De Blasio went back in time and once again made a man Sharpton associated with the hated Giuliani regime the city's police commissioner. It was déjà vu all over again.

That made it tough for Sharpton to know at whom exactly to aim his typically thunderous sermons. He was close to de Blasio, but deeply at odds with his police commissioner. Perhaps because of this, at that first Saturday speech about the Garner case on July 19, Sharpton's rhetoric seemed robbed of its usual bite. He sounded more like an elected official than an activist.

"This is going to be a real test to see where policies are in the city now and whether the change that we feel occurred has occurred," he said, looking pained.

This was just a year after famed Princeton University professor Cornel West had attacked Sharpton for being "the bona fide house Negro of the Obama plantation," ostensibly for not being tougher in calling for federal civil rights charges for vigilante George Zimmer-

man, the man who killed a seventeen-year-old black boy named Trayvon Martin in Florida.

Sharpton surely felt the sting of critics accusing him of being too
close to certain figures within the Democratic Party. A "let's trust the
process" approach with de Blasio in the face of the globally publi-
cized Garner killing would box him in even further.

But within a few weeks, Sharpton turned things around in a classic
demonstration of his skill as a political infighter, sacrificing the bum-
bling de Blasio to gain an advantage. As political chess moves go, it
was stunning to watch.

De Blasio was also in a highly awkward political situation. As a
candidate for mayor, he'd denounced Broken Windows policing tactics and called for an independent monitor, which the police department had long resisted. His embrace of police reform was perhaps the
element of his campaign that most galvanized the city's minority and
liberal voters.

But then he won and invited Bratton back to run his police department, which immediately brought outcries from his liberal allies. In
making the announcement about Bratton, de Blasio didn't seem to
know which notes to emphasize, criticizing the "overuse of stop-and-
frisk," a strategy that he said "too often alienated communities." But
he also said Bratton was a "proven crime fighter" whose accomplishments "just jumped off the page for me."

The Garner case was therefore destined to define de Blasio's administration. It would test all of his rhetoric about police reform. But it
would also test his loyalty to Bratton. In response to this conundrum,
de Blasio made a disastrous political miscalculation. He scheduled a
roundtable on July 31, two weeks after Garner's death, to discuss
police brutality issues. The roundtable was to include religious and
community leaders, who would sit down with Bratton and other police officials in what he clearly hoped would be a political love-in.

De Blasio was cooked before the meeting even started. For one
thing, the mayor's staff seated him flanked on one side by Sharpton
and on the other side by Bratton, leaving many line officers in the
NYPD with the impression that the hated Sharpton, who had railed
against police for decades and had compared prosecutors to Nazis,
had equal rank with Bratton. That single image essentially ruined
de Blasio with police leadership forever.

Then the show started, and it was a blowout in both directions.

Bratton had built a brilliant career out of impressing journalists and liberals alike with his ability to play the role of the thinking man's cop, the tough guy with brains and a surprising sense of culture who could hang out at uptown dining holes like Elaine's and be an entertaining eighth at a dinner party of liberal-minded celebrities. The act had never failed him before, and he tried it again now. He put on a smile and talked about how tragic incidents like the Garner case could be avoided with better attention to detail.

"Training is absolutely the essential catalyst for, out of this tragedy, finding opportunity," said Bratton.

"Systematic retraining will have a huge impact," de Blasio agreed. He went on to say, "It will help us to draw the police closer to the community, and the community closer to the police."

The mayor and the commissioner both apparently expected Sharpton to strike the same "We Are Family" note. But it went another way.

Sharpton had sat seething through the entire meeting. In his telling of the story, he was ambushed. "I didn't find out Bratton was going to be there until I was on the way to the meeting," he says. He recalls being on the way to the event when he heard from Rachel Noerdlinger, a former Sharpton aide who was then chief of staff to de Blasio's wife, Chirlane McCray.

"She said, 'Rev, I know I don't work for you anymore, but Bratton is going to be there. I'm telling you even though I know you might turn around,'" he recalls. "But I thought, if I turn around, then I'm showing up Bishop [Victor] Brown and other black leaders who'll look like sellouts. And I didn't want to do that. So I went."

In Sharpton's mind, de Blasio had set him up. De Blasio, he thought, had invited him to this meeting so that he could be photographed sitting next to the police commissioner, endorsing some vague plan to do better and pledging friendship and cooperation—"a kumbaya moment," as Sharpton put it, that would de-escalate political tensions in the city.

Sharpton decided to dispense with the kumbaya script. With Bratton one chair away, the reverend blasted Stop-and-Frisk and pointed out to de Blasio that his own biracial son, Dante—the one with the Afro—was statistically more likely to be a target of Bratton's chosen brand of policing.

"If Dante wasn't your son, he'd be a candidate for a chokehold," Sharpton seethed.

As far as "training" went, Sharpton wasn't having it. He told Bratton off to his face. "I also think, Commissioner, that the best way to make police stop using illegal chokeholds is to perp-walk one of them that did," he said.

Part of what happened was bad calculus on de Blasio's part. If de Blasio thought Sharpton needed an in with Gracie Mansion, he was overestimating his importance. "I was in with the White House now," Sharpton recalls. "I was talking police reform with Obama." Under the circumstances, Sharpton felt he had enough political capital to throw de Blasio overboard rather than participate in a sleazy photo op to save de Blasio's relationship with Bratton.

Only a part of the disastrous meeting was seen by the press, but it was bad enough. The mayor not only lost his tie to Sharpton—"We went through a period of just not talking for a few weeks after that," the reverend says—but he equally undermined himself with the police, who felt Bratton had been betrayed and set up to take a beating in the press.

A war in the media ensued. A week after the roundtable, Sharpton told *The New York Times* that he'd been totally unaware that Bratton was going to be at the meeting.

That wasn't exactly true. Sharpton did know, only, he says, he found out too late to do anything about it. But the mayor's office thought it could still use this discrepancy to bloody Sharpton. De Blasio's office had emails back and forth from Sharpton and Noerdlinger proving that the reverend knew Bratton would be there. This came out a few weeks later, when sources tipped off the *New York Post* to a "scandal" involving Noerdlinger.

Noerdlinger's presence on the city staff had always irritated the police rank and file, who didn't want anyone associated with Sharpton inside the administration. Now Noerdlinger became caught in the crossfire after Bratton was shown up at the roundtable. The *Post* was tipped off that Noerdlinger was supposedly dating a convicted killer who repeatedly called cops "pigs" in online posts and had been involved in a road rage incident that the paper described as "nearly running a cop off the road."

The paper also had details of email exchanges within the mayor's office. The most damaging was an August 7, 2014, note from Noerdlinger in which she explained why she was against outing Sharpton for saying he was unaware of Bratton's presence at the roundtable, when in fact he had been.

"I'm still not wanting to share any email with [Sharpton] to media because it will set us backwards with [Sharpton]," she wrote.

This made political sense, but when the news finally came out, it was spun as de Blasio bending over backward to "cover up" a rift with Sharpton. De Blasio had walked into two different media buzz saws almost simultaneously. Sharpton had blindsided him at the roundtable, and police "sources" now set him up for a beating in the Noerdlinger affair. Cops called for Noerdlinger's resignation. "Rachel's not going anywhere," the mayor's spokesperson responded.

None of this had anything to do with Garner's family members or their desire to see Daniel Pantaleo brought to trial. To them, this noisy and irrelevant political infighting threatened to drown out what truly mattered. Immediately after Garner's death, the public, including white voters, overwhelmingly saw him as an innocent victim and was, polls showed, outraged over what had happened. But Sharpton's presence in the case now allowed the police to direct public attention to him, shifting the narrative of the story back to ancient and familiar patterns.

For decades now, Al Sharpton's advocacy in police brutality cases, particularly New York brutality cases, has been a constant. Throughout the 1990s, 2000s, and early 2010s, Sharpton advised families and victims in more than fifty different police brutality cases. Whenever cops shot, beat, or choked someone, which was often, mayors and police commissioners learned to expect newspaper photos of Sharpton addressing angry crowds with a bullhorn the next day. He was a consistent thorn in the side of politicians like Rudy Giuliani.

He also showed remarkable consistency in recommending legal representation to the families of victims. Legendary New York investigative journalist Wayne Barrett worked on a story on this very subject for the website *City & State New York* after Garner's death, but he died before he could finish his research. What he did learn, however, was that in fifty-two different brutality cases between 1991 and 2014,* families that brought Sharpton into the fold ended up represented primarily by just four different lawyers.

The two main lawyers in Sharpton cases were famed litigators:

* In one of those fifty-two, Al Sharpton was himself the plaintiff.

New York–based Sanford Rubenstein and the late Johnnie Cochran. One or the other superstar attorney and Sharpton confidant sued the NYPD after such famed incidents as the Diallo case, the Sean Bell case (another unarmed black man, shot at more than fifty times by police at his bachelor party), and the Abner Louima case (sodomized with a plunger in a Brooklyn police precinct house).

The cases that didn't go to Rubenstein or Cochran during that period inevitably went either to Benjamin Crump, a highly respected African American lawyer who represented the family of Trayvon Martin, or to Michael Hardy, now the general counsel of Sharpton's National Action Network.

The Garner family was initially slated to be represented by Rubenstein, one of Sharpton's top-two heavy hitters, and the main one left now that the legendary Cochran had passed. The two were so close that Sharpton wrote the preface to Rubenstein's humorously self-admiring but light-selling autobiography, *The Outrageous Rubenstein,* which Rubenstein reportedly hands out like breath mints to office visitors.

Sharpton had a great many detractors in New York, especially among the white population. His reputation took a hit in the infamous Tawana Brawley case in the eighties, in which he'd accused white officials in a small upstate town of rape, accusations that later collapsed under scrutiny. He had also suffered the embarrassment of being outed as "Confidential Informant #7," a man who'd worn a wire for the FBI against mobsters and boxing promoters, among others (court papers said he "was a very reliable informant"). It was hard to imagine Dr. King or Malcolm X—the men whose legacy Sharpton implicitly claimed—ever working *with* the FBI.

But whatever feelings Sharpton aroused, several things were indisputable. One was that for many of these families, there was nobody else knocking on their doors with offers of any kind of help. None of Sharpton's many critics were offering to foot bills or line up legal aid for the families of brutality victims.

The other incontrovertible fact was that families represented by Sharpton's favored lawyers almost always scored major financial settlements.

Cochran, for instance, won the family of Amadou Diallo $3 million after the unarmed man was shot at forty-one times by police. The family of Alberta Spruill, a fifty-seven-year-old Harlem woman who died of a heart attack when cops mistakenly burst into her home and tossed in a flash-bang grenade, won $1.6 million from the city, in part thanks to Cochran.

Rubenstein won more than $7 million in settlements for victims in the Bell case, while Rubenstein and Cochran together helped Louima win $8.7 million and another black man shot after a chase, Dantae Johnson, win $2.3 million.

The record of settlements was extremely good. But just as remarkable was another statistic. Out of those fifty-two cases, only one, Louima's, resulted in a police officer actually going to jail. And the Louima case was rare because it involved a victim who survived.

Most of the rest of the cases resulted in acquittals, dismissals, or nonjail resolutions, or else charges were never even sought. In a few cases, investigations are still pending.

Whether this was by chance or design, the consistently huge settlements led to a debate within the legal community. Some lawyers wondered if Sharpton's circle was essentially leveraging the demand for justice for more money. There was never any evidence of this, but it was something that was talked about in courthouses.

There was a flip side to the argument. What if the practical truth is that real justice in white America is a loser's pursuit—and maybe money is the only consolation on offer for these families who'd lost their loved ones? If systemic change and true justice are nonstarters, is it wrong to focus on getting the families as much money as possible? Some civil rights lawyers reluctantly admit that these thoughts enter their minds.

"The only remedy the system really considers is money," says one. "You want to do more, but in the back of your mind you know they're just going to cut you a check in the end. That's in the best case. The one thing you can say about Sharpton is that the check is a lot bigger once he's involved."

Sharpton understands the question and insists he's always first looking for reform. "The goal is always institutional change," he says. But in an exhausted voice he adds, "We have to be pragmatic, too. There are realities."

He pauses and draws upon his celebrated facility for the memorable phrase. "The way I look at it is 'If you can't hit a home run, get on base.'"

Sharpton rose to prominence thanks in large part to his extraordi-

nary skill in using the commercial media to get his message out. In the
golden age of the New York City newspaper, nobody was better at
getting the press out to cover an event, or at delivering quotes tailor-
made for headlines.

But the twenty-first century's fractured media landscape presented
new pitfalls for Sharpton and other black leaders. With the rise of
right-wing media outlets on radio and cable TV, images of black politicians were often used to tweak and terrify aging white audiences.
Sharpton, one of conservative media's favorite villains, often engaged
and debated with right-wing show hosts, perhaps unwittingly reinforcing a WWE version of racial politics that by the end of the Obama
administration increasingly dominated a divided media landscape,
entrenching the most regressive voices.

For instance, the back-and-forth between Sharpton and figures
like Rush Limbaugh (who denounced him as a "race hustler") often
ended up becoming a mutually reinforcing PR campaign. Sharpton's
appearances with the likes of Fox's Bill O'Reilly (who was once a
featured speaker at an NAN convention), Sean Hannity, and Mike
Huckabee similarly raised eyebrows among media critics, who wondered at the symbiotic nature of these relationships. It was an odd
bargain for Sharpton: he'd play the heel for conservative entertainers
and politicians and get publicity and higher profile in return. But for
those conservatives, the payoff was more tangible. In the political
arena, any white, right-wing candidate singled out by Al Sharpton
usually had his base sewn up automatically and often prospered.
There was a long list of such politicians who used Sharpton's name
and face to secure votes, with Rudy Giuliani being one of his most
successful foils.

Dan Donovan, the Staten Island district attorney, was about to add
his name to that list.

Shortly after Donovan met with the Garner family members, a new
controversy sent the police brutality issue into overdrive nationally.

A police killing in the heretofore-little-known St. Louis exurb of
Ferguson, Missouri, where an eighteen-year-old African American
named Michael Brown was shot by a white officer, sent the country
spiraling into furious protests. There were street demonstrations in
dozens of cities large and small, from L.A. to Oakland to Denver to

Chicago to New York to Boston. Many involved people blocking highways and intersections.

One of the largest was in New York, where both the FDR Drive and West Side Highway were jammed with people chanting, "Mike Brown! Mike Brown!" This was a preview of larger demonstrations that were to come in connection with the Garner case.

Ferguson was "controversial" in a way the Garner case was not. There was no video of the shooting in Ferguson, so the case devolved into a battle of spin.

Ferguson police quickly released footage of Brown captured by a security camera in a convenience store shortly before his death. The footage appeared to show him stealing cigars and pushing a store employee into a merchandise rack. The manner of the video's release—in response to questions and protests about Brown's shooting—left many media viewers with the impression that Brown had been shot and killed in the course of being arrested for the robbery.

But that wasn't the case. Like Eric Garner and Jeff Thomas, Brown instead had almost certainly been stopped by the police officer who would kill him for yet another legally meaningless offense, in this case "blocking traffic."

Though there would be conflicting stories later on, the contemporaneous account by Ferguson police chief Thomas Jackson indicated that Officer Darren Wilson and his partner had decided to stop Brown and his friend, Dorian Johnson, simply because they were walking in the middle of the street.

During the course of the stop, Jackson said, Wilson "at some point" saw cigars in Brown's hands, which led to the attempted arrest. Once again, a suspect in a routine stop was conveniently waving probable cause around in the direction of a police officer.

Wilson stopped Brown and Johnson by positioning his police SUV in front of Brown in the middle of Ferguson's Canfield Drive. Something happened between the two men at that moment. Wilson testified that the unarmed Brown reached inside the police cruiser and attempted to grab the officer's gun. Other eyewitnesses say Brown never reached inside Wilson's car at all, while some said he punched Wilson.

Whatever happened in that quick altercation, Wilson responded by firing two shots at Brown from the front seat of his car. He hit him on the thumb with one shot and missed him with the other. Brown took off and ran east about 160 feet. Wilson pursued on foot.

Brown then turned around.

Some witnesses claimed the unarmed Brown had his hands up in surrender at this point. Others say he charged Wilson.

Wilson insisted he was attacked and spoke of Brown making a "grunting, like aggravated sound," one of many descriptions he would use that made Brown sound like an animal.

Wilson fired a total of twelve times at Brown, twice from his car and ten times from the street, hitting him on the top of the head, the eye, the chin, the neck, the thumb, his right breast, and three places on his arm.

The Ferguson case, too, followed a script, particularly in the media, where the victim was quickly villainized. Black brutality victims are almost always described as beings of superhuman strength, next to whom police are frail mortals. Dating back to the days of Emmett Till in 1955 and before, even children are inevitably described as "big for their age."

Brown was described as "no angel" in the press and caricatured as a physically imposing monster who had suddenly and inexplicably attacked an armed policeman, who had no choice but to shoot.

Wilson described Brown as a "demon" and said he felt like "a five-year-old holding on to Hulk Hogan."

The most crucial detail, however, was that Brown's dead body had remained facedown on the street, unattended, blood pouring from the head, for four long hours, until it was removed.

This was a grotesque continuation of the scene in which a dying Eric Garner had been left unattended in the dirt and grime of Bay Street for eight long minutes.

Regardless of what preceded the shooting, the picture of Brown's body encapsulated in one unshakable image the dichotomy in attitudes toward black and white life.

It was hardly a surprise that the Ferguson case reignited the nascent Black Lives Matter movement. This had begun two years before with the shooting death of unarmed seventeen-year-old Trayvon Martin at the hands of George Zimmerman, a neighborhood watchman.

Like the competing interpretations of the events in Ferguson, the very term "Black Lives Matter" was destined, absurdly in many respects, to become the locus of a furious nationwide controversy.

Black Americans may have hoped that the name would simply express the degree to which they felt a gap in basic respect, empathy, and rights.

White America instead mostly took it as a provocation. As in, *What, white lives don't matter? All lives don't matter?*

The relatively simple ask from black Americans was that white Americans take a moment to recognize what it feels like, say, to be told your son has been killed, but not told why or how, as happened with Trayvon Martin, or to watch a pregnant woman put in a choke-hold over a backyard barbecue, as happened to twenty-seven-year-old Rosan Miller in New York nine days after Garner's death. They asked white people to consider what it felt like to have your son's bleeding corpse left in the street for four long hours. But the request implicit in the name "Black Lives Matter" quickly flipped around into an absurd overreaction.

A growing population of Middle American conservatives (and even a sizable chunk of privately grumbling blue-state liberals) was getting good and ready to be open about how tired they were of being accused of racial insensitivity.

After Brown's death, tensions exploded onto the streets of Ferguson, where tens of thousands of people rallied for day-and-night protests. An increasingly defensive white America watched these protests with mixed feelings.

School days were canceled, the National Guard was called in, curfews were declared, and eventually a state of emergency was instituted as wide-scale racial disturbances of a type not seen since Los Angeles in the early nineties put the entire country on alert. There was a clear fear among Americans that the next time something like this happened, the black community might not just respond with protests but outright insurrection.

This historic series of protests, which cable TV covered round the clock for weeks like a live combat story, stoking fear and tension across the country, provided the background for Dan Donovan's looming decision about Daniel Pantaleo.

Until the Garner case came along, Dan Donovan had a rep for being a straight shooter. Heading into the Garner case, in fact, he was probably best known on the island for his political backbone.

In 2001, Donovan was still working as chief of staff for Staten Island borough president and local political mullah Guy Molinari, but
Molinari was, by then, ready to give up his fiefdom. Through his
powerful endorsement, Molinari essentially handed the position over
to his successor, one James Molinaro (who confusingly was not related to Molinari).

Like Donovan, Molinaro had worked in Molinari's office for years,
serving as his deputy borough president. And when Molinaro took
over the president's office, he at first made Donovan his deputy, until
Donovan left to become the district attorney in 2003.

Four years later, Molinaro's grandson, seventeen-year-old Steven
Molinaro, got in trouble. He was busted for assault, pleaded out, and
was granted conditional probation in lieu of a five-year sentence.
Later, he violated his probation by driving by the home of one of his
assault victims, a fourteen-year-old paperboy, and glaring at him.

This nasty case landed on Donovan's desk.

Donovan was in a very awkward spot. The expedient thing to do
would be to keep the case and somehow make it go away to the sat-
isfaction of the Molinaro family.

The alternative would be to recuse himself and hand the case over
to an independent prosecutor. Donovan here could keep his hands
clean, but then the grandson of a longtime political ally would be
dropped in the proverbial jackpot, exposed to serious consequences.

Donovan recused himself.

James Molinaro was furious and exploded in public. He took out
a full-page ad in the *Staten Island Advance* ripping Donovan for his
"senseless vendetta" against the Molinaro family, adding in a sub-
headline: "THIS INJUSTICE COULD HAPPEN TO YOU OR YOUR
FAMILY."

Donovan's decision was a portentous one. A special prosecutor
was brought in from Manhattan, who went all out on young Steven
Molinaro and sent him to prison for a five-year sentence.

This was politics at its most real and hard-core. Lawyers all over the
island quietly gave Donovan props for standing up to a political boss.

The Molinaro case established a pattern for Donovan. He would
earn a reputation for recusing himself from any case with which he
had even the remotest personal or political connection.

In just 2013 and 2014, he filed twenty-three different petitions asking for recusal, more than half of all such petitions filed by the five

New York City DAs. The cases involved someone whose wedding he'd once been invited to, a pro-Israel charity with which he had an unknown connection, an "acquaintance" who had donated to Donovan's campaign, and even a karate instructor who had taught the children of two of Donovan's staffers.

This same Dan Donovan was now faced with a historic decision. Would he ask to recuse himself from the Garner case? After all, if he'd been worried about the appearance of conflict in a case where the only issue was a couple of staffers having kids who took a karate class, wouldn't he recoil from a case in which he would have to investigate Staten Island law enforcement?

Maybe it was a stretch to say taking the Garner case would mean investigating his own office. But police and prosecutors work together constantly. If he had been willing before to sever a critical political relationship for the sake of the appearance of fairness, wouldn't he do the same now?

The reality is that prosecutors facing this choice virtually never recuse themselves. One semi-exception was the infamous Howard Beach racial assault case of 1986, which didn't involve a police assault but a gang of white kids attacking black youths. When Queens prosecutor John Santucci couldn't get one of the black witnesses to cooperate, he asked Governor Mario Cuomo to bring in a special prosecutor.

But as a rule, local prosecutors never embraced the argument that prosecuting police represented an inherent conflict, although this was becoming more of an issue in legal circles by the time the Garner case rolled around. Instead, prosecutors usually proceeded in one of two ways.

Occasionally, a "progressive" DA might keep the case and try to treat an offense committed by police like it was just another crime. Brooklyn's Ken Thompson would symbolize this approach that very year, in a case involving a rookie cop who shot a young black man in a project stairwell. Thompson went to his grand jury and got an indictment, infuriating police.

Donovan chose another, more typical path.

Adding to the pressure was the devastating August 1 report from the city medical examiner's office on Garner's death. The report declared

Garner's death a homicide, saying he died of "compression of neck (choke hold), compression of chest and prone positioning during physical restraint by police."

The city's police union chief, Pat Lynch, denounced the report as "political" immediately upon its release. Lynch was a red-faced loud-mouth with a barrel chest and a swoosh of horse-thick gray hair jutting straight up out of his forehead who looked like a central-casting caricature of a bully cop, like a pre-O.J. Mark Fuhrman, only without the introspection or writing talent. He was eager to insert himself into the case as a mindlessly belligerent advocate for the accused officer.

Lynch tried to use the media to paint Garner as street trash who had caused his own death by resisting arrest. He even went so far as to imply that Garner was killed by EMTs or doctors. Noting that the ME didn't use the word "asphyxiation," he said, "What they saw was compression to the neck, which is consistent with the medical treatment that Mr. Garner would have received by EMS."

Lynch would also be the first local character involved with the case to invoke what was quickly becoming a popular meme in national conservative politics: that brutality cases like the Garner incident or Ferguson were in large part the fault of liberal politicians who had instilled in their followers a disrespect for police officers.

This disrespect in turn led to people resisting arrest, which in turn led to deaths, was how the logic went.

In any case, Donovan waited out the ME's report, then waited another three very long weeks before making a decision about his involvement in the prosecution. On August 19, 2014, he announced that he wasn't going to ask for a recusal. He wanted to be the one who tried this case.

"I have determined that it is appropriate to present evidence regarding the circumstances of [Eric Garner's] death to a Richmond County Grand Jury," he said.

This was a legalistic take on the old commercial about Las Vegas. A district attorney who had punted more cases than the rest of the city's top prosecutors combined was now telling the world just the opposite: what happens in Staten Island stays in Staten Island.

All felony indictments in New York State require that a grand jury meet and vote to indict, a decision called a "true bill." Because of the sheer quantity of felony-level offenses, that means counties in New York raise grand juries as a matter of course.

These sitting grand juries consider felony cases in factory-style fashion and will sometimes hear four, five, six cases a day.

A former Staten Island prosecutor recalls how a typical presentation would go.

"Maybe you only have three witnesses," he says. "Somebody gets robbed. Then the person that got robbed comes in and says, 'This guy robbed me.' Then the guy that saw the robbery is coming in. The cop that picked him up comes in. And that's it," he says. "It's not complicated. How long is that going to take? A half hour? Forty-five minutes?"

The oft-quoted saying that a New York prosecutor can get a grand jury to "indict a ham sandwich" actually dates back to 1985, when the state's then chief judge, Sol Wachtler, used the phrase in an interview with *Daily News* reporting legend Marcia Kramer. Wachtler was complaining about the ease with which prosecutors could get indictments.

Nothing really had changed since then. The process still depended in significant part upon grand juries basically taking the prosecutors' word for it that their cases were solid. If grand juries were designed to be painstaking, in-depth evidentiary hearings, you wouldn't be able to get an indictment in forty-five minutes.

But by calling a "special" grand jury, Donovan removed all other burdens from his grand jurors. Instead of hearing a ton of cases, they would hear one. It would take a while. They would hear lots and lots of witnesses.

Which sounded great. Until you thought about it.

After all, why bother? If the all-powerful DA in New York can walk into a sitting grand jury and get an indictment based on a couple of witnesses and a pretty please, why complicate things?

If you think a crime was committed (and by taking the case to a grand jury, Donovan was formally signaling that he believed one had taken place), why not just walk into any normal grand jury with Ramsey Orta's video, call a few witnesses, and walk out with an indictment an hour or two later?

Donovan made contradictory moves. On the one hand, by not recusing himself, he signaled that he believed he could be objective about the case, that it was no different to him from any other case.

On the other hand, by calling a special grand jury, he was saying that there was, in fact, something different about the case, that this was not a normal crime.

He began to call witnesses.

Subpoenas dropped all over Staten Island, instantly igniting sidewalk controversies. By early September, Bay Street was divided on the wisdom of testifying against cops. A lot of not entirely legal things go on in and around Tompkinsville Park. Most everyone has a hustle of some kind. Drugs are sold and there's also more small-potatoes stuff, like bootleg smokes or fencing. And everyone has a past. It's a hard thing to contemplate trusting the authorities to put you under oath and not explore these matters.

Some people who'd been subpoenaed for the Garner trial were busted for minor offenses during this period. They began to gossip with their lawyers, telling them the word on the streets was that some people were now afraid to testify because it might mean trouble with their open cases.

Having heard some of this chatter, Christopher Pisciotta, the head of the Staten Island Legal Aid office, reached out to Donovan's office. His Legal Aid office had not only represented Eric Garner (most recently via attorney Joe Doyle) but was also located just a few blocks from the park. The lawyers there were familiar with a lot of the people being subpoenaed, and they knew many of them were nervous about testifying.

Pisciotta thought he would help Donovan out on this score. "Our idea was, if a witness was scared to come forward, we would represent them," Pisciotta remembers. "We would help work with the DA to make sure people weren't worried about anything but testifying."

Legal Aid also had had investigators on the scene and had information coming in all the time about who was where during the time of Garner's killing. Pisciotta wanted to share all of this stuff with Donovan.

He never heard back from the DA on any of it.

James Knight, the last person apart from police to speak to Garner, received a subpoena. He struggled mightily over whether or not to appear. Even though he was clean then, he had a natural trepidation about testifying against the police.

"It was a hard decision for me to do that, because I don't want to be targeted out here," he says. "But I talked to my girl and she told me do the right thing, do what you think is best. And I did."

James took a few days, then reluctantly decided to go in. At first he was heartened by the process. The investigators from the DA's office seemed to be genuinely interested in what kind of witness he would be, and James worked hard to convince them that he'd be a good one.

"I told them I'd been on drugs thirty-three years, but I'd been clean for seven," he says. He talked also about his work at the shelter. He remembers seeing one of the investigators look at James's last mug shot, then at the healthy, well-dressed, lucid, confident man he was now. He thought he saw genuine relief in the prosecutor's eyes.

"They showed me a picture of me when I last got arrested and they really looked at the difference," he says. "I thought these guys were really genuine."

But then on the allotted date, he went to the dull gray glass-and-steel court building just up the hill from Tompkinsville Park, and found the questioning to be far from what he expected. He remembers being shown a picture of the scene of the crime, a picture that among other things showed a piece of cardboard he and others sometimes used to sit on on the sidewalk.

"And they were like, 'What's that?'

"And I said, 'Cardboard.' And they said, 'What's that for?'"

James looked around the courtroom, which was mostly full of white jurors, and began to get a funny feeling. Why did anyone care about cardboard?

"Well," he said, "we sit on it."

"Why?"

He frowned. "If it's cold, or if you want to keep your clothes clean."

"I see."

James says in earlier interviews he had been asked about what he'd seen, had talked about the chokehold and other things. But once the lights went on for real, he got none of that. "Inside the grand jury room, they didn't ask any of those questions," he said.

They peppered him with more strange questions, and soon after that he was dismissed. He went home confused. "The more I thought about it, the more irrelevant the questions seemed," he said.

Fred Winship had also testified. The gray-bearded park regular was not young and healthy and cleaned up like James Knight and had been concerned about testifying. And his anxiety grew even greater, he says, when he found himself being prepped for his testimony by uniformed police officers.

"I'm being prepped, by officers, and they're involved in the whole situation," he says. "It's officers investigating officers."

Asked if he was intimidated, Fred says no at first. But then he shrugs. "Well, you know, you never know if something is going to come back on you," he says. "I had to tread lightly, so to speak."

When he got into the grand jury room, Fred was nervous to the point where he had trouble focusing. He can't remember how many black jurors or white jurors there were, except that one of the jurors was definitely a black man. Fred remembers that because he kept focusing on him to try to keep himself calm. "I was intimidated, you know? So I was looking at the black guy."

He blocked out the rest of the experience to the point where he doesn't really remember the questions, except to say that he felt they weren't asking the right ones. He left without any expectation that they would indict Pantaleo. "I felt like they were leaning in the direction of the police," he says. "I can't explain it."

Twan "Pure" Scarlett says he was another witness who didn't have much good to say about the experience. "They wasn't asking too much about shit," he says. "They was too busy laughing amongst themselves to ask."

When asked what questions he did get, Pure just shrugs. "It was full of shit, that's all I can say."

Because of the secrecy of the grand jury, some of its strange turns can only be seen in the negative space of the testimony that we do know about. For instance: the question of whether or not the prosecution argued that Officer Pantaleo used an illegal chokehold on Eric Garner.

Police chokeholds had been partially banned in New York City since 1985, when officers were instructed only to use them in a life-threatening situation. Then in 1993, after a twenty-one-year-old Queens man named Federico Pereira died of "traumatic asphyxia" after being choked by police, then commissioner Ray Kelly banned chokeholds with no exceptions.

Taisha Allen, who took the less-famous video of the aftermath of Garner's death, actually had her testimony about whether Garner was put in a chokehold altered twice, if one believes news reports. According to *The New York Times,* police had whitewashed her original testimony that Pantaleo had used a chokehold in the initial UF-49 internal report written immediately after Garner's death, quoting her instead as saying that police had brought Garner down "by his arms."

Now, in the grand jury room, she was once again instructed to alter her testimony—and not just about the chokehold. She tried to say that Garner didn't appear to have a pulse when he was left on the ground and they told her she couldn't say that. She told the *Times* that when she then tried to tell jurors about the chokehold, a prosecutor interrupted her.

"You can't say he put him in a chokehold," she was told.

That Taisha might have been told not to say Garner didn't have a pulse makes a little sense, since there was other evidence that he was alive after he left the street and was out of her sight, dying in an ambulance later on. Maybe prosecutors wanted to correct her on that score for consistency's sake. Maybe there were other witnesses who'd taken Garner's pulse who had other information.

But telling her she couldn't use the term "chokehold" was confusing unless it, too, would've been contradicted by other testimony.

After Garner's death, one of the few statements that came out of Officer Pantaleo's camp was an insistence by his lawyer that Pantaleo had not used a chokehold, that any contact with Garner's neck had been "incidental" and only part of a "takedown." Lynch had said the same thing, explaining that Pantaleo was only doing what shorter officers were trained to do when apprehending taller suspects.

Later, police experts whose qualifications were of varying degrees of dubiousness would surface in the press explaining that what Pantaleo had used was not a chokehold at all but something other than what it looked like to most of the planet.

"Police sources" had told the *New York Post* within days of Garner's death that it might have been a "submission hold," a fully legal maneuver that included techniques "like the headlock."

Had prosecutors called such experts to testify that Pantaleo had used a submission hold? If so, it would explain Taisha Allen being shushed when she tried to use the term "chokehold."

That would be a strange thing for a prosecutor to do, however, especially when aspects of the case hinged on Pantaleo using a chokehold—for which there was evidence, including Allen's original eyewitness testimony. A prosecutor honestly going after an indictment could have also drawn from experts on the issue, like for instance the commissioner himself, Bill Bratton, who had declared Pantaleo's maneuver a banned chokehold on live TV on July 18. To call in the so-called experts who were denying that it was a chokehold would have needlessly undermined the prosecution's own case for indictment.

On Bay Street, many of the grand jury witnesses defied instructions not to speak about their testimony and consorted with one another about what went on. There were differing opinions. Some, like Pure, thought the whole thing was a setup and laughed at the idea that Pantaleo would ever go to trial. Fred Winship mostly agreed.

As the fall wore on, James Knight and John McCrae sat down at their usual spot on Bay Street from time to time and worked out what the charge might be, according to what they'd read in the news. McCrae felt sure the cop was going to court.

"I actually think they're gonna do something," McCrae said.

"Got to," said James. "Four years, five years. Involuntary manslaughter. I'm not talking about no first-degree murder."

"Gotta do something," agreed McCrae, tapping his feet.

Weeks and weeks had passed. Then it was months. Garner had been killed in the middle of summer, and the grand jury had been called in August. Now fall was winding to a close and it was beginning to get very cold outside. The grand jury still had not made its decision. What was taking so long?

On November 24, 2014, a grand jury in Ferguson, Missouri, reached a decision not to indict Officer Darren Wilson. St. Louis County prosecutor Bob McCulloch, Dan Donovan's counterpart, announced that the grand jury had found "no probable cause" to indict for either first-degree murder or manslaughter.

McCulloch directly addressed witness accounts of Brown holding his hands up in surrender at the time of the shooting, an image that inspired the iconic nationwide "Hands Up, Don't Shoot" protest meme. He said the grand jury's decision meant that those witness accounts were "completely refuted by the physical evidence."

McCulloch spoke for nearly an hour and complained bitterly about the media, protesters, and multiple other factors, sounding like a man who was irked that so many people had expected him to get an indictment, despite the fact that he, as the state's prosecutor, was the one who was supposed to be disappointed.

While the death of Brown was a tragedy, he said, it was important not to act in response to a "public outcry or political expediency."

These were strange quotes coming from the prosecutor who'd presented the case to the grand jury in the first place. If he didn't think the case warranted an indictment, why had he tried for one? Was the whole thing a dog-and-pony show, designed to put an unpopular decision on the backs of anonymous grand jurors?

Residents in Ferguson pelted the local police station with bottles. In some neighborhoods there were reports of heavy automatic gunfire, and the situation was so volatile that airplanes were diverted away from the airspace over Ferguson.

President Obama was forced to make an ad-hoc, late-night statement. Appearing on TV just after 10:00 P.M., Obama had seldom looked more uncomfortable. The nation's first black president, desperately anxious to come across as a uniter and not an instigator, often seemed strained when he talked about race. And for good reason—he was in a nearly impossible situation.

The nagging suspicion among white voters was that Obama, beneath an outward façade of midwestern reasonableness and professorial logic, was a kind of double agent, a psyche in schism. Conservative media constantly presented him as the pre-Trump, left-wing version of a Manchurian president, raised in madrassas and weaned on socialism, who secretly hated white people, yearned to euthanize them, and took the White House with the sole aim of destroying traditional America.

The apotheosis of all of this was the preposterous birther contro-

versy, pushed by then peripheral political curiosity and reality TV star
Donald Trump. The Internet-driven furor over the president's birth
certificate led to huge numbers of Americans—41 percent in a 2016
poll—believing that Obama was not merely conflicted but not even
an American. He wasn't just black. He was illegitimate. An illegal
president.

If anyone could communicate the frustration black Americans felt
over Stop-and-Frisk and other neo-vagrancy laws that made black
people feel like they could be arrested anytime, anywhere, it should
have been Barack Obama. He'd made it all the way to the White
House and was still considered to be literally trespassing by a huge
plurality of the population.

But Obama chose not to go there. He didn't disavow the anger felt
by black America toward the police but also pleaded for restraint.

"In too many parts of this country, a deep distrust exists between
law enforcement and communities of color," he said. But "there's
never an excuse for violence," he added.

Even this passive-voice acknowledgment of the existence of mistrust would later be turned around by critics and presented as evidence of hostility toward law enforcement.

Protests raged for another day or two, but by Thanksgiving Day,
days after the grand jury decision, Ferguson was calming down. State
and federal authorities seemed relieved.

But the Garner decision was looming. There was excellent reason
to expect that a similar outcome from that grand jury would have
much farther-reaching consequences.

The Wilson-Brown case, after all, had not been captured on video.
But the whole country saw what happened to Eric Garner.

On December 3, 2014, the Garner family was put on alert by Sharp-
ton's National Action Network that news of some kind was coming.
From all over the city, Garner's relatives came to the NAN offices in
Harlem. Erica remembers sitting in the NAN offices, watching the
TV, waiting for word. "Reporters kept coming in and out, seeing
what was going on," she says.

Just after two in the afternoon, the word came in: the grand jury
had voted not to indict.

The family was outraged. They felt betrayed by Donovan, betrayed by the system, and were especially in no mood to hear a statement issued by Daniel Pantaleo's lawyers about how the in-hiding officer was feeling "very bad about the death of Mr. Garner."

At a press conference at the NAN offices in Harlem, reporters asked the family if they accepted Pantaleo's apology. "Hell, no," replied Esaw, in a response that went viral almost immediately. "The time for remorse for the death of my husband was when he was yelling to breathe."

She went on about Pantaleo, seething: "He's still feeding his kids, and my husband is six feet under and I'm looking for a way to feed my kids now."

It didn't take long for questions to be raised about the behavior of the Garner grand jury. Legal experts all over the country, but particularly in New York, almost universally expressed shock that the video had not resulted in an indictment.

Columbia law professor Jeffrey Fagan, for example, told reporters that "the video speaks for itself" and "appears to show negligence." However, he added, "if we learned anything from the Brown case, it's the power of prosecutors to construct and manage a narrative in a way that can shape the outcome."

Among the legal community in Staten Island, some local defense lawyers would have bet their lives against an eventual conviction. This was, after all, Staten Island. But most thought there would at least be an indictment.

One former Staten Island prosecutor watched the video over and over again. He doubted they would ever be able to prove intentional murder or even a lesser charge like criminally negligent homicide. But he thought it would go to court at least.

"I thought it would be a true bill, and then he'd be acquitted," he says.

Another defense attorney cited the aforementioned Sean Bell case, in which an unarmed New York man had been shot at fifty times by three detectives in the parking lot outside the strip club where he was holding his bachelor party.

In that case, the grand jury indicted, but then the three cops waived their right to a jury trial and put their lives in the hands of a judge named Arthur J. Cooperman. Cooperman acquitted all three.

"They've got so many different ways to do it," says the defense lawyer. "I thought it would be something like the Bell case. Indict Pantaleo, then it's just him and a Staten Island judge. That's what I expected. But no indictment at all, that was kind of hard to imagine, with the video and all."

President Obama, who'd played things right down the middle in the Ferguson case, was far less equivocal now.

"When anybody in this country is not being treated equally under the law, that is a problem," he said. "And it's my job as president to help solve it."

By the time Erica Garner went home from the NAN offices that night, protests had broken out all over the city. Many were spontaneous and involved dozens or hundreds, but in some places thousands gathered. On the Lower East Side, thousands made their way from Foley Square to Sara D. Roosevelt Park, merged with others on Canal Street, then stormed west to block the West Side Highway. Farther north, protesters marched to Thirty-fourth Street, where some three hundred people lay down for eleven minutes in a "die-in," which became the signature Garner-related protest. The protests spread to the point where crowds on the Williamsburg Bridge were blocking Erica's cab ride home. She was awed by the sheer number of people and right in the middle of the bridge jumped out of the cab to take a look, against the objections of her cabbie.

She went into the crowd and began talking to people. "I said, 'I'm Erica Garner. Thank you. I love you all so much.'"

She talked for a few minutes, then she remembered she had to get home. "They'd surrounded the car, and I asked them to clear up so I could go," she remembers.

The crowd parted, and Erica's cab drove straight across the bridge.

The city was still in shock over the announcement when the following day, December 4, brought another stunning piece of news. A Staten Island judge named Stephen Rooney issued an order approving a sealed ex parte request from Dan Donovan to release "certain limited information regarding the conduct of grand jury proceedings." Donovan had apparently at some point gone to the court and asked permission to release information about the Garner grand jury, with the aim of "assuring the public."

Because secrecy is so elemental to the grand jury process, information on proceedings is sealed and can only be released under certain criteria. What it mostly boils down to is that anyone who wants to unseal grand jury minutes has to have a pretty damned good reason. In the words of the relevant statute, a "compelling and particularized need" to allow the public access to information has to be demonstrated.

Donovan had apparently argued to Judge Rooney that such a need existed at this moment, and Rooney agreed.

"Somewhat uniquely in this matter," the judge wrote, "the maintenance of trust in our criminal justice system lies at the heart of these proceedings."

He added that we were at a "crucial moment in the nation's history, where public confidence in the evenhanded application of [our] core values among a diverse citizenry is being questioned."

Translated loosely, Rooney was saying that tensions were high and that he, Rooney, needed to release some information about what had taken place in the grand jury proceedings in order to keep millions of people from losing their minds and New York from turning into another Ferguson.

He therefore allowed Donovan to tell the media certain facts:

The grand jury sat for a total of nine weeks.

The grand jury heard from a total of fifty witnesses, twenty-two of whom were civilians. The remainder had been police officers, emergency personnel, and doctors.

Sixty exhibits were admitted into evidence. They included "four videos, records regarding NYPD policies and procedures, photographs of the scene and records pertaining to NYPD training."

By the afternoon of December 4, the whole country heard the new details Donovan had asked Judge Rooney to release to the public. In the media, this information was mostly presented as proof that Donovan's investigation had been thorough and fair.

But a few lawyers across New York City were quietly coming to a somewhat different conclusion.

They looked at the summary of the witnesses and exhibits and wondered: What kind of case had Donovan put on, exactly? Why all of those police witnesses? Why so much evidence about training procedures? Had Donovan called witnesses for the prosecution *and* the defense? If so, why?

Donovan was ostensibly after an indictment, and here he had a homicide, committed in broad daylight, captured on video. Even if the argument was for criminally negligent homicide—accusing Pantaleo of the overzealous use of a banned procedure—the case was not terribly complicated. Hell, the city's police commissioner had called it a chokehold on live television.

Yet Donovan had put on a case that reminded most criminal lawyers of a white-collar case, or a case involving government corruption, where jurors had to be led through an exhaustive evidentiary trail to see the crime.

That clearly wasn't the case here. There was a video of the victim being killed. So what happened?

See if this story sounds familiar:

A black male is killed by a police officer on the streets of New York in front of many witnesses. The murder triggers furious protests in the African American community. A white district attorney somberly pledges to investigate and convenes a special grand jury to consider charges against the officer.

But the grand jury takes an unusually long time to do its job. Dozens of witnesses are called to give more than a thousand pages of testimony in multiple secret sessions, facts we know because the district attorney himself goes out of his way to show the public what a thorough investigation he's conducted.

Still, there are whispers throughout that key prosecution witnesses and/or evidence is being excluded. And the city's black citizens are infuriated, if not exactly surprised, when the grand jury finally comes to a decision months after the homicide: no indictment.

This was the story of fifteen-year-old James Powell, a black teenager who was shot to death in Harlem on the morning of July 16, 1964, fifty years before the death of Eric Garner.

Powell had been involved in a confrontation with a white building superintendent who had threatened to turn a hose on him and two of his friends (and may have said something to the effect of, "Dirty niggers, I'll wash you clean"). When Powell chased after him, the superintendent fled, but an off-duty cop named Thomas Gilligan shot and killed Powell, claiming he saw him carrying a knife.

Two days after this incident, the city of New York exploded in protests. A three-day battle between police and protesters in Harlem, Bedford-Stuyvesant, and other neighborhoods ensued, leaving one dead and hundreds injured.

After the Powell shooting in New York in that summer of 1964, New York County district attorney Frank Hogan convened a special grand jury to consider charges against the police officer. Thomas Gilligan had at least one other shooting of a black youth in his past.

Hogan took a long time to consider the charges. The public was later told that he called forty-five witnesses who collectively gave 1,600 pages of testimony at fifteen secret sessions.

Despite the seeming thoroughness of the panel's investigation, he apparently excluded several key witnesses. Those included a visiting member of the Italian Ministry of Finance, an eyewitness who claimed Powell had been unarmed when shot.

On September 2, 1964, the grand jury returned its decision: no true bill. Lieutenant Thomas Gilligan would not be indicted for shooting James Powell.

The announcement sparked more protests. There were howls on the street of a cover-up. But over time, the story receded. And soon, nobody remembered what happened to that cop—what's his name again?—who shot that boy in Harlem. In order for patterns to repeat themselves, people first need to forget.

Staten Islanders had seen this same playbook before, too.

Two decades earlier, and thirty years after the death of James Powell, a man named Ernest Sayon, the son of Liberian immigrants, was asphyxiated by police. He died at the base of a tree on the 200 block of Park Hill Avenue in Staten Island.

This was in the middle of the rough-and-tumble projects that were home to many of Staten Island's famed rap collective, the Wu-Tang Clan.

Known as Kase, Sayon was a strapping twenty-two-year-old who sold crack and coke and at the time of his death was out on bail on charges of firing twenty bullets into an apartment building. He was a very different character from Eric Garner. Garner was almost universally liked, thought to be harmless, and considered to be something like the neighborhood mascot even by business owners.

Sayon was a hard-core banger who scared some residents of Park Hill, who gave him a wide berth. He was standing on his usual corner on April 29, 1994, when police drove by. Someone threw a cherry bomb, which the cops mistook for a gunshot.

A former Park Hill resident turned police officer named Donald Brown was the first man out of the car. He subdued Sayon at the base of a tree, perhaps using a chokehold. In an eerie precursor to the Garner case, Sayon gasped for air while multiple other officers then joined in, swarming over the rest of his body.

"Everybody's going, 'Leave him alone, leave him alone,'" remembers Charles, a Park Hill resident who knew both Sayon and Eric Garner. "The more people said, 'Leave him alone,' the more they whupped his ass."

Police eventually cuffed Sayon and threw him in the back of a van, where, according to local legend, other prisoners had to inform police that he was not breathing. Witnesses claimed it took police as long as seventeen minutes to take Sayon to a nearby hospital, where he died.

Though he might not have won any popularity contests, Sayon was one of Park Hill's own. Protests broke out in the projects that night. A crowd of hundreds formed spontaneously and marched toward the 120th Precinct.

Doug Brinson, the check-cash man, was one of the marchers. "There was a picture of me in the paper with my fist raised, I remember that," says Doug, who lived and worked in Park Hill for a time.

There was a long, tense standoff that night in Staten Island, but in the end, the police waited out the crowd. In the following days, city officials from Rudy Giuliani on down followed the brutality-scandal playbook to a T, promising a thorough inquiry and pleading for calm.

In yet another precursor of the Garner case, the medical examiner ruled Sayon's death a homicide, by asphyxiation.

Just as his Manhattan counterpart Frank Hogan had thirty years earlier in the Powell case, and just as Dan Donovan would two decades later in the Garner matter, Staten Island's then district attorney, William Murphy, convened a special grand jury to consider charges against the officers.

It eventually came out that Murphy called more than one hundred witnesses and took seven long months to present his case, at the end of which the twenty-three-member panel decided not to indict.

"We're enjoying pizza tonight," Officer Brown told *The New York Times* after being cleared by the grand jury on December 8, 1994. It was seven months after Sayon's death.

There was yet another brief flurry of protests, but soon it was over, and the Sayon case was forgotten almost everywhere, making it possible for the pattern to be repeated later on. From Powell to Sayon to Garner, from Hogan to Murphy to Donovan, very little in these stories ever changed, except for the names.

Apart from the Garner case, Staten Island that fall had been home to another bizarre controversy. The borough's congressman, a clodhopping, jockish Republican named Michael Grimm, had been hit earlier in the year with a twenty-count indictment on federal corruption charges. He'd been busted for concealing about a million dollars in wages from the IRS from his restaurant, a doomed Upper East Side eatery called Healthalicious that specialized in soggy ten-dollar salads.

After his spring indictment, Grimm refused to resign from office and commenced his reelection campaign.

He handled press questioning about his scandal with aplomb, at one point threatening to throw a NY1 reporter "off this fucking balcony" for asking about the case. He added, on camera, that he would "break [him] in half . . . like a boy."

Seeing a rare opportunity to gain a Republican seat, national Democrats poured $3.6 million of party money into the campaign of Grimm's opponent, Domenic Recchia, a former city councilman from the Brooklyn section of the Eleventh District. Recchia raised a ton of money of his own as well, ending up with more than $5 million total.

Grimm, meanwhile, was abandoned by national Republicans and limped into the race with a little more than a third of the resources Recchia had.

But Recchia proved to be a disastrous candidate whose answers to policy questions were so embarrassingly bad (he had to take a time-out and confer with an aide when asked what the Trans-Pacific Partnership was) that he ended up becoming a punchline on a *Daily Show* segment.

Recchia was whipped that November by thirteen points. Democrats in Staten Island couldn't even beat a guy who'd threatened to throw a reporter over a balcony on TV and was scheduled to go to jail for a million years moments after Election Day.

But that December, Grimm's incredible November triumph began to unwind.

Behind the scenes, Grimm folded in negotiations with the feds. On December 23, he pleaded guilty to a variety of misdeeds, including tax evasion, using undocumented labor, and lying under oath.

With characteristic goonishness, Grimm tried to hang on to his seat by his fingernails, pledging at first to remain in office even as a felon. But that plan, too, soon crumbled. On January 5, 2015, Grimm finally resigned, leaving a congressional seat open, along with room for a shocker plot twist to the Garner story.

Dan Donovan announced he would run for Grimm's seat. Whatever happened in that grand jury room had certainly not hurt his political career.

When Erica heard that Donovan was running for Congress, she was mortified.

"He was using my dad's body as a platform," she says.

Al Sharpton loudly opposed Donovan's run, opposition that became another key part of Donovan's platform.

"It would almost be seen as rewarding someone who has become the national symbol of what we are fighting," Sharpton told the *Daily News* after the possibility of a Donovan run hit the news.

He added: "How are we gonna send someone to Washington whose only national reputation is the guy who couldn't get a grand jury to indict on a video the whole world saw?"

Sometime later, the Donovan campaign would send out its first fundraising letter. Ostensibly written by his campaign chief, Ron Carara, the e-circular emphasized the name of Al Sharpton.

"Dear [Voter]," it began. Farther down, it read:

A recent news article revealed Al Sharpton's National Action Network is working under the radar and doing their best to hurt Dan's campaign. They were quoted saying they have to "tread delicately"

because they know how divisively they are perceived on Staten Island and in Brooklyn . . .

We don't need fringe agitators like Occupy Wall Street and Al
Sharpton dictating what's best for our nation or the 11th congressional district.

The invocation of Sharpton's name was absurdly transparent. The
letter referenced an article in which Kirsten John Foy, a spokesperson
for Sharpton's National Action Network, wondered aloud if it might
not be better to lie low in the congressional race. She said that NAN
had to "tread delicately" because, as she explained, "anything we
could do to excite our base can incite his."

Not only was this not an aggressive quote, it was virtually a kind
of public surrender. But for Donovan's purposes, it didn't matter. The
important thing was to make sure Staten Island voters knew that Al
Sharpton was on the other side.

Sharpton, meanwhile, insisted before Donovan announced his run
that even his potential candidacy "would energize those of us who
have been dealing with the whole protest movement since day one."

He made those remarks on December 30, 2014. He wasn't wrong,
but he wasn't particularly prophetic, either. In response to the announcement by Donovan's grand jury, the city had already come apart
at the seams.

ELEVEN **CARMEN**

On December 3, 2014, a little after 2:00 P.M., an activist named Carmen Perez answered her cellphone in an office in Midtown Manhattan. The call came from Michael Skolnik, a producer and political organizer who works with Russell Simmons, the pioneering hip-hop mogul. Simmons had by then become a model for politically active cultural entrepreneurs and was very interested in this case.

TV news stations were reporting that a grand jury had refused to indict Daniel Pantaleo. Skolnik, Simmons's liaison to the activist community, had an obvious question.

"What are we going to do?"

"We're gonna meet in my office," answered Perez. "And then we're gonna take the streets."

Within hours after Donovan's announcement of a nonindictment of Pantaleo, tens of thousands of people spilled out onto the streets. More would follow with each passing day. If ever there was a time to force change through protest, it was now.

But there was a problem. The Garner case, and the Ferguson episode that followed it, had exposed a vacuum of political leadership within the black community.

In Ferguson, digital-age activists like Black Lives Matter had surprised everyone by repeatedly massing in huge numbers. They rallied by the thousands to take on police blockades from all directions on the strength of messages flowing through Twitter, Snapchat, Instagram, and other online applications.

These crowds formed without top-down advance direction of the sort practiced by the older generation of civil rights leaders, people like Sharpton and Jesse Jackson. Those two had been the faces of such protests for decades, but in a subplot to the Ferguson protests, both were heckled everywhere they went by younger, more strident activists. Many of these confrontations became widely circulated YouTube hits, with titles like "Al Sharpton and Jesse Jackson Booed Off Stage in Ferguson Missouri."

Sharpton would later try to fight back, reportedly telling young members at an NAN gathering that new activist groups trying to drive a wedge between protesters and the old guard were "pimping" young people.

"It's the disconnect that is the strategy to break the movement," Sharpton said, according to *Capital New York* reporter Azi Paybarah, who obtained a recording of the meeting.

On tape, the reverend goes on: "They play on your ego. 'Oh, you young and hip, you're full of fire. You're the new face.' All the stuff that they know will titillate your ears. That's what a pimp says to a ho."

But it was no use. In a foreshadowing of the anti-establishment movements that would emerge in the Republican and Democratic Parties in the 2016 presidential race, younger protesters seemed convinced that old-guard warriors like Jackson and Sharpton were, in fact, the assimilated voices of the political establishment. They were accused of having grown fat off donations from celebrities and wealthy liberals and of doing little beyond pursuing financial settlements and/or directing votes to an ineffectual, untrustworthy Democratic Party. They were part of a structure that, for whatever reason, had clearly failed to change much on the brutality front over the course of many decades.

Carmen Perez and the activists in her group, Justice League NYC, stood somewhere in the middle of this dynamic. They were hardly lavishly funded. At the time of the Garner grand jury decision, the only person in the group pulling a salary was Perez, who got a little money from a union, the Service Employees International Union (SEIU).

But even the small amount of patronage the group received, and the fact that it had an office, exposed it to criticism from other criminal justice reform groups. Critics took issue with the group's relationship to celebrities (Justice League NYC was formed as a task force of the Gathering for Justice, an initiative of legendary singer Harry Belafonte); they even took issue with their clothes.

The Justice Leaguers were activists in their late twenties and thirties who, perhaps in an effort to connect with inner-city youth who

were the targets of a lot of their programs, dressed in the sweatshirts-
and-ball-caps look of people ten years younger. Over the phone lines
of their union-funded office, college graduates spoke in slang.

"[Justice League] is like an old person's idea of young people," is
how one rival protest-group member acidly described them.

But when nobody else emerged as the leaders of the enormous
crowds pouring onto the streets of New York in early December 2014,
Perez and her cohorts stepped forward into the middle of a once-in-a-
generation odyssey. For two extraordinary weeks, the crowds grew
across the city, to the point where something like revolutionary fervor
began to vibrate through the winter air.

Then, in a single moment of terrible violence, it receded.

Perez is a recognizable figure on the protest circuit. She has almond
eyes and long black hair that she wears in a variety of styles or (often)
under a black wool cap, which is never pulled down so far that you
can't see a trademark patch of shaved scalp over her left ear.

Originally from Oxnard, California, from what she says is a "gang-
infested" neighborhood, Perez got into politics early, "after my sister
got buried" (she died in a car accident). Carmen joined the Mexican
American civil rights activist group Barrios Unidos following a stint
at UC Santa Cruz.

She then moved east, where she ended up working as a canvasser
and organizer for Purple Gold, a youth group funded by the SEIU.

Perez is the prototypical community organizer. She's bright, asser-
tive, committed, and articulate, though it's a particular kind of locu-
tion. She speaks in the convoluted, difficult-to-master language of the
modern activist left, which features an evolving lexicon of appropriate terms and a whole mysterious separate dictionary of movement
phraseology.

She will talk about things like "silos" and "justice summits" or use
phrases like "doing change at a holistic level versus just the back end"
without always explaining what she means. And she talks with pride
about helping to raise the consciousness of incarcerated young people, for instance, a young man who'd turned in a poem at a Justice
League workshop.

"The first time he had read his poem, he said, 'I want to get an Uzi,

and I want to chill with my thot, and blah, blah, blah, blah, blah,' "
she says. "And I'm like, 'What's a thot?' "

"Thot" turned out to stand for "that ho over there." Perez hastened to expunge the term from the inmate's vocabulary.

The minute Perez got the call from Skolnik on December 3, she
dropped everything. Along with people like Julianne Hoffenberg, a
film producer who serves as the Gathering's director of operations,
and Rameen Aminzadeh, another filmmaker who became heavily involved in directing and organizing street protests, Perez made plans to
take a leading role in whatever was going on in the streets.

The activists, in recounting the history of a remarkable two weeks
during which the Garner story dominated the city and headlines around
the world, clearly share a kind of *esprit de combat* and emphasize their
friendship and closeness as part of their story. The "Justice League" tag
actually was dreamed up with a superhero connotation in mind.

"We all have these different powers, but when we come together,
we're really able to make change," says Perez, whose abilities include
being a basketball player and a dancer in rap videos once upon a time.
"That's why we're called Justice League, because we're superheroes, I
feel."

"We come together like Voltron," concurs Aminzadeh.

A stout, bearded, Baltimore-born filmmaker, Aminzadeh says he
has done everything from direct music videos to edit episodes of *Who
the (Bleep) Did I Marry?* He had just come to New York from protesting in Ferguson when the Garner news broke.

Like Aminzadeh, Julianne "Jules" Hoffenberg has an entertain-
ment background, having worked on everything from HBO documentaries to celebrity panels involving the likes of Liev Schreiber,
Sarah Jessica Parker, and Rachel Maddow.

All three recall the pressure and excitement of December 3.

"We stopped having ownership over our own lives," Hoffenberg
remembers.

"We stopped sleeping or eating," explains Perez.

"Everything happened that day," says Aminzadeh.

They set up a "war room" in their offices above the SEIU chapter
in Midtown Manhattan and then took turns going out on the streets
with bullhorns and cellphones, hoping to lead marches, block city
streets, and "shut things down."

The giant crowds that swallowed up the streets in those weeks reflected a strong impulse to do something about a very specific set of
policies and problems, including Broken Windows policing and the
lack of accountability for abusive police. Yet nobody quite knew what
to do with all of that anger and determination.

The only protest strategy most Americans are familiar with is the
sixties model, which in grainy TV documentaries always seemed to
involve big crowds of marchers headed toward a government building. Aspects of the old protest model have been romanticized over
time, leading to the sometimes-embarrassing phenomenon of well-off
college graduates bragging about getting arrested and confronting
"the man," usually a line cop who will work his whole life and still
owe money on a starter house in some dreary suburb somewhere.

A lot of modern protests will have the superficial characteristics of
old civil disobedience battles: blocked streets, people being dragged
off by police in riot gear, singing, candlelight vigils, etc. But the high-
stakes nonviolent tactics of Gandhi and King had some teeth behind
them, relying on economic strikes and nonparticipation campaigns
to apply pressure on people in power. Nothing like that kind of
highly organized battle for political leverage would take place in
New York. Instead, protesters and pro-police advocates would take
turns trying to seize momentum through the dissemination of images
in the media.

This was ironic because the Garner story began as a viral Internet
video phenomenon, and the protests surrounding it would end in
much the same way.

On the first night after Donovan's announcement, demonstrations
broke out all over the city. From the Barclays Center in Brooklyn to
the West Side Highway to Columbus Circle to the Williamsburg
Bridge to spots all over Harlem, the South Bronx, and Staten Island,
major roads, highways, and commercial centers were closed off by
furious protesters.

Some of these crowds were spontaneous, and some weren't. A
dozen or more organizations, from Black Lives Matter to Copwatch
to the Stop Mass Incarceration Network (a front group for the Revolutionary Communist Party, USA), had sprung to action. Many of

these groups actively disliked, even detested, one another and, behind the scenes, began vying with one another to seize a role as leaders.

Mostly, though, people just went out onto the streets spontaneously, massing in places like Union Square and Times Square and using intel from social media to seek out confrontations with the roving squads of police that set up in places like Rockefeller Center, the Seventy-ninth Street off-ramp of the West Side Highway, and Mount Sinai Hospital up in Spanish Harlem.

The Justice League crew involved themselves in all of these early demonstrations. Rameen, Jules, and Carmen even got arrested on the second day for blocking the West Side Highway. "There's an image taken of me that made national news," Carmen says.

Then they were involved with what Carmen calls "economic shutdowns" (they blocked entrances to Macy's and an Apple Store) and began planning other actions, like shutting down the George Washington Bridge and interrupting a visit of the British royal family.

But it wasn't until December 8 that the group assumed a central role in the ongoing demonstrations by leveraging its celebrity connections into a media coup.

While protesters continued to fill the streets that first weekend, Carmen called her friend dream hampton (a writer and activist who eschews capital letters in her name). hampton is a longtime friend of Jay Z (she's credited as collaborating with him on his autobiographical book, *Decoded*), and Carmen asked her if she would reach out to the music mogul for a favor.

She did, and before long the group was planning a stunt, this one involving the Brooklyn Nets, the NBA team that at the time still listed Jay Z as a minority owner.

Through Jay Z, the group reached out to then Nets guard Deron Williams, who agreed to wear a T-shirt reading "I CAN'T BREATHE" before a home game with the Cavaliers.

Hurriedly they got Rameen to design and print up the shirts, and in a detail that sheds light on how threadbare the group's organization was, they barely had the money to pay for the printing. "I don't think we even had two hundred dollars in the bank for the shirts," says Hoffenberg.

But they got the cash together eventually and rushed by subway with the shirts to the arena in Brooklyn, where Jay Z had made arrangements to bypass security. This was necessary because then Chi-cago Bulls star Derrick Rose had worn an I CAN'T BREATHE shirt on Saturday the sixth—two days before—a move that reportedly left the NBA less than pleased.

"So Deron, with Jay Z, had to get a security guard that was his buddy to meet these guys so that they could get in," Carmen explains. "We met Deron's security guard in the back entrance and snuck them to him. He took them inside to the players."

The Justice League crew stayed outside of the arena. Inside, Jay Z ended up having a picture taken with four Nets players who wore the shirts: Williams, former league MVP Kevin Garnett, Alan Anderson, and Jarrett Jack. Jay Z sent the photo to hampton, who in turn re-layed it by phone to Carmen.

Almost immediately, the picture of the Nets players went viral, and the Justice League crew was announcing the feat to a crowd that had gathered outside the arena. The fact that Prince William and Kate Middleton were at the game, trailed by the usual ten million or so Fleet Street photogs, made it an international public relations coup.

"You could see it on the big screens in the back in the Barclays Center," remembers Rameen. "You could see them playing ball, and so as she's announcing it, they're warming up, and people are seeing it. It was just something that was extremely inspiring to the everyday folk," he says. "There was a win here."

With these and other actions, Justice League made its way into the news stories in prominent enough fashion that they began to be de-scribed as the leaders of the mass demonstrations.

By Tuesday, December 9, city and state leaders were, remarkably, agreeing to hold meetings with Justice League members.

The planned meetings with Mayor de Blasio, Governor Cuomo, Attorney General Eric Schneiderman, and city council leaders were pitched to the media as the independent triumph of an autonomous youth-led movement that had protested its way into the corridors of power.

Hoffenberg herself downplayed the group's celebrity connections at the time.

"We haven't really used any of our Justice League members or ad-visory board members to make outreach to anybody in the govern-ment," she told reporters.

The whole situation was curious. As remarkable as it was to see

NBA players wearing the I CAN'T BREATHE shirt—and that moment meant a lot to Eric Garner's family members—there was something odd about the ease with which senior state officials were willing to enter into something very like official negotiations with this tiny group of heretofore unknown activists.

But it was happening. On December 10, a Wednesday, the Justice Leaguers met with Attorney General Schneiderman as well as members of the city council and afterward held a press conference at City Hall.

This solidified their status (in the media, anyway) as the leaders of the ongoing demonstrations. At the meeting with Schneiderman, the group issued a list of ten demands:

1. The immediate firing of Daniel Pantaleo.
2. The creation of a special prosecutor to investigate police abuse cases.
3. The city and state will draft legislation clarifying the rules of engagement on the street.
4. The city will create a comprehensive NYPD training program.
5. An end to Broken Windows policing.
6. An end to the mass criminalization of kids in the New York City school system.
7. The United States attorney general, Eric Holder, will expedite an investigation into the death of Eric Garner.
8. Passage of the Right to Know Act, requiring officers to identify themselves.
9. New York State and all localities to engage in complete transparency regarding profiling and police personnel issues.
10. Meetings for the Justice League with the attorney general, mayor, and governor.

The press conference at City Hall was attended by Russell Simmons, the rapper/actor Common, and several council members. Justice League member Cherrell Brown sounded like she believed it when she added, "I believe we will win." It was starting to look like they just might.

Then it all started to go sideways.

. . .

On Saturday, December 13, the protests continued on the Brooklyn Bridge. The Justice Leaguers were there for a while, leading chants on a nine-mile march that was supposed to end at One Police Plaza in Manhattan.

It took ten long hours to complete the march, and when the JL people got over the bridge, they found the way to police headquarters blocked at Foley Square.

So they knocked off for the day and headed to a Mexican restaurant called Gonzalez y Gonzalez, on Mercer Street between Houston and Bleecker. They drank margaritas, plotted their next move, and went home.

They woke up the next morning to surprising headlines.

"NYPD Cops Attacked During 'Peaceful' Protest," read the *New York Post*.

"Amid Assaults on Officers, New York Police Rethink Their Response to Protests," was the predictably less-interesting construction of *The New York Times*.

Rameen, Carmen, and Jules read in horror. The gist of the stories was that a rogue group of protesters, led apparently by a part-time English professor from Baruch College, had assaulted a group of police officers on the bridge.

The professor, a twenty-nine-year-old named Eric Linsker, was caught brandishing a trash can while people were tossing "debris" on cops stationed on the lower level of the bridge. When a lieutenant named Philip Chan tried to arrest Linsker, he fled, effecting his escape as another man in a mask punched Chan in the face, breaking his nose.

Linsker, not exactly a master criminal, seems to have dropped his backpack. Police looked through it and found a preposterous kit bag for an academic: three recently purchased hammers, a passport, a MetroCard, a mask, a debit card, and a pill bottle containing marijuana.

With half the city seized with revolutionary fervor over a race killing, in an instant it began to unravel because of a white liberal-arts professor who tried to throw a trash can at police and carried to the scene of the crime ID leading straight to his home. Who brings a passport to a protest?

In addition to Linsker and the man in the mask who punched Chan, six other people were involved in the attack, which also targeted another lieutenant named Patrick Sullivan.

The five included two women and three men, all engaged in obvious assaults of the police, punching and kicking and throwing the
cops to the ground. Police also insisted later on that the mob tried to
steal the cops' portable radios and tear away their jackets.

Worse still, there was video of the incident, posted to YouTube,
which blew the story into an instant media sensation. The video was
the worst kind, salacious and violent, but also not quite clear enough
to identify the aggressors.

This turned the story into a thrilling media mystery on top of an
outrage. Police issued wanted photos and began the manhunt for the
John and Jane Doe trash-can assailants.

"Male number two has a hat on and later on his hat falls off and
he has a receding hair line. He's seen kicking Lieutenant Sullivan,"
said NYPD chief of Manhattan detectives William Aubry. "Male
number three is the most disturbing as well as male number two. He
pulls the officers down to the ground, and then he proceeds to run
away."

When the Justice Leaguers began to see their names associated with
the march in news stories, they were mortified.

"The next day, everyone was like, 'Justice League was inciting a
riot with the police on the Brooklyn Bridge,'" recalls Hoffenberg.
"We were like, 'Wait. We were having margaritas.'"

"Worse than that, someone stole our megaphones," fumes Rameen, explaining that their bullhorns had disappeared at the Mexican
restaurant.

It wasn't long before the cops arrested Linsker. Reporters dug up a
poem called "Thwaites" he'd published in August that borrowed its
only notable line from Ice Cube:

Fuck the police
To rise as you
Disappear below current
Interpretations of observations
Fuck the police

This news came out at the same time as another viral video, this one
shot from the window of a home on Thirty-second Street that showed
a group of protesters chanting, "What do we want? Dead cops."

The same dynamic that was igniting the national furor against police brutality, the omnipresence of cellphone videos, was now being
flipped around to work against protesters. Now each side had its own
outrage videos that could be referred to endlessly and amplified in
their respective media echo chambers.

It got worse from there. Mayor de Blasio tried to condemn the
bridge attacks as an aberration from otherwise peaceful protests but
screwed up even that simple mission.

He called the bridge fracas, which again was entirely recorded on
film, "an incident . . . in which a small group of protesters *allegedly*
assaulted some members of the NYPD."

Police officials jumped all over the "allegedly." Ed Mullins of the
Sergeants Benevolent Association called de Blasio a "nincompoop,"
while Michael Palladino of the detectives' union fumed, "When cops
are the accused, the word 'alleged' never enters into the discussion."

After the bridge incident, the former NYPD captain Joseph Concannon lost it. That was the tipping point for him. He'd been following the entire arc of the story since Garner's death and had had
enough. He decided to lead pro-police marches.

A longtime dabbler in GOP politics, he asked the Queens Village
Republican Club for an advance.

"I said, 'Will you guys front me a thousand dollars? I need money
because I want to pull together an organization so that we can hold
pro-cop rallies,'" he remembers. "'These guys are getting beat up.
They're getting demoralized.'"

There was an irony in this. Concannon had no love for street demonstrators. He had spent large portions of his career on the other side
of marches led by Sharpton, who during the eighties became a symbol
of everything law enforcement hated and resented about "community
organizers."

In the old days most cops saw Sharpton as an overgrown hustler
who looked like a hustler—he wore huge gold medallions and velour
track suits—and who played the game of leveraging the media to the
cause of winning lawsuits against cops. The marches and anti-police
demonstrations of the eighties, in Concannon's mind, were just part
of the hustle.

Papers got sold, lawyers won lawsuits, victims got settlements, and
the reverend got a higher profile. Everyone won except cops like Con-

cannon, who were demonized in the papers and got more bottles and rocks thrown at them at demonstrations.

Now, years later, a new generation of demonstrators was taking over the streets of New York, and Concannon decided he couldn't stand on the sidelines any longer.

Concannon would go on to become something like the street proxy for the growing feeling of alienation and betrayal within the police ranks that sometimes found expression in the comments of people like Pat Lynch. His protests would capture the widespread disgust toward politicians that emanated from the ranks of the police, who felt that they were being pilloried for doing exactly what politicians not so subtly had told them to do.

To Concannon, the Garner story had to be viewed in the context of a long series of confrontations with police—and with the CompStat system that pressured cops to fix problems they had no real way of fixing. Concannon tells a story that he heard through police ranks, a version of which was also reported in *The New York Times*. To wit: a store owner first complained about "conditions," i.e., sales of cigarettes and drugs, to the commander of the 120th Precinct.

"And he basically threw up his hands and said, 'I have arrested this guy. I've been jostling him, I've been doing everything that I can legally do in my legal responsibilities. I can't do any more,'" says Concannon. "And they said, 'Hmm, okay.'"

In Concannon's telling, the citizen complaints then went to the borough commander, who dropped some CompStat on the precinct chief.

"They took it to the borough commander," says Concannon. "And the borough commander said, 'You like your precinct? Do you? You like being the CO of the One Two Oh?'"

Concannon described what that kind of call would sound like to a precinct captain.

"You want to keep that job, right? You don't want me to embarrass you in front of the entire city, in front of all your peers at One Police Plaza? You want me to put your precinct on the map, with a picture of [Eric] Garner standing in front of a store, intimidating people, saying, 'Hey, Precinct Commander, what are you doing about that?'"

Concannon became furious as he watched the politicians' response to the Garner case and then also to the Ferguson case. He believed that Bill de Blasio represented everything wrong with the political dynamic.

"He campaigned against the police department. He bludgeoned them at every opportunity he had," Concannon says. But after he got elected, Concannon says, "he knew he had a problem. He knew he needed to put a real cop in and not just one of his lackeys."

So publicly de Blasio was anti-police, but privately he wanted the toughest, most aggressive kind of policing. Oddly enough, in this at least Concannon was in agreement with a lot of the protesters. The only difference was what motivated them to go out on the streets. It all boiled over for Concannon after the bridge incident, when he first decided to hold his rallies. After the bridge incident, Concannon and most of the police union leadership targeted one person above all for their wrath: the mayor.

In the history of New York there has probably never been a mayor as politically accident-prone as Bill de Blasio was in his early days in office. He was the Chevy Chase of elected officials. He walked over and over again into punji traps of his own creation.

In early 2014, in a traditional Groundhog Day ceremony at the Staten Island Zoo, de Blasio dropped Chuck the groundhog, who later died. It wasn't quite shooting Santa Claus, but it was close.

Merely killing a groundhog on Groundhog Day would have been bad enough, but it later came out that the zoo also tried to cover up the death, insisting that the animal died of old age (sources told the *New York Post* the death was "consistent with a fall"). De Blasio was the only politician capable of turning even a Groundhog Day photo op into a murder and a cover-up.

The Garner case posed a serious challenge to de Blasio as a new mayor, and he fumbled it nearly from the start with his disastrous roundtable, which *The New York Times* dubbed "the healing that wasn't." In that single episode, he lost both the police and Sharpton as allies and soon found himself taking water politically in the ensuing scandal over Rachel Noerdlinger.

Now, as street demonstrations tore apart his city and set his police department against him, de Blasio froze. This was destined to be the defining moment of his administration, and he seemed to wander through each successive day with less and less of a plan, watching problems pile up without responses.

In the wake of the Brooklyn Bridge fiasco, for instance, police spokespeople pounded him on an hourly basis. But he seemed too paralyzed to answer.

One move de Blasio did make in the face of all this was to cancel a planned meeting with the Justice Leaguers, who responded by staging a protest at the mayor's holiday party outside Gracie Mansion on December 15. Protesters chanted "I can't breathe" and "Shut it down" while the mayor held a muted Christmas celebration inside.

The rapper Immortal Technique, a Peruvian-born artist who grew up in Harlem and spent some time in jail for an assault he committed while also trying to finish college, delivered an oddly moving and pointed impromptu demonstration at this protest.

Dressed in a Yankee hat and a plain black jacket, he told a story designed to refocus attention on the root of the problem. This wasn't about hating cops, he said, but rather about fairness.

"Don't tell us these racist lies, how we don't care when someone black or brown dies in our community, we only care when they're the victim of a white police officer," he said.

He paused. "My friend recently died. He left a hole in my heart. All right, a hole that can never be filled. And I'm speaking from my soul here. We *cared* when he died. We care when everyone dies.

"But you know what the difference is, bigots of the world? That when those people die, if someone catches the 'gangbanger' or the individual who's responsible for their murder on camera, he's going to jail ninety-nine point nine nine nine percent of the time!"

Applause broke out in the crowd.

"And when we catch an officer of the law, who's supposed to know the law, and in my opinion should be held to that law to the highest standards, ninety-nine point nine nine nine percent of the time we hear excuses instead of hearing accountability.

"And that's all we're saying. We want you to make it what you said it was on paper. Otherwise, it's a lie."

He went on, spoke more, and turned to look at Gracie Mansion.

"They think they can just close the door and have some kind of let-them-eat-cake Louis XVI party in there, while we starving out here," he said, before quickly catching himself.

"And when I say starving, I mean we got donuts. We starving for justice."

All of this was going on outside the home of a mayor who had been elected in large part thanks to his promises to reform the police.

De Blasio had gone from being the savior of New York liberalism to being Marie Antoinette in less than a year.

A few days later, Carmen and the rest of the Justice League activists were hit with a surprise. Mayor de Blasio sent word that he would, in fact, have a meeting with them.

"At one point it was supposed to be he was going to meet with everybody," says Jules. "And then it was like, 'We'll meet with ten people.' And then, 'We'll meet with eight people,' and then, 'We'll meet with six.' Then it was five."

At the meeting, when they brought up Broken Windows, de Blasio shrugged and said even discussing that was a nonstarter. He told them that Commissioner Bratton wouldn't budge on that. Everyone would just have to find a way to make that work.

The Justice Leaguers stared at one another in shock. Just like that, the central issue in the protests was officially off the table. What was de Blasio doing here?

To say that the mayor was an enigma would be an understatement. In the hours after the grand jury announcement, de Blasio had given an extraordinary—some would say politically unprecedented—speech talking about how he'd had to warn his own biracial son, Dante, about the dangers of his own police department.

He'd begun by referring to his conversation that night with Eric Garner's stepfather, Ben Carr, whom de Blasio characteristically misnamed "Ben Garner" and misidentified as Garner's father.

"It's a very hard thing to spend time trying to comfort someone you know is beyond the reach of comfort because of what he's been through," said de Blasio, adding, "I couldn't help but immediately think what it would mean to me to lose Dante."

He then talked about how he and his wife, Chirlane, had had to instruct their son in how to behave around police. "Because of a history still that hangs over us, the dangers he may face, we've had to literally train him as families have all over this city for decades in how to take special care in any encounter he has with the police officers."

Nothing de Blasio said was untrue. He was right that teaching children how to behave around police—no sudden movements, keep your hands visible at all times, etc.—was a ritual virtually all black families in the city had learned to go through over the years. After the Giuliani and Bloomberg years—almost two decades of hard insensitivity on police matters—hearing the mayor speak this simple truth was a breath of fresh air.

But to the police rank and file, de Blasio's speech was pure treason. It was as though he was describing an occupying force of unaccountable racists, not an army of cops that, incidentally, he personally commanded.

"He's the head of the police department and he's saying that!" roared the ex-captain Concannon. "Unbelievable."

A politician with keener instincts than de Blasio might have understood that the protests raging across his city were about two problems, one far more fixable than the other. And this sharper sort of politician could have defused the situation by diverting attention away from the one and toward the other.

A large part of the tension between protesters and police lay in the explosive and impossibly complicated argument about race that had long divided the whole country.

On one side sat a group of mostly nonwhite Americans who believed (or knew from personal experience) that institutional racism is still a deathly serious problem in this country, as evidenced by everything from profiling to mass incarceration to sentencing disparities to a massive wealth gap.

On the other side sat an increasingly impatient population of white conservatives that was being squeezed economically (although not nearly as much as black citizens), felt its cultural primacy eroding, and had become hypersensitive to any accusation of racism. These conservatives blamed everything from the welfare state to affirmative action for breeding urban despair and disrespect toward authority—in other words, these conservatives saw *themselves* as victims of malevolent systems and threatening trends but thought that nonwhite Americans were fully responsible for their own despair.

This basic disagreement animated virtually every major political controversy in America, from immigration to health care to welfare reform. It gave no sign of being quickly and easily resolved.

But the other controversy that caused de Blasio's streets to be

clogged with people that month involved highly specific sets of policies, including Broken Windows and the absence of a special prosecutor for police-abuse cases. These were immediately fixable issues.

If de Blasio was so concerned for the safety of his son, he had it in
his power to unilaterally end the practice of intrusive searches, mass
arrests, and summonses over ticky-tack violations that vastly increased the statistical likelihood of deadly encounters.

But he wouldn't go there. Apparently, his relationship with Bill
Bratton was too important to him. Faced with a fork in the road, with
a choice between keeping the status quo and changing a racially
charged enforcement policy, de Blasio took the fork.

He alienated the rank and file by talking about how his own police
officers were a threat to his son while simultaneously refusing to dial
down the City Hall/CompStat–generated pressure to make numbers
that was at least partly responsible for forcing cops into the role of
street bullies.

On a more mundane level, de Blasio alienated the cops by agreeing
to meet with the protesters. Then he would alienate the protesters by
blowing them off in the meeting. Every move the mayor made was a
self-defeating blunder.

The Justice League activists were perplexed and disappointed that the
mayor began the meeting by taking Broken Windows off the table,
but they went on. As they spoke, de Blasio interrupted them and
brought up the Brooklyn Bridge incident, asking for their take.

The activists quickly referred to their "Kingian nonviolence" platform and noted that they were not even there when it happened (they
left out the part about the margaritas).

"It was like, a two-second conversation," says Carmen.

Soon after, the forty-five-minute meeting wrapped up. The group
issued a statement.

"We were like, 'Great meeting, first step,'" Carmen explains.

Except that de Blasio spoke with reporters right after the meeting
and essentially tossed the group off a cliff, saying that Justice League
was ready to help police find the remaining bridge assailants.

"They will work with the police to identify anyone who seeks to
harm the police," he said. "So I thought there was real unity on that
point."

De Blasio either didn't know or didn't care that by announcing to the world that the activists would work with the police to capture protesters, he'd just sabotaged the group with the entire protest community. Twitter exploded with taunting tweets from all corners, including protesters and rival activist organizations.

One of the harshest denunciations came from Copwatch, a group dedicated to filming and observing police that was run by a young Puerto Rican from Sunset Park in Brooklyn named Dennis Flores.

Flores in the early 2000s had been beaten in a bogus arrest that went sideways, an incident similar to the Staten Island case involving Ibrahim Annan. When he later successfully sued the NYPD in federal court, he used his settlement to found Copwatch, which would later claim Ramsey Orta as one of its spokespeople.

Flores had heard the news coming from the mayor's office that Justice League would be working with the police to locate troublesome protesters, and he was furious. In his mind the Justice League meetings with state officials were a dog-and-pony show anyway.

"Harry Belafonte was a major backer of de Blasio's campaign, so that's how this happened," he says, echoing the complaints of several rival protest groups. "We've all been at this for years and we never get close to a meeting with the mayor, and they show up and get it right away."

As soon as he heard the news about the meeting, Flores tweeted out:

We have zero tolerance for people who collaborate with the police against people who want radical and/or social change. #stopsnitching

Flores had called the Justice Leaguers "snitches," a claim that was spun all over the Internet. The accusations of collaboration with police attracted enough press attention that Justice League was forced to put out a statement in response:

CLARIFICATION: @NYjusticeleague is focused on transforming the systemic racism within NYPD. We have NO relationship w/ them whatsoever.

It was an odd statement. "The group might have condemned violence while still maintaining an adversarial relationship with the police force," wrote Jacob Siegel of the *Daily Beast.* "Instead, its representatives said they weren't snitches and left it at that."

At the end of this trying day, the Justice Leaguers sat around in shock, devastated. The Chevy Chase of mayors had dropped a banana peel in front of someone else for a change.

"The mayor played a hand that worked for him," sighs Rameen.

Except that he really hadn't. Maybe the Justice Leaguers were always implausible as the would-be leaders of the protests wracking his city, but by blowing them up in public, de Blasio just ensured that he now had no one to talk to in the protest community.

And if he thought that wiping out a ragtag group of protesters would buy him some love from the police unions, he was about to find out otherwise.

Late in the afternoon of the next day, a Saturday, two police officers named Wenjian Liu and Rafael Ramos were sitting in a squad car in Bedford-Stuyvesant, at the intersection of Myrtle and Tompkins Avenues. Without warning, an itinerant loner named Ismaaiyl Brinsley walked up to the passenger-side window and pulled out a gun.

Before Liu and Ramos could react, Brinsley opened fire and shot both in the head, killing them instantly. He then ran down the street, entered the Myrtle-Willoughby subway station, and waited on the platform. As police closed in, he shot himself in the head with a silver-colored semi-automatic handgun.

Brinsley was twenty-eight and had been spiraling mentally for some time. Originally from Brooklyn, he'd bounced all over the Eastern Seaboard as a young person, growing up most of the time in Atlanta, living sometimes with his mother, sometimes in group homes, and sometimes on the streets.

He ended up drifting from town to town and getting arrested for a series of increasingly bizarre crimes. In one of his busts, he stole a pair of scissors, some condoms, and a power inverter from a Rite Aid. Police found him in the laundry room of a nearby hotel minutes later, trying to cut off his braids. In another case, he was caught threatening a Waffle House employee and trying to punch her.

He began the last day of his life in Baltimore. He went to the home of an ex-girlfriend in Baltimore who'd recently dumped him and put a gun to his own head. When she talked him out of killing himself, he shot her. She survived, but by then he was on his way to New York, having posted an ominous message on Instagram:

I'm Putting Wings On Pigs Today. They Take 1 Of Ours......
Let's Take 2 of Theirs #ShootThePolice #RIPErivGardner
#RIPMikeBrown.

Baltimore cops got wind of Brinsley's note and tried to alert the NYPD, but they only got the message just as Liu and Ramos were being killed.

As de Blasio trudged to a news conference to address the killings that evening, a number of police officers in attendance turned their backs on him.

Bizarrely, the decision by police to turn their backs on the mayor inspired the actor James Woods, of all people, to tweet out a hashtag, #TurnYourBack, that quickly circulated around the country. This would lead to hundreds of officers turning their back on the mayor during the funerals of the two slain officers.

Erica had been following the entire protest saga with great interest. At first, the sheer number of marchers protesting her father's death had inspired her. But she needed to figure out what she would do with that inspiration.

She felt the first inkling of a desire to start her own form of protest while sitting at the NAN press conference on December 3, listening to Al Sharpton give a speech about the nonindictment. Erica's thoughts had drifted at that moment. She didn't want to be just a prop at a press conference, the suffering victim. "I suddenly felt I had to do something that wasn't just speeches," she recalls. "I had to do something on my own."

As she watched the marchers flood the streets in the month that followed, she resolved to do more. "I figured, if they out there for my family, why shouldn't I be?"

And she began to have doubts that working within the system would get things done. The performance by the mayor was less than inspiring. At first, she'd been pleased by the speech that had so infuriated the cops, the one about how he worried about that son of his becoming a victim of police abuse.

But then she saw de Blasio bending and vacillating when the pressure started to pile on during the protests. He began to push his rhetoric in a different direction, as though anxious to appease the police force and white voters. And finally, after the deaths of Ramos and Liu, when the police openly defied him and turned their backs on him, de Blasio did nothing.

"I'd say that's the moment that hit for me," Erica remembers. "Just didn't like him when those officers turned his back twice, turned their back on him twice, and I felt like asking, 'Who do the police answer to?'"

She pauses. "I mean, if they don't answer to the commissioner, if they don't answer to the mayor, then who? That to me showed his weakness."

More and more, Erica began to see that if she wanted to accomplish anything in her father's case, she would have to do it without relying on political figures. She would have to do it herself.

The Patrolmen's Benevolent Association chief, Pat Lynch, gave a seething press conference that night after the Liu and Ramos funerals. Even by his standards, it was a doozy.

Lynch seemed incapable of empathizing with the victims of police violence and inevitably described such people as having brought their deaths and injuries on themselves.

Even when the victim had done nothing more than open a door of a housing project stairwell, as unarmed black teenager Timothy Stansbury had done in Bed-Stuy in 2004 before being shot, Lynch wouldn't hear of police being blamed. In that case, he called for then commissioner Ray Kelly's resignation after Kelly said there "appears to be no justification for the shooting."

In another case, Lynch defended a cop caught on video shoving a kid off a bicycle by saying the cyclist was an "anarchist."

In Lynch's mind, no police officer in history had ever been guilty of anything, and he repeatedly pooh-poohed the widespread anger over Garner's death as liberal propaganda besmirching the name of good cops.

Now, after the deaths of Liu and Ramos, Lynch was quick to describe the incident as the fault of a cop-hating mayor who coddled violent extremists who only posed as peaceful protesters but finally got what they wanted.

"There's blood on many hands tonight," Lynch said. "That blood on the hands starts on the steps of City Hall in the office of the mayor." He also pointed at "those that incited violence on the street, under the guise of protest."

Liu was the son of Chinese immigrants and had patriotically joined the force after 9/11. His mother would later tell a story of how he once found a little boy from Queens lost in their neighborhood. "He was hungry, so my son took him to McDonald's and fed him," said Xiu Yan Li. "He drove him home, back to Queens."

Ramos was the father of two and so devout that he was studying to be a pastor. His wife, Maritza, and his two sons would go on to spend the next years, like the Garner family, dreading anniversaries of the murder.

The Liu-Ramos murders essentially ended the nationwide demonstrations. Public opinion, which had tilted decisively in favor of police reform after the Garner grand jury decision, had swung around entirely. The country was now furious about the police deaths, and in yet another ancient pattern that surfaced and would repeat itself over and over again, the distinction between protesters and criminals blurred in the public consciousness.

Protesters of all persuasions found themselves paralyzed by grief and defeat. The Justice Leaguers knew it was over almost immediately, not just for them but for all the protesters in the city, and nationally as well.

"We felt defeated at that moment. We felt a lot of sorrow," Rameen remembers.

"Everything changed," Jules recalls.

"Everything," agrees Carmen.

There were some halfhearted attempts at different actions in the next days, but they petered out. The activists ended up spending Christmas on a toy drive.

On the night of the murders, a memo was circulated to many officers, ostensibly from the Patrolmen's Benevolent Association leadership, most likely from the pen of Pat Lynch. The memo asked officers not to respond to calls alone and then added something very strange:

> Absolutely NO enforcement action in the form of arrests and or summonses is to be taken unless absolutely necessary and an individual MUST be placed under arrest.

Whoever wrote this memo either had a keen sense of irony or was completely deaf to the subtleties of language. After having railed for weeks against citizens for protesting, the police were now going to engage in a protest of their own by limiting themselves to "necessary" arrests.

Which raised the question: What exactly was an "unnecessary" arrest or summons? And why had the police been handing them out to begin with?

Capital New York got hold of a recording of Lynch talking to union members at a nonpublic meeting at this time.

"If we won't get support when we do our jobs, if we're going to get hurt for doing what's right, then we're going to do it the way they want it," he said, not realizing he was being recorded. He went on:

"Our friends, we're courteous to them. Our enemies, extreme discretion. The rules are made by them to hurt you. Well, now we'll use those rules to protect us."

Lynch clearly seemed intent on making sure police would no longer aggressively engage their "enemies" on the street, instead asking cops now to follow what he called the "stupid rules" as a way of showing the public how necessary it was to defy them.

A month of December that began in furious protests against police brutality ended in an unprecedented police slowdown, what the *Post* called a "virtual work stoppage." The numbers were staggering. From December 22 to December 27, police made 66 percent fewer arrests versus the same period the year before, while summonses (including traffic summonses) were down 94 percent.

It was not clear exactly at what or whom the stoppage was aimed: the protesting public who needed to be reminded of the essential nature of police, a president who'd angered many police after Ferguson, or a mayor who had made enemies of the rank and file by palling around with Sharpton (and by talking about how he'd warned his own half-black son, Dante, to be careful around cops).

Whatever the plan was, it didn't really work, as the public mostly seemed pleased not to be ticketed so much.

The police protest lasted nearly three weeks, until January 13 or so of the new year, when the *Daily News* pronounced it over.

"So long to the slowdown," the paper cracked.

Commissioner Bratton said that while he was still "concerned" with the "levels of activity," which had been down 38 percent in the week of January 5–11, things were now returning to "normal."

The story, however, was not over.

Throughout the month, as protests raged on the streets, another line of opposition was quietly developing in the offices of a number of New York lawyers.

Since Dan Donovan had announced the results of the grand jury and petitioned the court to release information about the case he'd presented, several groups of attorneys, independently of one another, began to ask themselves a question: If Donovan could violate the sacrosanct principle of grand jury secrecy for the sake of "assuring the public," why should he be the only one?

A judge had let the DA release secret information for the plainly self-serving public relations objective of maintaining confidence in the efficacy of his office. Why didn't the public have an equal right to know if that confidence was misplaced?

As it happens, five different groups of lawyers, each with different relationships to the Garner case, all had the same thought more or less simultaneously. All five ended up making an effort to try to unseal the Pantaleo grand jury.

The five groups included New York's Legal Aid office, the office of Public Advocate Letitia James, the *New York Post,* the NAACP, and the New York Civil Liberties Union (NYCLU).

Their individual reasons varied slightly, but each essentially wanted to get to the bottom of the mystery of what had happened inside Donovan's grand jury. Many of them suspected that Donovan had thrown the case and believed that the public had a right to know.

Christopher Pisciotta's Legal Aid office was the first to go to Rooney's court. Having represented Garner in the past, their office was blindsided by the December 3 decision.

"It was very moribund in the office, and everyone was quiet and depressed," Pisciotta says. "A lot of our attorneys had contact with Garner, and with the video there was an assumption that we'd get justice." Disappointed, Pisciotta reached out to Tina Luongo, head of criminal defense for Legal Aid in New York, and they sketched out a motion together.

"You have more than enough in the public eye to support a charge, so why'd you call fifty witnesses?" Pisciotta remembers thinking. "Was the DA seeking an indictment or fashioning a defense?"

Pisciotta stayed up most of that first night, studied the case law surrounding grand jury secrecy, and before long was ready with the motion. But when he went to Rooney's court, he was hit with a huge surprise.

The judge's clerk refused to accept his brief unless it was filed under seal.

In other words, the motion to unseal the secret proceeding had to be secret itself. He could not tell the media what his office had done and couldn't discuss it with other organizations.

Pisciotta and the rest of the Legal Aid team thought this was crazy. How was it fair to ask lawyers to keep the whole thing secret? He and his team pondered raising a public fuss but ultimately decided to go along.

"We made a strategic decision that it was more important to get this done for justice, rather than making this about PR," he says. "So we filed, and the court accepted the motion."

Ludicrously, this secrecy meant that none of these organizations initially realized that the others were trying the same thing. Had it not been for a quirk in the résumé of a lawyer in the public advocate's office, it's possible that none of the five petitioners would ever have heard about the others. It's even possible that the entire effort to unseal the Garner minutes would have remained completely secret from the public.

The public advocate is the second-highest elected office in the city of New York and serves essentially as a kind of government ombudsman, an elected official keeping watch over other elected officials.

The advocate's job is to keep his or her doors open to the public, listen to complaints, and pursue concerns aggressively. De Blasio was the city's public advocate before becoming mayor, and the current officeholder, Letitia "Tish" James, was not only the first woman of color to hold citywide office in New York but had kept open lines of communication with the Garner family. When James's lawyers went off to Rooney's court to file their motion, they were stunned by the demand that the motion itself be kept under seal.

The two attorneys working for the public advocate were Jen Levy, the office's general counsel for litigation, and Matthew Brinckerhoff, of Emery Celli Brinckerhoff & Abady, probably the city's most prestigious civil rights firm. The lawyers thought Rooney's demands for secrecy were ridiculous and confounding. The problem was that there didn't seem to be anything to do about it, given that the order meant you couldn't even mention the problem to any other living soul.

"You couldn't tell reporters to come and then get them to guess what had happened," Levy remembers. "As in, you know, if I blink once that means yes, twice it means no."

Frustrated, Levy and Brinckerhoff put their heads together to think of a way around Rooney's dictum. By coincidence, both had been tenant attorneys once upon a time and remembered a tool they'd often had to use to force courts to swiftly reconsider the sometimes-unsound ex parte orders of judges.

"As a tenant lawyer, sometimes you have clients who are at risk of being evicted the next day," remembers Levy. "If they get a denied order, then it's important for them to have some ability to seek an immediate appeal."

The tool, they recalled, was Civil Practice Laws and Rules (CPLR) provision 5704(a), aka "Review of ex parte orders by Appellate Division." Rule 5704 allowed them to go over the heads of judges to the state's appellate division to ask for reconsideration of an order.

Levy and Brinckerhoff filed their motion under seal, then went to the appellate division and asked for a review of Rooney's order. They won.

While the advocate's office was making their 5704 appeal, the NYCLU, led by veteran civil rights lawyer Arthur Eisenberg, went to Rooney's court with their own motion. Soon after, the NAACP and the *Post* joined in. While the streets of New York were consumed for weeks by protests, another more concentrated battle was coalescing around the Garner grand jury.

What had happened in the 139 days between Garner's death and the grand jury decision? What was said in that room?

This puzzle over a secret legal proceeding quickly became another powerful metaphor for the underlying problem of American race relations. Just as there was no way for anyone to really know any person's true feelings about race, there was no way to ever be completely sure about what had gone on in a grand jury hearing.

Prosecutors insisted that the process had been on the level. The family—and most of black and immigrant New York—was convinced that something dirty had gone on in that room. On the most mundane level, the effort to peek inside the Garner grand jury was merely a huge legal challenge, intellectual safecracking that would require finding a way around a bedrock concept in the Western legal tradition, grand jury secrecy.

But on another level, the five legal petitioners were engaged in a profound historical mystery. The sealed Garner grand jury proceedings became a stand-in for the Pandora's box of American racism. The effort to open it was symbolic of the larger argument about what exactly was going on behind the walls of American race relations—what was really happening inside our homes and offices, inside our own minds.

Were we a postracial society, as so many people claimed? Or was there something crooked and evil just below the surface? Opening the grand jury proceedings could allow the country a rare glimpse at the truth.

TWELVE JIMMY

On May 31, 1971, in a small city called Benton in southern Arkansas, a young African American woman named Clementine Russ, a newborn baby in her arms, stepped into a shiny green Delta 88 Oldsmobile with her husband, Carnell.

The two had met more than half a decade before in a furniture factory in Monticello, a small town an hour or so to the south. Carnell had been overcome by the sight of the stunning young woman incongruously dressed in goggles and a white work shirt who worked the rip saw a few feet over from him on the factory floor. He'd courted her almost from first sight.

Clementine for her part was less impressed at first. But eventually she gave in to the burly young man who lied about his age (he said he was older, to impress her) and was always testing her patience, dirtying up her clean work clothes by putting his grease-covered hands around her waist.

"He just wouldn't give up," she remembers, thinking back. "I got to liking him. He was funny and always carrying on."

Now it was years later, and they were married and had a large family. Clementine sat in the front of Carnell's new car with their week-old daughter, Fashunda. Five of her other children—Roosevelt, Curtis, Sylvia, Joyce, and Verna—were in the backseat.

Clementine's grown cousin, Denton "DeeDee" Lambert, sat next to her on the bench front seat.

Although there were nine people inside, Clementine remembers that it didn't feel crowded in the car. They were planning on a ninety-minute drive to the southeast, from Benton to Monticello. They left Benton around four in the afternoon. Carnell was due back to work at the factory at midnight that night.

On the way, the family detoured into the town of Pine Bluff, where Carnell stopped at a record store called Yancy's. Inside, he bought a new 45 from an R&B band called Billy Butler and Infinity.

The name of the record was "I Don't Want to Lose You."

After the quick stop, the family piled back into the car and headed for Monticello. On the road between those two towns lay Star City. Although they'd been married there, the town had a bad reputation among black people in southern Arkansas. Clementine remembered years before not being allowed inside the town laundromat. The family didn't intend to stop there.

About six miles before Star City, along a grassy two-lane highway that is today called Route 425, Carnell rounded a slight turn and came over a hill, beginning a long descent toward the town.

A few moments later, he heard a siren. A white Arkansas state trooper named Jerry Mac Green was behind him, signaling for him to stop. Carnell pulled over.

Trooper Green ostensibly stopped Carnell for speeding, although the real offense may have just been driving too nice a car. He didn't trust the man to pay his fine later, so he demanded that Carnell drive into Star City and pay a "bond" on the spot.

On the way to Star City, Trooper Green called in for backup. He was met in Star City by two other men in uniform, a Star City police trainee named Norman Draper and another town cop, a Mississippi native with a history of violence named Charles Lee Ratliff. The three men demanded that Carnell come into the police station, where they told him he needed to pay twenty-three dollars before he could leave town.

Carnell came back out to the car to ask Clementine for the money. Years later, Clementine would remember that the three officers followed closely behind and hovered under a nearby tree as her husband leaned inside the car window to ask for money. It was as though they were afraid Russ might try to run.

Carnell took twenty-five dollars from Clementine and walked back toward the jailhouse with the three men. She remembers watching him walk away, around and behind the courthouse, for the last time.

Inside the courthouse, Russ paid the money, then made what proved to be a fatal mistake. He asked for a receipt.

There are differing accounts of what happened next, but they all come back to the same thing. Outraged by Carnell's insolence, Ratliff ended up shooting Russ between the eyes.

From her seat in the car, Clementine didn't hear the shot. But she remembers watching an ambulance arrive and circle round the back of the building. Nobody told her anything for a good long while.

Eventually Trooper Green exited the police station. He walked slowly across the courthouse lawn, past Clementine, and went to his car, never looking over at Carnell's car. Finally, Clementine sent her cousin DeeDee to ask what was going on.

"I said to DeeDee, 'Go down there and ask them what happened to Carnell,'" she said. "But just as he was fixing to get out the car, [Green] came back up here."

Green had gotten out of his car but remained on the driver's side of the vehicle, so that the police car remained between him and the Russ family. From a distance, he signaled for cousin Denton.

"He made for DeeDee to come over," Clementine recalls. "And he said something to DeeDee, and he had this look on his face. And I knew something was wrong. I don't know how I knew, but before I got out of the car I was a nervous wreck. And that's when [Trooper Green] told DeeDee to take the baby."

By then, Green and DeeDee had come over to the car. Clementine, knowing and yet not knowing, was shaking and trembling all over. DeeDee took week-old Fashunda from her, and Green finally broke the news.

"Your husband said a smart word," is how Green explained Carnell's death.

Half a year later, in January 1972, an all-white jury took eight minutes to acquit Charles Lee Ratliff of voluntary manslaughter.

Clementine remembers sitting in the courtroom in a fog, dizzy at how fast it all happened. "I didn't know what was happening," she says now. "It was unreal."

After Ratliff's acquittal, the Russ family filed suit against everyone they could think of for the wrongful death of Carnell Russ.

An elderly judge named Oren Harris was chosen to hear the Russ lawsuit. Harris had represented southern Arkansas in Congress for nearly a quarter of a century. He had been Clementine's congressman.

While serving in that capacity, he'd signed the infamous Southern Manifesto against the *Brown v. Board of Education* Supreme Court decision forcing the integration of public schools. The document accused integrationists of trying to upset the "good" relations that existed between white and black people in the fifties.

Three days into the trial, the man who'd signed that document tossed the Star City mayor, the six aldermen, and Officer Draper from the suit. Proceedings were allowed against Green and Ratliff only.

Ratliff, Clementine remembers, represented himself in court. He was laughing and winking at people in the gallery and generally gave the impression that he wasn't too concerned about the case.

"He was very arrogant," says Clementine now. "He acted like he knew he didn't have to be worried about nothing."

Once again, an all-white jury was seated. The jury took three hours this time instead of eight minutes. They found Ratliff and Green innocent.

Clementine's NAACP lawyers, George Howard Jr. and James Meyerson, were frustrated by the results. They decided to look for another way to fight the case.

Howard and Meyerson, the former black and the latter white, couldn't have been more different. Howard was a measured, serious, academic presence whose whole life had been about breaking barriers. After serving in segregated units in World War II, he returned home and became the first black student to live on the campus of the University of Arkansas at Fayetteville.

He was for a time the only black lawyer in Pine Bluff and went on to become the first black person in Arkansas appointed to the federal bench. Many years later, he would be the presiding judge in several of the famed Whitewater corruption cases, including the trial of Susan McDougal.

Meyerson, meanwhile, was a thin, quirky, unbuttoned character, a courtroom brawler given to soaring rhetorical flourishes. A former Syracuse Law classmate of Joe Biden's, he played a unique role as a white lawyer within the NAACP, where he served as the assistant general counsel for the whole of the seventies. He was probably best known for helping to negotiate the pardon of Clarence Norris, the son of a slave and the last living member of the Scottsboro Boys, nine young men who'd been falsely accused of rape in 1931.

His legal partnership with the stately Howard was a bit of a good cop/bad cop routine, with Meyerson playing the role of the unpredictable courtroom presence.

The two men had been through tough times. In the 1972 desegregation case *Alexander v. Warren,* about the firing of a black teacher named Travistine Alexander, anti-integration protesters in the Arkansas town of Warren were so vociferous that the National Guard had to be called in to escort Howard and Meyerson to and from the courtroom.

In the Russ case, Meyerson and Howard decided to focus on a law passed by Congress in 1948, giving the federal government the power to intervene if a person was harmed by a "deprivation of any rights, privileges, or immunities secured or protected by the Constitution."

That law, 18 U.S.C. § 242, was a kind of magic bullet, a legal trump card that gave the federal government the right to step in and act if local governments failed to uphold the constitutional rights of any person.

In the case of Carnell Russ, the fact that Charles Lee Ratliff had been brought to trial at all ostensibly blocked the federal government from pursuing the matter. This was true even though the "trial" had been a fairly obvious fraud. Under current law, any local proceeding, even a sham trial, obviated the need for federal action.

The policy against "dual prosecutions" was based upon an interpretation of the law elucidated in a memo by then deputy attorney general William Rogers during the last years of the Eisenhower administration. It seemed to Meyerson that the Rogers policy made no sense if the first prosecution was not a real one. The federal government clearly had a tool to make things right in the Russ case, but Rogers was keeping 18 U.S.C. § 242 holstered.

So Meyerson huddled up with Howard and decided to try something off the wall. They filed suit against Edward Levi, the attorney general of the United States, for failing to conduct an investigation into the possibility that Russ's rights had been violated under 18 U.S.C. § 242 and/or other laws.

Essentially, they were suing the federal government for failing to use its power to tame corrupt local city governments.

On September 3, 1976, an African American judge named Barrington Parker handed down his ruling. It was a blowout for the NAACP. He ruled that the NAACP and the Russ family had standing to sue.

After this change, the federal government for the first time openly claimed purview over local criminal cases. It asserted its right to step in and reprosecute if state or city governments were too backward or corrupt to do it themselves. Star City, Arkansas, became the birth-place of the modern federal civil rights investigation.

Characteristically, this enormous intellectual and legal victory in Washington did little for Clementine Russ personally. Though she won the right to see one, there never was a successful civil rights pros-ecution of anyone in Star City. Meanwhile, her own civil lawsuit dragged on endlessly.

It was only in April 1979, eight years after her husband's murder, that a jury finally awarded Clementine Russ $288,000 in damages due her from Charles Lee Ratliff. At the conclusion of the case, one white lawyer in the courtroom approached her with a huge smile on his face.

"You should be happy," he said. "No black person in Arkansas has ever gotten that much."

Miss Clementine waited for her money to arrive.

Thirty-five years later, as she sat watching TV in rural Arkansas, a news story caught her attention. A man named Eric Garner had been killed in New York by police. As her family had once done, Garner's family was now headed to court to demand answers.

As she watched, Miss Clementine was sitting in the same small home near the railroad tracks she once shared with her husband Car-nell. She sat in the living room, not far from where her husband used to leave his work clothes while he slept. Ratliff had never paid up, then had disappeared out of state, then apparently had died. So no-body had paid her a dime yet. She was still waiting. Nearly half a century had passed.

The north side of Staten Island in the winter always seems colder than everywhere else in the city. Tompkinsville Park rests at the base of a hill overlooking New York Harbor, and the wind here rushes up from the water's edge and bites at the ears and eyes. When Eric Garner worked here he struggled to find any way to stay outside and shel-tered from the wind at the same time. He would come home from a day standing in the cold and collapse, his massive body exhausted from the energy-sapping cold.

Up the street from Tompkinsville Park rests the city court complex. It's on higher ground and feels even colder here than the park. Febru-ary 5, 2015, was a particularly frigid day, too, a bitter Thursday at the outset of what would prove to be the third coldest February in the city's history. Protesters—not many, due to the extreme weather— gathered outside the courtroom that day, carrying signs that read, "End the New Jim Crow!" and "What Are They Hiding?" and "Open the Grand Jury Records!"

Inside, a heretofore little-known judge named William Garnett entered a small, oppressively lit courtroom packed with press, Eric Garner's friends and family, and a large and plainly nervous assembly of court police. With a swipe of the gavel, the judge opened the proceedings.

"Part twenty-two, the Honorable William Garnett presiding," shouted the clerk.

"Please be seated," said Judge Garnett, a pale and narrow-shouldered man with a carefully trimmed sweep of metal-gray hair.

The tension in the room was palpable. This was the day that arguments would be heard on the matter of the unsealing of the Garner grand jury proceedings.

Staten Island's fancy new court complex had not yet been completed. The hearing was held in a shabby little room with worn benches that any of the other four great city boroughs would have been embarrassed to present to the world in a case with so much media. The dozen or so court officers lined the yellowing walls of the little room and glared defiantly throughout, silent symbols of the borough's inferiority complex.

Erica was there, and Jewel, and Esaw and Miss Gwen, staring forward at the judge, all of them anxious, but also with an air of preemptive disappointment; they weren't expecting anything to come of this. Their mood was further soured from the start, as they almost didn't get seats—the press had gotten in and packed the courtroom early, and the court officers kept telling them the room was full.

"I had to explain to them that we were the family," Erica remembers. "It got to the point where voices were raised."

Finally, seats were found for them, parked behind the multitude of lawyers arguing on their behalf. Five in particular would speak that day.

Matthew Brinckerhoff of Emery Celli Brinckerhoff & Abady, arguing for the public advocate's office, had a dark mop of curly gray hair and a goatee. He was probably best known for winning a $50 million settlement for an astonishing sixty thousand New Yorkers who'd been illegally strip-searched before arraignment on minor violations. In another universe, Eric Garner, who claimed he was strip-searched on the streets of Staten Island, might have been one of his living clients.

Art Eisenberg, arguing for the NYCLU, was another prominent civil rights attorney in a city full of them. He was tall, with a broad forehead and a wizened, faintly ironical expression. The silver-haired Chris Pisciotta, a quiet man in Coke-bottle glasses, represented Legal Aid. Then there was Alison Schary, representing the *New York Post,* who as a media rights expert was one of the few lawyers in the room whose expertise rested outside civil rights or criminal justice.

Dark-haired and quick-witted, Schary within a year would be sucked into another monstrous national controversy, representing *Rolling Stone* in its infamous face-plant exposé of campus rape at the University of Virginia.

The last of the five, representing the NAACP, was James Meyerson, the onetime counsel of Clementine Russ.

Now in his seventies, Meyerson was still doing the same kinds of cases. His co-counsel on the Russ affair, George Howard Jr., had passed away in 2007. Meyerson's presence testified to the fact that in nearly half a century since the Russ case, very little had changed with the passage of time except the names on the docket.

So here he was again in another shabby provincial courtroom where the fix was probably in, awaiting the inevitable disingenuous ending that is a consistent feature of these cases: the moment when a judge or a prosecutor sighs and tells the family that the law says there's nothing they can do.

Meyerson was no pessimist, however. The thin, bespectacled, silver-haired lawyer had grown over the years into a sentimental and confirmed eccentric, given to elaborate expressions of well-wishing and friendship. He signed his emails, all of them practically, with a remarkable tagline:

> As always, I do hope that, all things considered, you and yours are well. Be strong; keep the faith; keep thinking positively; and keep hope alive. I wish you and yours, now and forever more, much peace, health, happiness, hope, joy, productivity, good will, strength, courage, kindness, good luck, respect, dignity, honor, wisdom, and prosperity—spiritually and in all ways and every way.

In court, however, this quiet sentimentalist was an unpredictable, extroverted, weirdly confrontational personality. He rubbed people the wrong way—not just legal opponents, but sometimes allies as well.

He would go his own way in this case, too, alone among the five lawyers arguing for the unsealing of the Garner grand jury records. The others—Legal Aid, the NYCLU, the *Post,* and the public advocate's office—planned a semi-coordinated assault based on the scant legal precedent governing the opening of grand jury proceedings.

They focused in particular on the 1970 case *People v. DiNapoli.* In this case, New York's Public Service Commission, a government body charged with overseeing state utilities, sought to gain information from a grand jury that had indicted a group of mobsters for rigging bids for public contracts.

DiNapoli boiled down to the state wanting to see the grand jury proceedings in order to find out the extent of the bid rigging. That information would tell them whether or not some Con Ed customers were owed a refund on gas and electric bills.

The *DiNapoli* case established the standard for granting access to grand jury information. The Public Service Commission had proved a "compelling and particularized need" to break the seal of secrecy. Trying to use *DiNapoli* to open the Garner grand jury was an absurd fit, like using a tweezer to bust a bank vault. The Garner case was about broad, biblical themes of justice and fairness. *DiNapoli* meanwhile was a narrowly material case about remuneration. To convince a Staten Island judge that anyone in the Garner affair had anything like the "particularized" interest the Public Service Commission had in *DiNapoli* was almost a practical impossibility.

The deck was stacked against the petitioners, but four of the five planned to give it the best possible shot anyway. Lawyers like Pisciotta, Eisenberg, Schary, Brinckerhoff, and Jen Levy (who worked with Brinckerhoff on the public advocate's argument) pored through the books and carefully prepared Hail Mary arguments they hoped would sway Judge Garnett.

Privately, they were hopeful, but going into court that day, some of them were very worried about a potentially serious complication: Meyerson.

The NAACP lawyer, who seemed in person like a cosmic ambassador from the twelfth chakra of kindness, had planned his own strategy, and everyone was worried about what he might say.

. . .

Judge Garnett did not look like a happy man behind the bench. He had been a prosecutor in Staten Island in the eighties but had spent most of his career as a judge in Brooklyn. Then, just months after returning to Staten Island to serve as a judge, he had this terrible case dropped in his lap thanks to a sleazy-looking maneuver by his predecessor.

The original judge in the Garner case, Stephen Rooney, had recused himself on December 17, citing the need to avoid the "potential appearance of impropriety." Apparently Rooney's wife, Kathryn Rooney, was the board chair of the hospital where Garner had been taken after being choked.

It took Rooney an awfully long time to remember this conflict. The judge had sworn in the Garner grand jury months before, and on December 4 had done Dan Donovan a solid, granting his motion to disclose limited information to the public. After that, he'd tried to keep the entire effort by the five petitioners to unseal the grand jury proceedings secret.

Only when that effort failed, and a higher appellate court guaranteed that some judge in Staten Island would have to face the wrath of the community in a public hearing, did Rooney suddenly have an attack of conscience about his wife's conflict.

By then it was nearly three months into his relationship with the case.

Rooney's maneuver left Garnett to face the public anger over the grand jury's decision, and the latter didn't seem particularly pleased about it. In his opening remarks, the sleepy-looking, pink-faced judge with a tightly combed helmet of dark-gray hair told the assembled they would limit the discussion to section 190.25 (4) of the state's Criminal Procedure Law, governing the release of grand jury records.

"I just want everyone in the courtroom [to know that] Grand Jury secrecy is embodied in the Constitution of the State of New York," he said. "Amendments to our Constitution are affected by a vote of State legislature, and then are submitted to the voters at the next general election."

Some of the petitioner attorneys shot unhappy glances at one another. It seemed like the judge was letting them all know that if they didn't like the law, they could always change it at the ballot box. In the meantime, he seemed to be saying, he might have to interpret the law as it was, and they might not like it.

Brinckerhoff, representing the public advocate's office, went first.

"Your Honor," he said, taking a deep breath, "this case presents two unique and compelling circumstances [that] certainly did not exist in the cases that are relied upon by the district attorney in this case."

Those two unique factors, he went on, were the fact that the crime was on video and that the district attorney himself had already broken the seal of grand jury secrecy.

Garnett interrupted him. "Did the DA ask for testimony to be released or ask for permission to give a summary of the scope of the grand jury investigation?"

Brinckerhoff answered back: How should I know? Donovan's application to Judge Rooney had been made under seal.

"As far as I know, that has not been disclosed to anyone," Brinckerhoff went on. "I have never seen the application."

Garnett reddened. If he'd even read the news stories about the case, he should have known that. There were a few whispers to that effect in the back of the courtroom.

The judge glanced in the direction of the murmuring, then refocused on Brinckerhoff, who by then was in the middle of arguing that the Garner case presented "unique and compelling circumstances that get us past the threshold question."

Garnett snapped awake and interrupted again. Yes, he said, this case is compelling. But that's not the issue here. The issue is, what's your client's *particularized* interest in this case? Why should the public advocate get to look at this material?

Brinckerhoff wrestled with the judge, trying to convince Garnett that the public advocate had a "particularized" interest because, for instance, she had the power to introduce legislation to correct a problem discovered in the grand jury.

The judge wasn't impressed. What legislation would she introduce? Specifically? And why does she need to get the grand jury minutes to do so?

Brinckerhoff fought back, reminding the judge that the district attorney had obtained permission to release information for the sake of reassuring the public and that the public advocate had the same interest and responsibility "as a government official who is interested in these issues and wants a full record."

Garnett didn't seem convinced and kept asking what was Brinckerhoff's best argument for a "compelling and particularized need," a phrase that was already eliciting frowns in some parts of the courtroom.

The lawyer tried over and over again to talk about the urgent general interest in finding out what was rotten in the case, noting that "it is very atypical for the grand jury to sit for this many witnesses in any case, any case at all, or to be provided presumably large reams of material. Usually a prosecutor focuses only on inculpatory evidence."

Garnett again interrupted. "Isn't that something in favor of the DA?" he asked. "Instead of just focusing on the inculpatory, isn't that the DA's duty to be fair?"

This line led to more whispers in the back of the courtroom. The judge's line about Donovan not just "focusing on the inculpatory" seemed to imply he might also have focused on the *ex*culpatory, which was exactly what everyone suspected. That the judge didn't see the problem with that was very odd.

And what did he mean by "fair"? Since when did prosecutors worry about being fair to people they were trying to indict? The prosecutor, after all, has the power to not present a case to a grand jury at all. If he thinks an indictment isn't "fair," he doesn't have to try for one.

But if he does think it's fair, then what is he doing presenting exculpatory evidence? The whole thing was strange.

Brinckerhoff concluded by trying to explain to the judge that there was a widespread belief, not just in New York but nationwide and worldwide, that there was a conflict of interest in Staten Island. He insisted that a district attorney who works regularly with the police cannot be trusted to investigate the police.

A former Staten Island prosecutor, Garnett stiffened at this. He interrupted Brinckerhoff to ask if he was talking specifically about Staten Island. "You seem to suggest that this was unique to this county, and not to other district attorney's offices," he snapped.

Brinckerhoff had stumbled onto one of the most pressing fixations of Middle American thought. You could reduce an enormous quantity of the content on Fox News and afternoon talk radio to a morbid national obsession that could be summarized on a T-shirt: *Are you calling me a racist?*

Brinckerhoff had not, in fact, made any such accusation with regard to Staten Island in particular. But the judge had taken it that way, which indicated a belligerent sensitivity—or bias—that might have been worth exploring in open court.

Instead, Brinckerhoff hastened to reassure Garnett.

"No," he said, in response to the question about whether his complaints were unique to Staten Island. "And I apologize if I left that impression because that is not at all what we're saying. The distinction—"

"I have your argument," snapped Garnett. "Thank you very much. We'll move on now."

The Brinckerhoff exchange set the pattern for the entire day. Each successive lawyer would stand up and explain to Judge Garnett the very good reasons why the grand jury records should be opened, why this was in the public interest, and why it was particularly appropriate given the fact that the district attorney himself had already done the same thing.

And in each case, the judge kept shooting them down, mainly by asking the attorneys what their compelling and particularized need was.

Each lawyer would make a valiant and wordy effort to show such a need, but the judge mostly yawned the whole way through.

When Pisciotta of Legal Aid began his presentation by noting again that Donovan had "conceded that the public needed to know what happened behind the doors of the grand jury," Garnett cut him off immediately.

"Put that aside, what is the Legal Aid Society's compelling and particularized need to have these grand jury minutes?" he asked.

Pisciotta began by saying that his office had represented Eric Garner, which the judge liked, because that was very particular. But the more he parried with Pisciotta, the more it came out that Legal Aid, like the rest of the petitioners, was basically hoping to get to the truth so that the public could know what had happened.

PISCIOTTA: What we're asking is this community, the Staten Island community, be aware of what happened behind the Grand Jury doors so that they—

THE COURT: You're telling me, you're here on behalf of the community?

The community was everyone, and by definition, *everyone* couldn't have a particularized need. Garnett didn't seem impressed.

Art Eisenberg of the NYCLU came next, and at first, it sounded like he was coming with similar arguments. He talked about the need to inform the public and then mentioned also that opening the Garner grand jury proceedings was necessary in order to have a broad public conversation about grand jury reform.

The judge appeared to move just a hair above absolute boredom with these arguments, but he was jolted awake when Eisenberg hit him not with pleading rhetoric, but with a piece of clever lawyering.

Eisenberg brought up a 1983 case involving a request by the district attorney of Suffolk County to open up grand jury records involving an investigation into corruption in a county sewer project.

Judge Jacob Fuchsberg ultimately denied the DA's request to unseal the grand jury proceedings, but Eisenberg noted that in Fuchsberg's opinion, the key issue was whether the DA could have gotten the information he needed somewhere else.

"As we read it [in] Judge Fuchsberg's decision in the Suffolk County case," Eisenberg offered, "particularization refers to the issue of whether the information is otherwise available through some other source."

Garnett was obviously concerned:

THE COURT: The word particularized, you say in Suffolk, was interpreted to mean the unavailability of any other source of the material?
MR. EISENBERG: Correct.
THE COURT: As opposed to a nexus between the movant and the material?

Correct, said Eisenberg.

The judge seemed rattled. He was in lawyer hell, relying upon a definition of "particularization" that required a "nexus," and here was some attorney blithely telling him he could have particularization without a nexus. Anarchy!

The two lawyers talked a little bit longer about whether or not a nexus was required and whether one existed in this case.

Then they moved on to the question of the five "*DiNapoli* factors." Apart from the compelling and particularized need standard, *DiNap-*

oli had also outlined five reasons grand jury records needed to be kept secret.

These included things like the prevention of flight by a defendant about to be indicted, the protection of an innocent from unfounded accusations, the assurance to witnesses that their testimony will be kept secret, and so on.

To disclose any information from any grand jury, a judge needed to be convinced that none of these five *DiNapoli* factors existed. More hurdles.

Eisenberg dutifully went through and explained why the Garner case passed this test, slogging through each of the five *DiNapoli* factors, a subject that held the judge's keen attention.

Meanwhile, the Garner family struggled to stay awake. Erica, seated behind the lawyers, rolled her eyes. This hearing was drifting further and further from the story of her father's death. Forty-five minutes in, it had devolved into something very like a discussion in a foreign language, with two lawyers blabbering about nexuses and particularization and the fifth *DiNapoli* factor.

Eisenberg, meanwhile, looked relieved. He'd covered all the bases, steaming through the whole *DiNapoli* test and even seeming to dent Judge Garnett's faith in particularization.

Still, his whole argument in the end was really the same one made by the other lawyers: we need to open the proceedings so we can find out what happened. He finished with a quote from Justice Brandeis, who said, "Sunlight is the best disinfectant."

Pausing, he looked up at Garnett. "We urge the court to cast some sunlight on these proceedings."

Schary, the *Post* lawyer, also did her best, insisting that the newspaper, too, had a nexus, and a compelling and particularized need, and didn't upset any *DiNapoli* factors, and so on.

Garnett looked at her with dead eyes. In his final analysis, Schary represented a newspaper that was after some copy that would smear Staten Island. An unimpressed Garnett basically asked her if her particularized need was to do a big story.

"You could do a ten-part series," he quipped.

Schary stared back, mute for a moment.

. . .

That left Meyerson.

When called, the bespectacled NAACP lawyer shuffled to the lectern and paused, the way an actor does before jumping into character. And he did seem to physically jump into his argument.

Meyerson's courtroom persona is a weird, physically dynamic, herky-jerky sort of performance art. He turns this way and that, and his grandiose delivery vaguely recalls an outpatient playing a pipe organ. He took a deep breath and began.

"Thank you, Your Honor," he said. "Let me start out last, but not least. Let me try and start out from the beginning, so that we don't drown in the abstractions of law, as the abstractions can drown us."

There was no mistaking Meyerson's point, which seemed aimed at the other attorneys behind him as much as at the judge: You've all been making legal chit-chat. Let's focus on what we're actually talking about.

One could feel the discomfort emanating from the front of the room, where the lawyers sat.

"This case didn't start today," he began. "It started on July seventeenth, when an unarmed African American man was choked to death by a group of white New York City police officers, one of whom was Officer Pantaleo."

There was some nodding among the family members.

Meyerson went on: "At that point, there was an audio recording and video recording in which that African American man was crying out for help, if you will," he said.

"When he said, 'I can't breathe,' that's another way of saying, 'Help me.' And nobody, none of those white police officers standing around, did anything. And the white police officer continued to choke him, as the video shows, and then brought him to the ground with the assistance of the other white police officers and compressed his chest."

Meyerson went through all the familiar elements: that the medical examiner had ruled the death a homicide, blaming both a chokehold and a compression of the chest, that chokeholds had long ago been banned by the NYPD, and that there were widespread calls for Dan Donovan to recuse himself.

This, he said, was because there was "a perception, a belief, even if wrong, a very deeply held perception and belief by segments of the community, largely African American, that fairness and justice could not be achieved."

That segment of the community, he said, believed that accountability was impossible if Donovan proceeded, because "the police officers involved are members of his prosecutorial family."

Garnett was playing along so far. When Meyerson mentioned that Governor Andrew Cuomo had refused requests to name a special prosecutor in the case, Garnett parried back, asking him if a special prosecutor would have gotten a different result.

Meyerson shrugged. He didn't know. He told the judge that he couldn't stand there and say that an independent prosecutor would have gotten an indictment. What he could say is that lots of people would have felt a lot better if there had been a special prosecutor.

Punctuating his argument with large, controlled gestures, Meyerson reiterated that there's always a problem when local law enforcement is asked to investigate their own.

"They are members of that prosecutorial family," he said, again invoking a metaphor of kinship, and then looked straight at the judge. "Just as *you* are a member of, not the prosecutorial family, but the criminal justice system in this county."

Garnett bolted upright in his chair, immediately uncomfortable.

"Maybe I should have started at the beginning," Meyerson said, as the courtroom filled with whispers.

"We're asking that *you* disqualify yourself and this court itself be disqualified. That you refer to the presiding judge of the Appellate Division, or Judge Lippman, as the chief administrative and chief judge of the state, and ask that this case be reassigned for the purposes of this proceeding . . ."

There was a hush, and then murmurs all through the court. Meyerson went on:

". . . which didn't start today. It started a long time ago."

Meyerson's argument was: Screw the law, screw the *DiNapoli* standard, and screw your particularized need. This court is illegitimate and Your Honor is illegitimate.

A local newspaper reporter would later compare this moment to Al Pacino's celebrated "You're out of order! You're out of order! The whole trial is out of order!" speech from . . . *And Justice for All*.

Garnett flushed to his roots after being called out in his own courtroom by an NAACP lawyer.

"Where do I fit in this perception?" he stammered. "Aren't you just prejudging the district attorney and aren't you prejudging me?"

"If you're asking me, am I asking you whether you could be fair, that's an irrelevant question," Meyerson snapped. "I don't know. I'm assuming you can. I'm assuming you can. It is immaterial to the equation, if you will, if there exists within a large segment of the community a belief that because of your relationship with the criminal justice system, in Richmond County, that you can't be fair, whether you can or not."

Garnett had done his homework about all the cases pertaining to section 190.25 (4) of the Criminal Procedure Law. He had an answer for every volley each of the other attorneys had thrown at him when it came to the strictly legal question of how and when and under what circumstances a grand jury's minutes may be made public.

But the judge was momentarily speechless when the hearing turned in the direction of his own legitimacy.

Meyerson wasn't accusing him of being biased, just saying that lots of people in Staten Island might think he was simply because he was part of what was perceived to be a racist county's racist system of justice. Meyerson's argument was that for the African American community to be satisfied in this particular case, they needed a different judge, which made perfect sense and really had nothing to do with Garnett personally.

But Garnett, unsurprisingly, took it personally. The judge now set out to defend his honor, rather than argue the issue at hand, which was whether or not the community was entitled to an impartial hearing.

"I'll tell you right now, the vast majority of my career has not been in this county," said Garnett, sounding wounded.

"But you are sitting here," retorted Meyerson.

"I sat as a judge mostly in Kings County, in Brooklyn," he said.

The line "as a judge" was telling: he was taking care not to mention to the courtroom that he'd been a prosecutor in Staten Island for nine years.

"I've only been here since November," Garnett went on.

The significance of this moment was that rather than a lawyer trying to persuade the judge of something, the judge was now pleading his own case to Meyerson.

Meyerson wouldn't let go. He pushed Garnett some more and reiterated that the case was not about fine legal abstractions but about brutal, obvious reality. He argued that if the case had been about a white man choked to death by a black man over a cigarette while the black man's friends watched and did nothing, the killer would have been indicted long ago.

"That African American and probably his friends would have been arrested," Meyerson thundered. "And in the proverbial New York minute, the prosecutor would have convened the grand jury, and in half a day, with the videotape, with the medical examiner's report, and with some report saying chokeholds cause people to die, and the audio saying, 'I can't breathe,' would have gotten indictments for some form of homicide."

Finally, Meyerson told the judge another story about another case he'd been involved with, ages ago. It was the story of Clementine and Carnell Russ.

"Going back to 1971," he said, "a young African American and his family on Memorial Day weekend were driving on a highway outside of Star City, Arkansas. Former president Clinton was then the attorney general in the state of Arkansas. And his people represented some of the defendants in that case."

Describing Carnell Russ, Meyerson went on:

"He was shot between the eyes at point blank range when he went in to post a bond for a speeding ticket, and there was an argument whether or not he should get a receipt." He paused. "His family was sitting outside in the car."

Meyerson then told the story of going all the way to Washington to sue the attorney general for failing to investigate Russ's death. The NAACP in that case, he said, had been "injured because of the defendant's failure to undertake a sincere and meaningful investigation of Carnell Russ's death. We could substitute Eric Garner's death here."

And a federal judge ruled that the NAACP had standing to sue in that nearly exact case because the state had indeed failed, and the NAACP, an organization founded for the exact purpose of defending African Americans against being lynched, or shot between the eyes over a speeding ticket, or strangled over a cigarette, had a clear interest in securing the civil rights of its clients.

"And so we say, Your Honor," he concluded, "that the NAACP has a specific and compelling interest in this matter."

Meyerson went on like this for a while, then sat down. His basic point was that these cases have been going on for decades if not centuries and have so often played out to no result locally that the federal government had to assert the power to step in. When he was done rehashing all the old tales of hangings and shootings and murders, the gallery went silent for a minute. The room felt full of ghosts.

A few weeks before this hearing, Dan Donovan had shocked the North Shore of Staten Island by announcing that he was running for Congress, to fill the seat of multiple felon Michael Grimm.

The governor was a few weeks away from calling a special election for May 5. Seemingly, Donovan would want to capitalize on any opportunity to get his face in front of voters. But he was nowhere to be found in the hearing, electing instead to have Assistant DA Anne Grady stand in his place.

Grady, a thin woman with red hair and an anxious, rabbity disposition, had an unenviable task at the hearing. Her boss, after all, had only weeks before argued to a judge in a sealed motion that the grand jury needed to be unsealed.

Now he wanted Grady to argue the exact opposite in public.

It was a delicate balancing act and everyone present would have understood if she had just punted her rebuttal time and offered some forgettable, boilerplate remarks on behalf of the DA's office.

But Grady went in the other direction. When the five petitioners were finished speaking, she launched into a strident and defiant monologue in defense of the district attorney's position. She spoke quickly and bounced from point to strange point, talking, for instance, about the importance of secrecy in protecting sources.

Why, she said, just look at Deep Throat, the source in the Watergate case. How long did they keep his identity secret?

It was hard to imagine anything having less to do with a police murder on the streets of Tompkinsville than Watergate, but Grady nodded her head in emphasis as she made the point, as if the whole courtroom was with her.

Garnett grew impatient and asked her to move on. She did and eventually made it to the strangest point of all. She had been listening to all of these petitioners' arguments about the need to inform "the people" about what had happened in the grand jury, and clearly those arguments had grated on her. She now waved a hand in the direction of those other lawyers and offered her take.

"The Legal Aid Society, as they are the public defender, suggests that the segment of the public with the need for disclosure is New York City's indigent criminal defendants," she says. "The NAACP says it represents people of color, to use their expression, who have a higher risk of interactions with the police."

She went on: the public advocate, she said, claims to represent all citizens of New York City, as does the NYCLU.

She took a deep breath. "I submit, Your Honor," she went on, "that the only 'public' with legally cognizable interest in the case are the residents of Staten Island, the county of Richmond."

A low hum rose in the courtroom as Grady went on to reiterate that the only public with a legitimate interest in the case was the citizenry that had voted in the borough's elected officials. They, and the grand jurors who had already spoken in the case, were the true public, and they'd already had their say.

"The public has spoken," she said. "And that public body has said an indictment should not be returned."

She concluded, bitterly, "I suggest [that the] interest that the non–Staten Island segment of the public asserts to critique the work done by the members of the Staten Island grand jury is simply of no moment."

Those last three words, "of no moment," hung poisonously in the air. It was the age-old argument: we don't need outsiders coming in to tell us our business. The argument was as old as America, a country where southern white resentment over anyone telling them how to deal with "their" blacks was written into the Constitution.

The hearing went on for a little longer, but about two hours in, Garnett mercifully gaveled it to a close. It had been a tense, unpleasant affair, with lots of genuinely hurt feelings.

Jewel Miller glared back in the direction of the DA's table as the crowd filed out of the courtroom, still focused on Anne Grady's argument. "What the fuck did she mean, 'We're the people'? Like they're the only people?" she said, shaking her head. "That shit is crazy. Staten Island is crazy."

Erica was seething, too. "Literally I wanted to just get out of my seat and run up and snatch that lady's wig off," she says. "The only thing I could see was the back of her head. It was just a whole lot of nonreasons that she was giving. It was so disrespectful."

. . .

Five days after the Garner hearing, on February 10, an interesting thing happened across the bay, in Brooklyn. A cop was indicted by a grand jury for killing an unarmed black man. Back on November 20, just before the Garner grand jury rendered its fateful decision, a Chinese American rookie police officer named Peter Liang shot and killed twenty-eight-year-old Akai Gurley in an East New York project tower.

Liang and his partner, Officer Shaun Landau, had been conducting a "vertical" search of a tower in a place called the Pink Houses. It's a project with a tough reputation for drugs and violence. Verticals were another innovation of the Broken Windows/Stop-and-Frisk era. A pair of cops would enter a tower, ascend staircases at opposite ends, check each floor, then finally meet on the top floor to compare notes. On the way, they would stop people, ask for ID, empty pockets, and, as they saw it, stop suspicious characters and gather intel.

Daniel Pantaleo had done such duty in Staten Island. Project residents in New York for the most part deeply resented these searches. The idea of having to bring ID with you to empty trash pissed people off. Even worse was the notion of having to deal with police patrols in what most people considered their own hallways.

The practice, yet another Broken Windows gambit with an Orwellian name—it was called Clean Halls—would eventually become the focus of a lawsuit, after people across the city reported a wave of absurd arrests.

Jaleel Fields was eighteen years old when he got busted during a vertical patrol in his own project home, not far from where the Gurley incident took place. In that case, Fields simply got on and off an elevator that happened to have two patrolmen in it. During the elevator ride, police got into an argument with another young man, and Fields made the mistake of laughing and telling the boy he didn't have to talk to the police.

Ultimately the cops got angry and arrested Fields for the catchall offenses of "obstructing pedestrian traffic" and "obstructing government administration." They claimed, among other things, that the skinny young man had prevented people from entering the elevator.

Fields caught a rare break. His lawyer, Martha Grieco, had the extreme good fortune to get a tape from the public housing authority showing Fields not only not blocking traffic but standing aside, almost like a doorman, to wave other people into the elevator.

"You just get used to it," Fields says now of how the police operate. "That's just the way they work."

The paradox of Broken Windows is that it relied upon enhanced contact with people to be effective. No longer just sitting in cars driving in circles, no longer even just pacing sidewalks, police were going up stairwells and crisscrossing hallways, stopping people indoors. Obviously they only did this in certain neighborhoods, i.e., "where the crime is."

Add in a statistical imprimatur to secure a certain number of tickets and arrests and you had a highly combustible situation. Cops went into buildings looking to bust people, and people expected to be messed with in their own hallways. More things could go wrong. The Gurley case went wrong.

Liang was ascending a staircase on November 20 with his hands on his weapon when, two floors below, a door opened. Gurley walked through with his girlfriend, Melissa Butler. The young couple was just going outside.

Liang panicked and fired a shot that ricocheted off a wall and hit Gurley through the heart. He then went down the stairs toward Butler, who was kneeling in a pool of Gurley's blood, trying to resuscitate him. Instead of helping, Liang just kept walking. The two officers did return to the scene but only stared at Butler as she tried to administer CPR. Liang said he didn't know if he could do CPR better than Butler, so he didn't intervene.

The case proceeded almost as an exact inverse of the Garner affair. Whereas Bratton had quickly thrown Pantaleo in the soup, describing his takedown as a chokehold, in the case of Liang he immediately called the death "accidental."

Meanwhile, Brooklyn district attorney Ken Thompson, an African American, proceeded exactly as Donovan had not. He asked the grand jury to hand out a spate of serious charges, and he worked fast. On February 10, the grand jury complied, hitting Liang with second-degree manslaughter, criminally negligent homicide, second-degree assault, reckless endangerment, and two counts of official misconduct.

Cops and ex-cops across the city were furious. Many felt sure Thompson had pressed for an indictment solely to avoid a riot in his borough. One of those critics was Joseph Concannon, the ex-captain and leader of the pro-police marches, who fumed over the "waterfall" of felony charges.

Concannon had his own history with vertical searches that informed his view of the Gurley case. He remembered being a rookie in the 114th Precinct and doing a vertical at Twenty-first Street and Broadway, in the Astoria section of the city, in a building where a "man with a machete" had been reported. He and a bunch of other police reached the floor in question, and sure enough, there was a guy waving a machete around.

"We're all trying to say, 'All right, how do we get a machete away from this fucking idiot?'" he says, remembering. "And one of the senior guys goes, 'Very easy. Here, watch this.'"

Concannon pauses.

"He goes down, he starts talking to the guy, and then he body slams him against the wall. The machete flies away, and everybody is okay at the end of the day. I was like, 'Okay. I guess that was a plan.'"

Concannon explains the parallel.

"This guy Liang, he's a rookie cop. He enters probably one of the most dangerous housing projects in the city. He's probably scared to bejeesus. It's not his culture, it's not in his line of thinking. All he knows is the briefing that he's been given, and he's probably been given a healthy briefing about what's going on there.

"He's going down the stairs in blackout conditions. There's no light." Concannon pauses and playacts Liang's reaction.

"Okay, you want me to go to a housing development?" he says. "That's fine. You want to go with no lights? Yeah. You're a cop, don't worry about it."

Concannon shakes his head. Nobody can imagine what it's like to be in that situation, he says.

"This is a young guy," he says. "This could have been me in that parking lot. This could have been me shooting this guy with the freaking machete in a hallway." He pauses. "I don't know if you know what it's like to be in an apartment hallway with six cops, with only your gear and your uniform on. It's like fighting Godzilla for space."

Concannon inadvertently had cut right to the heart of the problem. Liang was scared. He was a nervous visitor to an alien culture. His conception of life in the Pink Houses came entirely from a police briefing. This to him was only a dangerous place, not a place where people raised kids, fell in love, watched Giants games, told bad jokes, and ate Christmas dinners. People who lived there had no identity for him apart from the fact that they were potential threats.

A cop ascending a staircase in a white neighborhood who was so pre-terrified of the residents that he pulled the trigger at the first sound he heard would be derided as a paranoid lunatic.

Similarly, the idea that a fat white guy selling hot smokes on a street corner was a grave threat would be laughed at as absurd. But a 350-pound black man is plausibly described in the press as someone who scared pedestrians, a threat needing to be defused.

Try to imagine a world where there isn't a vast unspoken consensus that black men are inherently scary, and most of these police assaults would play in the media like spontaneous attacks of madness. Instead, they're sold as battle scenes from an occupation story, where a quick trigger finger while patrolling the planet of a violent alien race is easy to understand.

Concannon was so mad about Thompson's grand jury that he began arranging for a demonstration in support of Liang. His take on the situation was that Kenneth Thompson was a plant, a guy with "history."

"Al Sharpton, the whole nine yards," he said. "He is not an inconsequential member of the NAN network."

For the protest, he had a huge amount of cooperation from the city's Chinese American community, which rallied to Liang's cause.

March 8, 2014. It's a little more than a month after the Garner hearing, on a bitterly cold Sunday afternoon. About three thousand people gather for a demonstration outside City Hall at the southern tip of Manhattan.

Most of the people gathered here are Chinese. They stand in the freezing cold and hold up signs that say things like "SUPPORT P.O. LIANG" and "NO SCAPEGOATING."

In a strange twist on the racial tensions already swirling around this issue, many in the crowd insist that Liang would not have been indicted if he had been white. In this sense it is both a pro-police protest and an antidiscrimination protest, which puts it in a new category of the city's racial dynamics.

"Not fair," says one of three middle-aged Chinese women who had come to the protest together.

Why is it not fair?

"Because Peter Liang is Chinese. Okay?"

The three women frown and walk away.

"He was doing his job. Accidents happen, but he was not trying to kill anyone," says Tso Chung, forty, who stood nearby.

He goes on: "Other officers, when they do things, they [are not indicted]."

Chung cites the Garner case as one such example.

It was a tale of two grand juries. The borough with the white district attorney had taken forever to get no indictment from a special grand jury. The one with the black DA had taken little time at all to get murder charges from a regular grand jury. There had been little call from protesters for Thompson to recuse himself from the Gurley case, even though he was in exactly the same situation Donovan had been in with Garner. Both men were perceived as having acted out of racial solidarity. Both were judged to have done the right thing by their respective constituencies. In war what matters most is not right or wrong, it's whose side you're on.

One person who didn't necessarily think Thompson did the right thing was Meyerson, who in the days after the Liang protests sat down in his office and pondered the whole strange case. Meyerson's take on Thompson was the same as his take on Donovan, that law enforcement can't be trusted to investigate law enforcement.

"I actually think that it's great that Ken Thompson got the indictment, but my position from the outset was that Ken Thompson should have disqualified himself," Meyerson said. "As progressive as he may be as a district attorney, we can never forget that he's still a district attorney."

Meyerson was still waiting for an answer from Judge Garnett after the Staten Island hearing. He didn't seem to be on the edge of his chair in suspense. The outcome seemed predictable. Still, he was troubled. The Garner case had raised thorny questions about what path any attorney should choose to take in a legal system that may not be functioning correctly.

Meyerson talked about a line from a book by Thomas Oliphant called *Praying for Gil Hodges,* about Jackie Robinson's Dodgers. "Every important American story is punctuated by race," the author wrote. Racial tumult is buried deep in the body of American society.

Because of slavery and the fallout from it, it is, Meyerson reflected, our original sin. But we're unable to face it.

Like prisoners of ourselves, we seem doomed to repeat patterns over and over. Meyerson talked about the Kerner Commission of the late sixties, convened by LBJ to study the causes of race riots. LBJ had hoped to learn that some instigator or group was conspiring to turn otherwise patriotic black Americans to riots and protest. But the commission found just the opposite.

"The Kerner Commission said that the trigger point [of riots] is that police are viewed as an occupying force in black and brown communities," he said. "Fifty years later or forty-five years later, whatever it is, in Ferguson, reports will say the same thing, that police are viewed as an occupying force. Everything's changed and nothing has changed."

In nearly half a century of litigating police abuse cases, Meyerson had become fixated on the idea that the law was becoming a thing too much of itself, self-deceiving and disentangled from morality. He cited Edmund Burke, the British parliamentarian from the 1700s known for his support of the American Revolution. Burke, he said, worried about the "separation of the law from the right . . . what's more important than what lawyers tell you you should do is what reason, justice, and humanity tell you you ought to do . . . You ought not to separate these things out, because when you begin to diverge those two, you are leading yourself down a very dangerous path."

This, he said, was the issue in the Garner case. There was the law, and then there were the facts of what happened. "A guy got killed," Meyerson said. "That gets lost on everybody."

Meyerson believed that the mere fact that Judge Garnett was focused on inane issues like *DiNapoli* proved that the discussion had moved too far from the matter at hand. He kicked himself for not saying so.

"One of the things I wanted to say but failed in courage to say it was, 'Judge, the fact that we're having this abstract discussion and you're asking these questions in fact makes my point why you should be disqualified.' I really regret not having said that."

Meyerson understood that the other lawyers, whom he all respected, disagreed with his approach in court with Garnett. He knew they felt their best shot was to argue the law, such as it is. He'd gone another route.

"At the end of the day," he said, "I turned to Matt [Brinckerhoff] and I said, 'You know, whatever the nature of the exercise I engaged in, maybe it will guilt him into something.'"

It didn't. On March 19, Garnett quietly issued a decision shutting down the effort to unseal the grand jury. As expected, he wrapped his arms around the doctrine of compelling and particularized need and held on for dear life, using it to strike down all the petitioners' requests.

"What would they use the minutes for?" he asked. "The only answer which the court heard was the possibility of effecting legislative change," he wrote. "That proffered need is purely speculative and does not satisfy the requirements of the law."

Dan Donovan, by then deep into the process of running for Congress, was quoted in the press saying that he would "adhere to Judge Garnett's well-reasoned decision." He said this without irony, as if there was a chance that he might suddenly decide not to adhere to it and break open the files for public view.

The petitioners appealed, and Meyerson and others sought several new avenues of attack. But for most people following the case, the suspense was over. Staten Island had circled the wagons. Unless the federal government intervened, nobody would ever find out what went on in that grand jury room.

THIRTEEN DANIEL

Just before Christmas 2011, a young African American video producer named Charles Roberson got in his car on the North Shore of Staten Island and drove toward a 99-cent store. His plan was to get detergent there, then go to a local laundromat to do his laundry. He knew there was a special at the laundromat, like maybe the machines were half off if you got there before noon, so he was in a bit of a hurry.

He had just bought detergent and was about to take his laundry out of the car when, out of nowhere, he heard police telling him to freeze. Roberson ended up with his hands on his car's trunk and his pants and underwear pulled down around his ankles. A young white officer was strip-searching him in broad daylight.

"I felt the wind, it was cold," he recalls. "I'm like, 'Why are you doing this?'"

Roberson felt that there was something a bit off about the officer, like he was looking for an excuse to go off. "I kept thinking, 'This guy is unstable. He's going to hurt someone.'"

The group of police tossed his car, popped his trunk, found nothing illegal. Finally, after a lot of profanity and groping, they told Charles to get the fuck back in his car and leave.

Charles did so, his head spinning. He felt violated and furious. He wanted to sue, press charges, do something.

Charles had a female friend who convinced him to walk into the 120th Precinct to complain. He walked up to the desk and began to tell the desk sergeant a story about being strip-searched in the street. Suddenly, as he was talking, the young cop who'd strip-searched him walked past in the corridor.

Charles pointed. "That's the guy! That's the cop that pulled my pants down!"

As he pointed, Charles's friend went to the front desk and asked for the name and badge number of the officer. She wrote it down:

Pantaleo, Daniel. Badge #13293

Roberson confronted Pantaleo, who told him he was "just doing his job" and that he'd been stopped because he was seen coming out of a "known drug location."

"The ninety-nine-cent store is a known drug location?" Roberson asked, incredulous.

They parried a little more, then finally Charles asked one last time: "Why did you need to pull my pants down? What was the point of that?"

"I was just doing my job," Pantaleo said. "You went to the spot."

For a long time, the incident rattled Roberson. The stop was one thing, but the strip search, whose sole point seemed to be to humiliate him, was too strange to make sense of.

"I wondered, did this guy's girlfriend leave him for a black guy or something? Did he want to see what I was packing? I don't know why he did it."

Three months after Roberson's encounter, in March 2012, Pantaleo and three other officers stopped three black men on Jersey Street, not far from where Eric Garner lived. He ordered the three men—Morris Wilson, Darren Collins, and Tommy Rice—out of the car to be searched.

The stop appeared to be a classic fishing expedition, albeit a more successful one than the stop involving Roberson. Pantaleo and his fellow officers said they spotted crack and heroin in "plain view," on the backseat of the car, which gave them cause to arrest all three.

In fact, all three seem to have been rousted out of the car before police saw any drugs.

Once the men were outside the car, police searched them. Wilson had the drugs on him. The other two men got the Charles Roberson treatment. According to a lawsuit later filed by Collins and Rice, "Pantaleo and/or [another officer] pulled down the plaintiffs' pants and underwear, and touched and searched their genital areas, or stood by while this was done in their presence."

Pantaleo and the others took them back to the precinct after that and repeated the whole ritual, forcing them "to remove all of their clothing, squat, cough, and lift their genitals."

Wilson, in a plea deal, later admitted to having drugs on his person. Collins and Rice were charged, but their cases were dismissed down the line. It was a humdrum case of test-a-lying and fishing with dynamite: stop a whole car, fudge the probable cause, violate a right or two or three, charge everyone, let the courts sort it out.

Long after charges had been dropped against Collins and Rice, their lawsuit finally went through. The NYPD ultimately had to pay out $30,000, or $15,000 for each man strip-searched.

In 2012, it seems, a young black man from Staten Island named Rylawn Walker contacted a lawyer named Michael Colihan and told a story about having weed planted on him by a cop named Daniel Pantaleo. The incident took place at 225 Park Hill Avenue, the exact spot where Ernest "Kase" Sayon had been killed.

Colihan, a one-man operation who'd sued a lot of cops over the years, didn't see anything unusual in Walker's case at the time. He'd seen plenty of cases of cops "flaking" suspects, either planting stuff on them or massaging the probable cause. This looked like a run-of-the-mill flaking.

He sued the NYPD on Walker's behalf along with two other plaintiffs, alleging civil rights violations, and ended up settling for $15,000 in that case, too. Later on, Walker's brother, Kenneth Smith, also filed suit over the same incident, also claiming to have been jailed for nothing by Pantaleo that night. Colihan remembers reading about the Garner case and being struck by the name of the officer.

"I thought, 'I know that name. It's an unusual Italian name,'" he says.

Then it hit him.

"I have an open case with that guy."

Despite being infamous around the world thanks to Ramsey Orta's video, Pantaleo throughout late 2014 and early 2015 remained an almost perfect cipher. He didn't speak to the press, his grand jury testimony was secret, and the city had mostly settled the lawsuits he'd been involved with before he ever got a chance to be deposed. Apart from what the police told the press, there was little available about his past.

The public was told that Pantaleo grew up on the South Side of

Staten Island, on the white side of the Mason-Dixon Line. This is a part of the city where there is an empty chair at the dinner table somewhere on almost every block, a testament to how many firefighters and police from here died during 9/11. These neighborhoods are intensely patriotic and proud of their contributions to the city. The families are close-knit, politically well organized, and resentful of the "city problems" they feel they pay to clean up with their tax dollars.

Pantaleo's father is a retired New York City firefighter, his uncle a city cop. Daniel went to Monsignor Farrell High School in Staten Island and moved from there to the College of Staten Island.

He joined the NYPD in 2006, beginning his work in what was called a "condition unit." Basically this meant doing Broken Windows stuff, making quality-of-life arrests.

After the Garner incident, Pantaleo hunkered down at his home on Elmira Street on the South Shore, saying little to anyone, even his neighbors, who naturally were interrogated by reporters on a regular basis in search of any kind of clue into his behavior. But even when the neighbors talked, the mystery of Pantaleo only deepened.

"He's like a shadow," an elderly neighbor told the *Daily News*. "He's in and out."

"I've never seen him at all," added an MTA worker named Donald Petosa.

On Bay Street, there was little debate. Pantaleo was talked about like the Bogeyman of Staten Island, a drug-planting, crotch-grabbing monster who should have been stopped years ago. The park regulars and inhabitants of nearby projects who claim to remember him describe him as young, inexperienced, and with more muscle than brains. "Motherfucking hothead" is how McCrae described him.

In the courts and in police circles, it was different.

"I can't believe it was him. He was one of the *better* ones," was a common observation in the halls of Staten Island criminal courts. Lawyers pointed to the "relatively small" number of federal abuse lawsuits that had been filed against him.

"What's he got, two, three?" offered one attorney, shrugging. "There are guys on the force with a dozen, fifteen, even twenty lawsuits."

On the day after the announcement that Daniel Pantaleo would not be indicted, Pat Lynch, the bombastic union chief, issued a full-throated defense of his officer. Lynch's defiant remarks came to be known among some wisecracking reporters as the "literally an Eagle Scout" speech.

"[Pantaleo] is a model of what we want a police officer to be," said Lynch. "He's a mature, mature police officer, motivated by serving the community. He literally is an Eagle Scout."

Lynch added that Pantaleo had had "very few" citizen complaints against him in a career spanning some three hundred arrests.

What kind of number was "very few" to someone like Pat Lynch? What was in Pantaleo's file?

From Thomas Gilligan, the man who'd shot James Powell in Harlem half a century ago, to Charles Lee Ratliff, the man who'd shot Carnell Russ in Arkansas in the seventies, through the present, the officer with a lengthy abuse history who should have been removed years before a fatal incident has been a consistent character in brutality stories. Was Pantaleo the latest?

In late February, Erica for the first time saw a copy of the lawsuit her father had written by hand in Rikers Island, the one about being groped and digitally penetrated on the streets of Staten Island. The sight of her father's miserable handwritten missive made her physically unwell but also galvanized her to continue the fight on his behalf. It was too late to prosecute a lawsuit for the groping incident, but there were other things she could do.

By then she had been leading weekly marches and meetings on the Staten Island Ferry, but now she also filed Freedom of Information requests with the city, seeking information on the background of Daniel Pantaleo. Hers was the second major effort in this direction.

On December 18, 2014, two weeks after Lynch's Eagle Scout speech, a young Legal Aid Society lawyer named Cynthia Conti-Cook had also submitted a Freedom of Information request to the Civilian Complaint Review Board, or CCRB, the city agency in charge of processing and investigating complaints of police abuse. The CCRB was also, at least theoretically, in charge of disciplining officers in noncriminal situations.

If Dan Donovan's grand jury was the first black box in the Garner case, the personnel file of Daniel Pantaleo would be the second. This was no surprise, because the bureaucracy the city had built to deal with bad police behavior was designed to be impenetrable. The CCRB in particular turned out to be an organization so complicated that even the most skilled lawyers had difficulty understanding how it worked. As multiple people connected with the Garner case would discover, it was a maze where citizen complaints went to die.

In the years before Eric Garner's death, the residents of heavily po- liced neighborhoods in New York had demanded the creation of an independent inspector general, someone who was not a cop to over- see the police department and help rein in abuses. The city council pushed for the idea. But the mayor, Michael Bloomberg, denounced the plan as one that would "outsource management of the police to unaccountable officials." Police Commissioner Kelly likewise blasted the very idea of an IG, saying it would imperil the lives of police.

The council nonetheless passed a bill—and overrode Bloomberg's angry veto—to create a new IG's office, its first appointment falling to new mayor Bill de Blasio. Philip Eure (pronounced "yore") seemed to have the perfect résumé for the job. Tall, affable, and African Ameri- can, he'd come up from Boston's tough Roxbury neighborhood to go to Stanford and then Harvard Law. For ten years he'd managed a similar operation in Washington, DC, called the Office of Police Com- plaints.

The New York job, especially in light of its famous/infamous Stop- and-Frisk program, was a massive challenge he was eager to take up. He would be heavily funded and tasked with hiring a staff of about fifty, who in turn would be given free rein to investigate the problems of one of the world's biggest police departments.

He was still hiring staff when Garner was killed. Immediately, Eure, whose offices didn't even all have working phones yet, was thrust into the middle of a perilous national controversy—and a dicey political situation.

"If we don't do something, people will talk" is how Eure recalls the dilemma. "But at the same time, we didn't want to replicate the work of the Staten Island DA, the feds, the Internal Affairs Bureau, or any- one else." He pauses. "So we settled on a systemic review."

Eure decided to look at the question of how the city had handled complaints of police chokeholds in the past. He soon dove down into the bureaucratic rabbit hole with the Garner family and the Legal Aid lawyers.

. . .

In New York, if you get beat up by the police, there are really two places to complain.

The most common destination is the CCRB. The organization is supposed to be an independent civilian agency, with no ties to the police, as unthreatening to walk into as the DMV or an emergency room. If you have a problem with police, you're supposed to call them up and explain: I was walking down the street, police stopped and questioned me, then they knocked me down and broke my finger, etc.

The CCRB takes your info down, then conducts its own investigation. When they're done, they make a presentation to a three-member panel of CCRB members.

After that presentation, the CCRB panel makes one of six recommendations: substantiated, exonerated, unsubstantiated, unfounded, officer(s) unidentified, and miscellaneous.

"Exonerated" means the CCRB agrees that the officer did it but finds that he or she was justified.

"Unfounded" means they have positive evidence that the cop didn't do it.

"Unsubstantiated" means they don't think there's enough evidence to say one way or the other.

"Officer(s) unidentified" is self-explanatory: maybe it happened, but we can't figure out which officer knocked your head against a radiator.

And "miscellaneous" usually means the CCRB found the officer involved isn't on the force anymore, so whatever.

But if it's "substantiated," it moves on. Typically, that means the commencement of a proceeding before the Administrative Prosecution Unit, which is basically a court within the police department.

The APU holds trials, but it's not a court of law. It's what's called an administrative law court, which exists entirely within the executive branch, rather than the judicial. In the case of the New York City APU, technically everyone present at a hearing, from prosecutors to judges to defenders, is a member of the police department.

This makes it an odd choice for judging police misbehavior, but the APU hears all substantiated cases of police misconduct. If, at the end of these "trials," the APU court determines the officer is guilty, it makes a recommendation for discipline. This can be as serious as dismissal and as trivial as "instruction" or "command discipline," which can be just a talking-to from your precinct chief, who might not even really care.

But the APU's ruling isn't final. All rulings in favor of discipline are sent in the end to the commissioner's desk. The commissioner, in turn, can unilaterally decide to overrule everyone.

This long and winding system means that any complaint has to complete a series of extraordinary hurdles before an individual police officer is punished. Within each one of those hurdles are multiple sub-hurdles.

For instance, even if the initial investigators believe your complaint and recommend action, you still have to get past a three-member panel of the CCRB, which tends to be stacked against the public.

The CCRB has thirteen members. Five are chosen by the city council, with one member coming from each borough. Another five are chosen by the mayor, and three are chosen by the police commissioner.

The composition makes it sound like the system is weighted in favor of the city council, which tends to advocate for individual citizens.

This setup is deceptive, though. Every three-member panel must have one council-appointed member, one mayor-appointed member, and one commissioner-appointed member.

This means that as far as individual abuse complaints are concerned, the opinion of the police themselves carries as much weight as the mayor and the city council.

And if your mayor-appointed panel member has been chosen by the likes of a Bloomberg or Giuliani, that would mean your complaint would have to survive the review of both a direct police appointee and the appointee of the mayor, who is the titular head of the police department and usually a strong ally of the commissioner.

If by some miracle, however, your complaint makes it past these first two barriers, it then has to survive the judgment of an NYPD trial commissioner, another police-appointed official, at the APU court.

And if by an even greater miracle your complaint impresses even this police-paid judge, it has to survive the direct veto of the police commissioner, who is usually inclined to dismiss any charges, especially since these proceedings rarely play out in public.

When Eure did his chokehold study, the numbers he dug up were mind-boggling.

He focused specifically on ten recent instances of chokehold complaints that had been substantiated by the CCRB. The incidents included the case of a man who'd been walking his bicycle in the park when police attempted to frisk him for no reason and ended up putting him in a chokehold. In another case, a man who was carrying a newspaper in a public housing elevator ended up on the ground, with a nightstick under his neck, gasping for air, when police decided to search him.

Eure's report covered the period 2009 to 2014, but he wasn't saying that there were only ten chokehold complaints during that time. On the contrary, the number of complaints of chokeholds since the practice had been banned in 1993 was extraordinarily high.

Only a few of them, like the Ernest Sayon case, ever made it to the papers.

Eure's report claimed that between 2009 and 2014, there had been 1,082 complaints alleging 1,128 chokeholds by NYPD officers. Of those complaints, the CCRB fully investigated only about half, or 520 total. And of those 520 complaints, the CCRB substantiated just 10. So the vast majority of chokehold cases were never substantiated and died somewhere in the exonerated/unsubstantiated/unfounded/officer(s) unidentified/miscellaneous piles.

Eure decided that there was still a point to be made just with those ten.

"There are hundreds, if not thousands of unsubstantiated chokehold cases," Eure says. "But we focused on this discrete set of substantiated cases as a way of putting attention on the baseline problem."

Eure found that in nine of the ten cases he examined, the CCRB recommended the strongest possible punishment, departmental charges. But in all nine of those cases, the cop in question ended up getting off with either no punishment at all or a maximum of five vacation days lost.

In six of the nine cases, Commissioner Kelly personally overturned the CCRB's recommendation, including one case involving a teenager who had been choked by a sergeant while handcuffed to a rail inside a police station.

Essentially, out of more than one thousand chokehold complaints, roughly 99 percent of the cases simply disappeared. Of the remaining 1 percent that actually made it all the way through the disciplinary process, nine out of ten ended with either no punishment or a max of five days of vacation lost. Another officer died before his case could be resolved.

In five years, the department had never once really punished an officer for a chokehold.

After the election of Bill de Blasio, all of this was supposed to change. He appointed a new chief of the CCRB, Richard Emery, a legendary civil rights attorney in New York. Newspapers described his appointment as heralding a "more muscular" CCRB, and indeed, that's what most people expected. Emery had become famous for, among other things, rooting out and then suing over mass abuses in the police ranks. His most famous case had probably been a 2010 affair involving people arrested for misdemeanors like fare beating or pot smoking and subjected to public cavity searches—what was it with cops and cavity searches?—on the way to Rikers Island. He was the partner of Matthew Brinckerhoff, the man who had argued on behalf of the public advocate's office in the grand jury hearing.

The trim, silver-haired, fashionably dressed Emery came out with strong statements on the day he was introduced (coincidentally, the same day Garner was killed), saying the CCRB had never "fulfilled its promise."

But one person at least had reason to be suspicious of Emery's comments.

Tracy Catapano-Fox was a former Queens prosecutor and former clerk of the Queens Supreme Court who since June 2013 had held a very senior position at the CCRB, serving as its executive director. As befits a former prosecutor, the tall, sandy-haired Catapano-Fox is quick-witted and a sharp arguer.

She had thrown herself into her new job at the CCRB with considerable energy and was looking forward to Emery's arrival, among other things because of a brewing sexual misconduct issue involving some of the board members that she'd hoped would be cleaned up.

But very quickly after Emery arrived, she found herself feeling disillusioned. For one thing, Emery had wondered openly if the CCRB should even be investigating Stop-and-Frisk complaints. This seemed like an odd position for a famed civil rights champion to take. Worse, he didn't seem concerned that there might be a problem with the way the city was reporting Stop-and-Frisk statistics.

Only a year before, the city had lost the landmark Stop-and-Frisk lawsuit. By January 2014, de Blasio was settling with the plaintiffs, agreeing to widespread reforms that the mayor believed would "turn the page" forever on the infamous practice.

Even before de Blasio took office, police were already claiming that Stop-and-Frisk was a thing of the past. Among other things, they insisted that stops had declined 94 percent by the last three months of Michael Bloomberg's administration.

Catapano-Fox had seen those statistics and was dubious. She knew, from the CCRB's records, that people were still complaining of being harassed. Her suspicion was that police were perhaps doing the same things they'd always done but simply not filling out a UF-250 form every time. There was no way it had dropped that much, she thought, noting that, at the time, the CCRB had not seen any significant decrease in complaints.

When she went to Emery with her concerns and pleaded with him to do a study to see if the 250s matched up with the complaints, she claimed that he balked. In her lawsuit, she talked about having made "numerous complaints to Emery and the Board about his attempt to have the CCRB stop accepting or substantiating 'stop and frisk' complaints."

Emery denies that this conversation ever took place and insists that he himself later became concerned about the possibility that the stops had not declined as much as advertised. He was never able to establish this statistically. The point of this odd story is not to adjudicate who was correct, Catapano-Fox or Emery, but rather to point out that there was significant concern even within the CCRB that what many people in minority neighborhoods already suspected was true: that the reported 94 percent drop almost certainly didn't really mean the end of Stop-and-Frisk—that in fact things were much the

way people in places like Bay Street said they were, basically un-
changed.

Catapano-Fox and Emery also clashed over a plan that he came up
with shortly after his arrival. His idea was that every substantiated
CCRB complaint would first go to Emery and to the Department Advocate's Office (DAO), which is charged with "prosecuting" the internal police trials for ninety days before proceeding to adjudication.
During that time, Emery and the DAO could "reconsider" the CCRB's
recommendations.

This proposed new additional hurdle in the already hurdle-laden
CCRB process would have allowed the CCRB chair to feel out the
police commissioner to see if he or she intended to actually discipline
the officer in question if convicted.

If the commissioner indicated that he or she had no interest in disciplinary action, then the CCRB could change its recommendation to
"unsubstantiated" or "unfounded" or whatever. Emery described this
seemingly Orwellian proposal as "front-loading" the recommendation process to avoid the issue of recommendations that were "routinely altered by the police commissioner."

Catapano-Fox didn't think any of these ideas made any sense and
said so. Emery, for his part, insists that the new procedure was an
important reform that gave the CCRB more credibility, since its recommendations weren't being overturned as often.

Whatever the case, Emery ultimately fired Catapano-Fox. She sued
him for wrongful retaliation on the same day she was dismissed. The
city later settled the case for $275,000.

Emery, like many of the city's well-known civil libertarians, was put
to the test politically by the Garner case. He was close friends with
Bill Bratton. He had known him for decades and had been a close
political ally, among other things encouraging him to run for mayor
as a Republican in 2001.

Emery also had a son who worked under Bratton in the NYPD's
counterterrorism unit, which was run by a former WNBC reporter
named John Miller. The former newsman was one of the country's
most powerful terrorist chasers, and Emery's son was one of his ana-
lysts.

Before his arrival at the CCRB, Emery had been known as an abuse victim advocate. In fact, he had a reputation for being one of the great victim advocates and civil rights lawyers in a city full of them. But the CCRB job seemed to weigh on him, and many of his admirers in the legal community began to wonder if he'd changed after taking the job.

For instance, after taking the post, he began comparing reform of the police to "space exploration," i.e., a long and open-ended journey possibly to nowhere. Also, in a statement that seemed a bit strange given his job description, he complained that punishing cops was counterproductive.

"Police officers, for the most part, really respond to rewards, not only discipline. They don't do that well with discipline," he said. "Discipline is kind of a wasted effort in many respects, I'm afraid."

One of the people who saw Emery's remarks was Cynthia Conti-Cook, the Legal Aid Society lawyer. "I thought that was an odd thing for a person in charge of disciplining police to say," she remembers.

Nonetheless, she had hopes that the Freedom of Information Law request she sent to the CCRB on December 18, 2014, requesting access to Pantaleo's complaints file, might produce some answers in the Garner case.

She was wrong. Less than a week later, on December 24, she and the Legal Aid Society got a letter back from Emery's CCRB essentially telling them to stuff it.

"Dear Ms. Conti-Cook," the letter from a CCRB lawyer named Lindsey Flook read. "Pursuant to the Freedom of Information Law, I am respectfully denying your request."

Flook cited a catchall shield for police in Freedom of Information requests, Section 50-a of the New York State Civil Rights Law.

If the CCRB is a maze within which citizen complaints essentially die of exhaustion before police can be disciplined, the civil and criminal code is nearly as bad. Where police personnel files are concerned, it is an endless series of loopholes and cutouts designed to shield police behavior from public scrutiny.

Passed by the state legislature in 1976 as an exemption to the 1974 Freedom of Information Law, for instance, Section 50-a held that police records in most all cases were exempt from FOIL. It said "all personnel records used to evaluate performance" of police shall be considered "confidential" and could not be released "without the express written consent" of the officers.

This preposterous loophole meant anything that the government deemed "personnel records used to evaluate performance" of police couldn't be released unless the officers themselves personally approved. The city added that any request about Pantaleo's history amounted to an "unreasonable invasion of privacy." This was an odd word to use given that the on-duty behavior of police officers is entirely a public concern.

Legal Aid fought back, formally petitioning the court to order the release of a summary of Pantaleo's file. The main piece of information they were after now was how many complaints against Pantaleo had been substantiated by the CCRB.

"We seek only a few sentences summarizing the existence, number and outcomes of civilian complaints concerning on-duty conduct by an active officer," Conti-Cook wrote.

Not gory details, just a number. Given how many hurdles a complaint had to go through to be substantiated by the CCRB—think of Eure's remarkable study on chokeholds—how high a number could that be, anyway?

The CCRB responded that the release of even that much information would be "inherently stigmatizing and subject to abuse."

Now joined to the case, Pantaleo himself argued to the court through his attorney that he had already suffered hardship and threats because the press had published information about one of his CCRB cases, the Rice/Collins groping case.

The judge in the case, Alice Schlesinger, wasn't impressed. She didn't think CCRB records were Pantaleo's problem. Without passing judgment on Pantaleo's actions in the Garner matter, she noted it was likely that "any adverse reactions expressed toward Mr. Pantaleo" would "have their roots in the video of that incident, which speaks for itself."

So Judge Schlesinger ordered that the CCRB release the summary. Coincidentally, that order came on July 17, exactly a year after Garner's death.

Both the city and Pantaleo appealed, however, and the case was tied up in court for another year and a half. By the summer of 2016, both sides were still months away from making oral arguments in the case. Years of pitched legal battle over a single number. Even the release of that much information was too much for the city to bear.

. . .

There was a bizarre twist to this part of the case. While Legal Aid was fighting the CCRB for disclosure of Pantaleo's complaint history, the CCRB itself, and Emery, had petitioned a Staten Island court for disclosure of the Pantaleo grand jury minutes.

This was a separate and distinct petition from the one filed earlier by the likes of Meyerson and the NAACP, the *Post,* the public advocate's office, Legal Aid, and the NYCLU. Those were outside entities asking for a look in the tent. In this case, a city agency was asking for a look at Pantaleo's grand jury case, not to publicize it, but to use it.

The CCRB under Emery at the time was preparing to prosecute Pantaleo in APU, that internal police court. The CCRB, Emery says, was planning to push for an APU prosecution of Pantaleo in this proceeding once his grand jury investigation had been completed, and once the U.S. attorney had decided whether or not to file civil rights charges. But the Department of Justice, Emery says, requested that the CCRB put a hold on the APU case until the department finished investigating.

Even though Emery's CCRB was not disclosing Pantaleo's records at the time—he says because the law barred him from doing so—he nonetheless petitioned the Richmond County Supreme Court for Garner's grand jury minutes in May 2015. "We needed that material to properly assess how to discipline him," he says.

Emery says the CCRB would have had a much better chance at the grand jury minutes than the five petitioners who went to court in February. "We were a government agency, we weren't going to make it public, and we had a particularized need," he says. "This was a different case with much better precedents."

Nonetheless, the judge—Judge Garnett, the same judge who shot down the other five petitioners—refused the CCRB's request to open the grand jury minutes formally. The denial came down on August 20, 2015. Emery, after meeting with the rest of the CCRB, wrote a letter to the city's corporation counsel, Zach Carter, asking permission to file an appeal.

Carter quickly squashed this final effort to get the Pantaleo minutes. On September 4, 2015, he wrote to the CCRB and reminded the board that he had the authority to bar it from filing an appeal (and in fact had had the authority to bar the original motion to Judge Gar-

nett, and would have, had he known about it). In strong language,
Carter basically told everyone to cut it out:

> As to your Chair's suggestion that the CCRB adopt a formal resolu-
> tion requesting authorization to appeal, that is unnecessary under
> the circumstances. Your Chair has voiced his disagreement with my
> position on this matter on your behalf and by this writing, I have
> responded.
>   . . . There may well come a CCRB case in which the rules pro-
> tecting grand jury secrecy should yield to CCRB's compelling and
> particularized need for evidence unavailable from other sources—
> but this is not that case.

Not seeing an explicit order not to appeal, the board met again and
voted 5–3 to file an appeal. Emery told Carter of the decision. Carter
quickly wrote back and formally ordered the board to shut it down.
"I do not authorize an appeal of the above-referenced decision," he
said, and that was that.

The story of what happened inside the Pantaleo grand jury was
such a closely held secret that the city was afraid to disclose it even to
the CCRB. This was despite the fact that the CCRB was fighting with
all its might to keep any information about Pantaleo from reaching
the public's ears. With this strange exchange of memos between
Emery and Carter, about which the public knew nothing, the last attempt to get at the Pantaleo grand jury minutes was snuffed out.

Emery stepped down as the head of the CCRB in April 2016, a
day after he was sued by yet another female CCRB employee, this
time for allegedly saying "I don't know why everyone is acting like a
bunch of pussies" after a board meeting. He'd also gotten in hot
water with police earlier that year after characterizing criticism by
police unions as "squealing like a stuck pig." Police union officials,
unsurprisingly headed by Pat Lynch, went crazy over the line. Emery's tenure at the agency had been brief and, from a public relations
standpoint, no picnic. He was probably relieved to return to private
practice.

Some time later, Emery would reflect on his time at the CCRB. His
tenure at the agency had been dominated by the Garner case. Garner
had been killed, after all, on Emery's first day on the job. "It hovered

over everything," he recalls. "The whole time I was there." And even as he took criticism from lawyers and activists who blasted his CCRB for not releasing Pantaleo's records, Emery was burdened by knowledge about the case he couldn't share at the time.

During the course of his agency's preparation for a possible prosecution of Pantaleo in a police trial, the NYPD had made some nonpublic investigatory materials available to the CCRB. Corporation counsel Zach Carter had even made reference to this in one of his letters to Emery and the CCRB, in which he castigated them for seeking access to the grand jury minutes. "[The] NYPD ultimately relented and provided access to evidentiary materials in July 2015, including tape recordings of the interviews of the target, Officer Pantaleo, and other witnesses," Carter wrote on September 17, 2015.

As CCRB chief, Emery therefore had access to materials that none of the many police critics following the case had. He had seen the autopsy photos. "Just horrifying," he recalls. He also had been able to review some of the investigatory materials, and says they left him without much doubt about the matter, at least in terms of the internal CCRB prosecution he ostensibly would have led.

"There was a very strong case that I would have pursued, seeking the most serious form of discipline for Pantaleo," he says now. Without elaborating on the specifics, he says that his review included "the autopsy photos, the medical examiner's report, and a very skillful interrogation of Pantaleo by IAB [Internal Affairs Bureau] investigators."

Emery is quick to point out that he's not offering a judgment on whether or not Pantaleo could or should have been indicted criminally. He could speak only of Pantaleo's vulnerability to police discipline. On that score, though, he says he had no doubt.

"Those three things," he repeats, referring to the autopsy photos, the ME report, and the IAB interview, "made it a very strong case for the most serious discipline, in my view."

Perhaps, if he had remained in office long enough to conduct a prosecution of Pantaleo—APU trials at One Police Plaza are public, even though the public rarely attends them—Emery's tenure might have been remembered for bringing some of that information to light. But he never got the chance to show how his office would have responded to that opportunity.

In June 2017, there was a quiet announcement in the *New York Post* that the CCRB had moved to substantiate an excessive force complaint against Pantaleo. The paper noted that this decision could result in "an administrative NYPD trial," which left open the possibility that some of this evidence might still see the light of day. But it was also possible that a deal could be reached that would keep the lid on everything. Three years after Garner's death, the case was still a maze of dead ends. Virtually every avenue that might have led to disclosure of what police and prosecutors knew remained closed.

In late spring, a series of envelopes began showing up on Erica's doorstep.

Inside each one was a denial of her FOIL requests. Some of the city's letters used language that seemed cut and pasted from the arguments the CCRB had thrown at Legal Aid.

Releasing the information requested, the city told Erica, would constitute an "unwarranted invasion of privacy" and "could endanger the life or safety of any person." It also would "interfere with law enforcement investigations and judicial proceedings."

Erica was floored by the language. Her father had been killed by a police officer with a history of abuse incidents. If her request was "unwarranted," what would have constituted a warranted request?

"It didn't make any sense to me," she said.

While the fight over Pantaleo's records was going on, a similar battle was taking place in the city of Chicago over another police killing, involving a seventeen-year-old named Laquan McDonald. McDonald had been shot sixteen times by police on October 10, 2014, while the Garner grand jury was hearing whatever case Dan Donovan was putting on.

Chicago police said McDonald was shot because he had lunged at cops with a four-inch knife while they were investigating break-ins at a trucking yard.

But there were questions about the case from the start. In April 2015, the FBI launched an investigation into the case. Days later, the city approved a $5 million settlement to McDonald's family, but still no one really knew what happened.

In May, a Freedom of Information Act request was filed by a free-lance reporter named Brandon Smith, who like Conti-Cook was part of a project aimed at compiling data about police abuse complaints. His was one of sixteen different efforts to obtain police video of the incident.

It wasn't until November 19, 2015, more than a full year after McDonald's death, that a judge ordered the release of the video, over the objections of Chicago mayor and former Obama chief of staff Rahm Emanuel.

The video was finally released on November 24 and showed that McDonald was clearly walking away from police when he was gunned down. A single officer, Jason Van Dyke, shot him all sixteen times.

Virtually simultaneous with the release of the video, Van Dyke was charged with first-degree murder. The horrifying video by then was just the latest in a series of gruesome scenes that had gone viral since the death of Garner.

Those included the killing of twelve-year-old Tamir Rice in Cleveland, shot for carrying a toy gun by police who began firing seconds after arriving on scene; unarmed Walter Scott, shot at eight times after being pulled over for a broken taillight in North Charleston, South Carolina; Freddie Gray, who had his spine broken in a police van in Baltimore; Dajerria Becton, a bikini-clad fifteen-year-old girl thrown to the ground by a white officer named Eric Casebolt at a pool party in McKinney, Texas; Sandra Bland, a twenty-eight-year-old black woman found hanged in a cell in Waller, Texas, after being detained for an illegal lane change; and countless others.

The FOIA request leading to the release of the video was clearly a major reason that Van Dyke was charged with murder at all. Law enforcement had lied repeatedly in that case, claiming an assault that never happened. It was only when it couldn't be denied anymore that charges were filed.

And there was one additional detail that came out as a result of the FOIA request: Van Dyke had at least twenty different civilian complaints on file, including an excessive force case for which the city paid out $350,000. The database project Smith was involved with showed that as many as 402 different Chicago officers had twenty or more complaints on file, with one officer having a high of sixty-eight.

When the McDonald video was released, and news of Van Dyke's history became public, protests engulfed the city of Chicago.

But halfway across the country, in New York, the history of the officer in the most infamous case of all remained secret.

Within a month or so after Eric Garner's death, his stepfather, Ben Carr, began to frequent the spot where Garner died. He and others, including fellow North Carolina native Doug Brinson, set up a memorial with candles and posters and other items at 200 Bay.

A little Plexiglas box containing flowers and cards would remain for years. Carr would frequently come by with a bottle of Windex and a rag, shining and cleaning it for hours, pouncing on even the smallest speck of dust. If anyone spit on the sidewalk near the spot, he would immediately douse it with bleach and mop the whole sidewalk in a fury. The shrine became his personal mission.

His presence raised eyebrows among the Bay Street regulars, who didn't know quite what to make of him. Some were resentful that he occasionally told people to behave this way or that near the box. Others just learned to steer clear of the spot when he was around.

Standing at the box in the days after the Laquan McDonald video went public, Carr told a story about his youth.

One night in the late 1950s, when he was about twelve years old, Carr crouched in the bushes near his house, waiting, a rifle in his hands. This was in rural Rocky Point, North Carolina, right around the time of the historic *Brown v. Board of Education* decision desegregating America's schools.

"I had a twenty-two and an eighteen-shot rifle," he said. "I got my first gun when I was eleven. We used to go hunting for squirrels and rabbits."

Carr lived in a cul-de-sac off Route 117, a little looping road called Pennsylvania Avenue, where both blacks and whites lived. "All the families worked at the sawmill," he said. "We was all poor."

During the Brown case, a tall, broad-shouldered, then-little-known lawyer for the NAACP named Thurgood Marshall had lampooned the argument made by white America that chaos would somehow ensue if black and white kids who already played together were allowed to go to school together.

"They play on their farms together, they go down the road together," he said. "But if they go to elementary and high school [together], the world will fall apart."

Marshall might have been talking about the rural Carolina neighborhood where Ben Carr grew up. Not only did the boys and girls on Pennsylvania Avenue play in one another's yards, the white and black parents watched and disciplined one another's children.

"The white parents would whip our asses, and our moms would whip their asses," he says now, laughing. "If we needed something they would loan it to us, and if they needed something, we would loan it to them. We lived together and it was cool."

But one of the black residents on the block was a local teacher (Carr calls him "the professor") who had the gall to go work for the white public school when integration began. The rednecks in town didn't like it, and one night, they burned a cross on his lawn. Carr remembers seeing the flames licking the night air.

The black men on the street doused the fire and then set up in the bushes by the side of the road with rifles, pellet guns, and any weapons they could get their hands on. "We knew that they liked to come back and burn your house down," he says. "It didn't matter if you were in it."

Because the stretch of Pennsylvania where he lived was a U-shaped road, it was a good spot for an ambush. "If you came in," Ben says now, "we got your ass."

Ben waited in the bushes with his .22 that night, but they never came back. Did he know who they were?

"They wore masks," he said. "But we knew who they were."

Decades later, he stood on Bay Street and traced a finger right down the middle of his face, recalling the men in masks who had burned a cross in his neighborhood when he was a child.

"They had two faces. One with the mask and one without."

The fight over personnel secrecy, he said, was the same thing.

"Back then they had masks," he said. "Now they have uniforms. Then they hid behind the masks. Now they hide behind the uniforms. We know their faces, but we don't know nothing else."

Not long after, Carr had a mild stroke while driving a car and nearly lost his life. He stopped coming around the spot so often. Except for the little Plexiglas box, it was as though nothing of note had ever happened here.

FOURTEEN RAMSEY

Friday, February 19, 2016, just after noon. Ramsey Orta, famous for his phone-camera video of the last moments of Eric Garner's conscious life, is holed up in an apartment somewhere in the Bronx. He is wanted by police, but he's not sure what to do. Afraid for his life, he's thinking of running.

The previous Sunday, he and his new wife, Bella Eiko, got into an argument at their place in the Baruch Houses, on the Lower East Side.

The two had married very quickly after meeting the previous year, and their relationship ran very hot and very cold. Sunday had been one of the cold days. They had a dispute, things got ugly, and the back-and-forth spilled out into a Duane Reade. This led to police being called and Bella being grilled by detectives.

Bella Eiko is a striking young African American woman who'd only just moved from Oakland and had a young child from a previous relationship. She had a pleasant manner but sometimes seemed anxious. She would smile and say one thing in a tight, staccato rhythm one minute and frown and sigh out the opposite a moment later.

In the station, she says, police told her she couldn't make arrangements for her son until she gave a statement.

"I panicked," she says. "I was under duress. I didn't know what I was saying."

So she "gave police what they wanted," eventually making a statement about being threatened by Ramsey. The story may have had a few truths in it, but it was clearly also true that Bella, who was active in the Black Lives Matter movement, did not want to help the police by giving evidence against her famous husband. She seemed mortified and conflicted by the whole situation.

She almost immediately recanted, but the deal was done. Police moved swiftly to obtain a warrant to grab Orta off the streets. Already one of the planet's most oft-arrested people, Ramsey was about to head back to jail one more time. But before the police got their warrant, he split uptown and set himself up in a friend's apartment in the Bronx, trying to win himself some time to think things through.

On the phone from his hideout, a wired and freaked-out Orta gave a frenzied history of his eighteen-month saga as the suddenly famous amateur videographer who had brought the mother of all global controversies down on America's biggest police force. He sounded very much on edge.

He explained that he expected to be arrested at any minute and feared for his life. Although he'd told his story a hundred times, he seemed frustrated that he was still misunderstood. More than anything, he was worried about what might happen to him in custody.

"What I'm asking for is for help," he said. "I'm in a very, very dangerous situation, where I actually had to shoot a video to explain that if I died, it wasn't suicide."

He took a deep breath and paused to look outside.

"Where do you want to start? Because I could start from two years ago, or I could start from now," he said. "This shit has been going on since I took this video. Everything hit the fan from that moment."

He started at the beginning.

Orta traced his troubles back to the night Garner was killed. After shooting the video he'd returned home to play video games in his bedroom when police drove by his place, shining a spotlight in his window.

"It was a warning," he said. "I didn't see it at the time, but it was."

His serious legal problems started a few weeks later. Late at night, just outside the Richmond Hotel, a flophouse up the street from where Eric Garner was killed, police stopped Orta and a young girl. He'd been in a room at the Richmond with a seventeen-year-old named Alba Lekaj, whom Ramsey now says he did know, although he told reporters otherwise at the time.

Police said they caught Orta handing her a gun and arrested him.[*]

***

* Orta would go on to have interactions with countless reporters in the next eighteen months, and many of those relationships ended the same way. Journalists would tie themselves into knots trying to present him as the innocent victim of a racist manhunt, not seeming to grasp that he could be technically guilty and railroaded at the same time. So they tended to flee the first time one of Orta's explanations for an arrest didn't add up.

Orta's account of the case was all over the place. He not only had to worry about talking himself into jail, he had to worry about what his then wife, Chrissie, would think about him being in a hotel room with a seventeen-year-old girl. He gave multiple explanations for what went on in that hotel. The one he settled on ultimately was that he was in there doing business. "She was an addict," he says. "I was selling her drugs."

When Orta and Lekaj came out of the hotel, two plainclothes police approached them and started to question them. These two officers swore that Orta slipped Lekaj a .25 caliber Norton pistol at that moment.

This is the problem with the Stop-and-Frisk era. There are so many cases where police clearly invent the reasons either for a stop or a search that it makes it hard to know what the truth is in any arrest where the evidence is the say-so of a police officer.

Was Jeff Thomas swallowing a baggie of crack? Was Eric Garner really selling cigarettes before he was killed? And did an experienced criminal like Ramsey Orta actually slip a pistol to a seventeen-year-old girl in direct view of two plainclothes police?

Whatever happened, the encounter as written up by the arresting officers didn't make much sense.

Police claimed that Orta wasn't being targeted that night. They said they were "conducting enforcement operations" in the Bay and Victory neighborhood where Garner worked. They added that they saw him and Lekaj going into a "known drug prone location," i.e., the hotel, which gave them the probable cause to stop them.

Now, from his hideout in the Bronx, Orta completely denied everything, pointing out that his prints weren't on the gun. He also insisted that the fact the gun wasn't loaded was important. "If I'm such a master criminal, what am I doing with a gun with no clip and no fucking bullets?" he says.

Orta's lawyer at the time was a Staten Island–based attorney named Matthew Zuntag. Zuntag had represented him in other cases and had Orta's trust. Zuntag tried to contest multiple aspects of the gun case, among other things by trying to organize a DNA test to prove Orta had never touched the weapon. But there were multiple delays, and by the new year he was still waiting.

"I'm stuck," he told reporters after a court hearing on January 22, 2015. Orta by then had started to become a cause célèbre among lefty protesters, who saw him as a symbol to rally behind in the emerging national movement.

They packed his January hearing, many of them wearing "Black Lives Matter" and "I Can't Breathe" buttons, and followed him after court in a short march to the spot where Garner had been killed.

Haltingly, Orta was trying on political activism for size, realizing that his name meant something to people.

But even as he stood on Bay Street with protesters that January afternoon, Orta had already caught another bust. Unbeknownst to him, he'd become the target of an undercover drug operation almost as soon as he'd bailed out on his gun case.

Throughout that fall, a group of at least nine people connected to the Tompkinsville Park scene where Eric Garner lived and died had been targeted for undercover drug buys. The Staten Island police, embarrassed around the world, were striking back with a wide sweep, with Ramsey the biggest catch.

Orta remembers the undercover agent who got him. He was suspicious right away because the guy was white and talked too much.

"He was going on and on about how he liked to party in Atlantic City and all that," Orta says. "I remember thinking the guy was suspicious. But he was shooting up right in front of me, so I thought he had to be okay."

Police ended up capturing scenes on video of Orta directing Mr. Atlantic City to Michael Batista, Orta's brother, who allegedly gave him drugs.

There is also a scene in one video involving his mother, Emily Mercado. In it, Orta tells his mother on the phone, "G'head, Ma, pass it." The grainy film shows her handing a paper bag to the man before counting some money.

Later on, police would charge Orta with an incredible thirty-four separate charges in just this one case, including nine sales. Although it would be extremely unlikely to happen, prosecutors could theoretically have asked for ten years on each sale.

In a detail that would later send Orta's paranoia levels through the roof, the evidence for seven of those nine sales was supposedly on videos where the audio containing the alleged drug deals was missing. Authorities said they had to alter the videos to protect the identity of the undercover agent.

When his lawyers asked what was going on, authorities replied only that "seven of the sales were captured" but promised that "the defendant can set up a mutually convenient time for a viewing of the unredacted video."

But they never set up the viewing.

Significantly, the police made most of these undercover buys before December 4, when the nonindictment in Pantaleo's case was announced and New York City blew up in protests. But the arrests weren't made until long after the furor from that grand jury decision died down.

The buys in Orta's case supposedly took place on November 18, 2014. But Orta was not actually busted until February 10, 2015. Shortly after sunup, Staten Island cops burst into his Staten Island home with the bravado of soldiers raiding Entebbe.

The door flew open and Orta, who was already awake, suddenly saw officers tearing through his house. The first thing he noticed was a weird detail.

"I expected them to be waving guns, but they were flashing cameras at me," he said. "They was like, 'You had the camera, now we got the camera.' It was fucked up."

He watched as officers tore through his house.

"When they came in I was already up," he says. "They hit the door and started bringing everybody to the living room."

Orta says he tried to explain to police that his then wife, Chrissie Ortiz, wasn't up yet.

"Listen, my wife is not dressed. Let her get dressed," he said.

"Fuck your wife," he says they said.

Then they kicked his bedroom door down.

"Now my ex-wife is standing there naked, pussy all out, tits all out," Orta recalls. "And I'm telling him, 'Officer, you're not supposed to be doing this. You're sitting there getting off on my wife.'"

"Fuck you," the officer said.

"Now my wife is screaming," Orta remembers. "I had to wait until a female officer came into the house for her to put clothes on. They didn't even allow her to get dressed. Like, my little brother witnessed my ex-wife butt-ass naked while they searching the house."

Police didn't find anything else in the house, but they did bring Orta in. They also arrested other members of his family, including his mother, on drug charges.

The arraignment in Staten Island was a tense affair, attended by still more protesters, with Ramsey screaming that it was a frame-up and his mother in obvious distress. The glee of the authorities over Orta being arrested on the strength of an undercover video was palpable. A "police source" summed it up for the *Daily News* just as they had for Ramsey.

"He took the video," the source said. "Now we took the video."

The fact that it could just as easily have been the Easter Bunny as a low-level drug dealer like Ramsey Orta making the video of Garner's murder was lost on the department.

The *News* quote showed that police saw the whole narrative as one more skirmish in the ongoing war between Them and Us. While Orta may not have been innocent as a general rule, he was certainly an innocent bystander when it came to his role in making the Garner video.

The police, however, made it absolutely clear that they saw a connection between Orta's criminality and the fact that he'd taken the film, and they were determined to have the rest of the world make that same connection.

After that hearing, Orta ended up on Rikers Island on the drug charges. His unit was put on lockdown shortly after he showed up. As a result, prisoners were not allowed to help in preparing their food, as was customary.

During this time period, the unit was fed a meatloaf dinner. Orta ate it but noticed that the meat contained a funny-looking bluish-green substance. He quickly began to feel unwell but didn't think anything of it at the time. He even joked about it in phone conversations with his family.

"I said, 'There's something weird about this food. There's like these green pellets in it. Maybe they're trying to kill me by poison,'" he says. "But I was joking."

Next thing he knew, though, other inmates in his unit were experiencing vomiting, stomach pains, dizziness, nosebleeds, diarrhea, and other symptoms. This led to a lawsuit in which nineteen men from Orta's unit accused the city of putting rat poison in their food. Orta says he was shocked when he found out that there were many brands of blood-thinner-based rodenticides that actually come in blue-green pellet form.

"I'm from the projects. Rat poison to me is a big-ass box that says 'POISON' on it," he said. "I never heard of no pellets."

That incident terrified Orta, who later became convinced that he was the intended target of the poisoning. He was still recovering from that incident when he caught some jailhouse gossip about his lawyer, Zuntag.

Apparently one of the Rikers inmates, also represented by Zuntag, had tried to buy his freedom by giving evidence against Zuntag for bringing drugs into the jail.

"Basically the inmate had snitched on Matt," Orta said. "He had his sister bring the drugs to Matt. She was basically testifying against Matt for her brother, the one that was locked up."

Normally, no lawyer caught up in a drug case could help his or her cause by serving up a low-level street dealer. But Ramsey was no longer just another small-time dealer. He was famous and a prize.

Orta immediately wondered if his lawyer might now be tempted to get out of his own problems by trading on their relationship somehow. He even wondered if his cases had already been messed up. Holed up in his friend's Bronx apartment nearly a year later, he still wondered about that.

At the time, though, he fired Zuntag and had his family set up a GoFundMe account to get him new lawyers. They raised twenty thousand dollars and set about looking for new help.

Because Orta was a high-profile figure by then, he and his family had received tons of letters already from criminal attorneys willing to take on his case, so they had a lot of names to go through.

Orta ended up with two well-known criminal attorneys with a reputation for taking on cops, Ken Perry and Will Aronin. They came on his case and immediately set about getting him out of Rikers. Soon after that, a relieved Orta bailed out, having lost a significant amount of weight.

Almost immediately, he was arrested again, this time in Manhattan.

"I go into a store, and when I come out, the police grab me and say I did a robbery," Orta says. "Then they're saying I had a knife that was found on someone else, and they're saying I did a robbery for ten dollars."

Orta pauses. "Then they got to the station and they say they found Percocet in my jacket pocket. They didn't find it until I got to the station. So now I'm being charged with possession also."

He sighs. "Come on, man, you think I'm gonna rob someone of ten dollars? That shit is insulting."

Orta around that time began to draw parallels between the way he had been treated and the way Daniel Pantaleo was being treated. The two men had somehow switched fates. Pantaleo had actually killed Eric Garner, but it seemed like Orta was somehow stepping into what should have been Pantaleo's role of the man being hunted for the crime.

Orta was still under near-constant surveillance, while Pantaleo enjoyed twenty-four-hour police protection. Then it came out that Pantaleo was reportedly training for a career as an MMA fighter. The news turned out not to be true—fake news, before fake news was famous—but it was on the Internet, and Orta, like a lot of people in and around Bay Street, believed it and saw it as still more evidence of the double standard.

"They're chasing me and Pantaleo is going to be fucking choking people for a living or whatever? Shit is crazy," Ramsey said.

On September 15, 2015, which Orta noted would have been Eric Garner's birthday, he had a court appearance in his drug case. When he got there, he discovered that his brother and codefendant, Michael Batista, had had all of his charges dropped. He immediately began to suspect that his brother had cut a deal to give Ramsey up.

"He done, he ain't got no charges, no nothing," Ramsey said. "Like, where the fuck his charges went if he got wrapped up in this secret indictment with me?"

Subsequently, authorities let him know that they had new evidence against him, apparently recordings of jailhouse phone calls between himself and Batista that were incriminating. Orta insisted that couldn't be.

"I've been doing this Rikers Island shit for so long that I know not to talk over those phones," he said. "The only conversations they have over those phones is me and my wife fucking talking dirty to each other. Normal locked-up shit."

Perry and Aronin at the time were filing motion after motion on the gun and drug cases, trying to tilt some leverage back in Orta's direction to make a possible deal more favorable.

According to their math, by February 2016, Orta was facing charges that could easily have landed him in jail for twenty years or more. They began to talk to Orta about taking a single deal to make all the cases against him (and, ostensibly, his mother) go away if he would just do, say, five years.

Orta didn't like hearing from his own lawyers about any deal. What he heard was them telling him in one breath that all of the cases were flawed and then arguing for a deal in the next breath. He started to get suspicious. Of everybody.

Meanwhile, Orta was increasingly stressed out by his fame. After more than a year, he'd been unable to find any way to navigate the immense double-edged celebrity the Garner video had brought him.

He was never sure what to do with his new status. Should he make money off it, become an activist, or what? The pressure to do something seemed to throw his whole life into disarray. Life was much simpler when he was a small-time drug dealer nobody cared about.

He tried to get involved in an organization dedicated to monitoring the police called Copwatch, but his commitment waxed and waned. One thing he was sure of was that if there was a way to play being Ramsey Orta that involved getting rich, he hadn't found it.

"If you look at the pictures throughout the whole two years since I took the video, I'm still wearing the same clothes in each picture," he said. "I mean, let's just be real. I didn't make no money."

He sighed. "The thing is, this is not about the money. I don't give a fuck about the money. This is more about my life."

And what was his life supposed to be now? All over Staten Island and beyond, people had opinions. Some said he had a responsibility now to stay out of trouble, not give the cops any headlines. There were a lot of whispers of this sort on Bay Street, where some people close to Garner were pissed about his arrests.

"Ramsey, dude, throw a little shade on it" was how one of Garner's close friends put it.

But was it Ramsey's fault he kept getting arrested? Was he a true victim or just a criminal who had a bad habit of getting caught? Was he being persecuted and singled out by police, or was he a villain and an abuser of women who was finally getting his comeuppance? The reality was that all of these things might have been true.

In conversation, Orta was a great storyteller, tremendously candid, raw and foulmouthed about his criminal past. He cut a thrilling figure for reporters and foreigners, who seemed to flock to him. He was constantly surrounded by European film crews, magazine writers, documentarians.

But he was also just an ordinary street kid facing a hundred years in jail, and so there were limits to what he could say without talking himself into a long sentence. He wanted to be completely honest and couldn't. Nor did he want his protestations of legal innocence to be misinterpreted as a desire to be put up on a pedestal.

Call it a triumph of racially charged propaganda and dog-whistle reporting that Orta eventually resorted to using the infamous cliché newspapers often slapped on the victims of police abuse.

"I mean, I'm no angel," he said.

The awkwardness reached a height on January 18, 2016, Martin Luther King Jr. Day. At the small but beautiful Trinity Lutheran Church in the Sunset Park section of Brooklyn, Orta was given the Martin Luther King Community Service Award, presented by Copwatch, the activist group he had begun working with.

Also receiving an award that day with him was Kevin Moore, the Baltimore man who'd made a similar cellphone video of police arresting Freddie Gray. Moore, a burly, broad-shouldered man with long dreadlocks and a cheerful disposition, stood at the rear of the church with the sullen, stressed-looking Orta.

The church was not filled, but the people who were there represented decades of constant struggle against police brutality, mass incarceration, and the drug war. There was Dennis Flores, leader of Copwatch, the man who'd been embroiled in an argument with the Justice League folks. Flores was trying, best he could, to mentor Ramsey, be a friend to him, and help him use his name for something good.

Also in the crowd was Javier Nieves, a former state assemblyman who'd once helped stop a prison construction project that was being pushed by erstwhile liberal-hero governor Mario Cuomo after he'd undertaken the largest prison construction campaign seen in the industrial world since Stalin.

The room was filled with such people, who had all taken part in hard-fought political action campaigns with profound relevance to the life and death of Eric Garner. And Flores took the stage and asked all of them to salute Ramsey.

"Police violence is something that continues to exist, from Dr. King's day to today," Flores said. "And we are honoring brother

Ramsey Orta and brother Kevin Moore. It is important for us as a
community to build support for them, because they are targets, just
like Dr. King was a target."

Orta looked like he might turn green when he heard himself compared to Dr. King.

Still, he kept his cool. He read a brief statement of thanks and
meekly accepted his award, a little wooden statuette in the form of a
camera.

A few weeks after that, the incident with Bella happened. Now Orta
had cause to freak out even more. He explained that after the fight
with his wife, he saw that details of his case had been leaked almost
immediately to local papers.

"Sources" had told the *Daily News* that Orta had waved a knife at
his wife and said, "I'll kill your ass."

Then he saw a story in *Vibe* that took a year-old quote from his
aunt, Lisa Mercado, speculating that Orta was suicidal.

"He was always an outspoken person. He's not anymore," the article read. "He talks about, 'Maybe I should just kill myself. I'm just
hurting my entire family.'"

Orta nearly jumped out of his seat when he read that.

"That shit scared me," Orta said. Now, he was not only sure police
had leaked details of his case to the *News,* he was convinced that they
were also spreading word to other publications that he was suicidal.

"Now if something happens to me in jail, they can just say he was
depressed or whatever," he explained. "Like, where the fuck is this
coming from, on the day I'm supposed to turn myself in? That's what
blew my mind. This is why I'm running, because now I'm scared."

Orta had other concerns. Though they'd gotten him out of Rikers
a year before, he'd begun to seriously wonder whether or not his well-
heeled pay lawyers, Aronin and Perry, were really on his side. He felt
they were pressing him too hard to deal.

Among other things, he said, they'd come to him with a proposal
that maybe he could shave some years off his future jail term by doing
a humiliating joint press conference with some senior Staten Island
law enforcement officials.

The idea they presented was that upon surrender, Orta would sit next to all of the officials who'd been pilloried in the press as a result of his video, hang his head, and admit to being a criminal.

He would be a captured trophy for the likes of former DA Dan Donovan and perhaps even Daniel Pantaleo, who in Orta's understanding of the fantasy presser would also be invited.

Ramsey thought it was crazy. As it happens, the Staten Island district attorney's office also thought it was a crazy idea. They later confirmed that "an offer of this type was put on the table by Mr. Orta's defense team" but that "such an offer would never be entertained by . . . this office."

Perry and Aronin said only that as defense lawyers, they were duty bound to explore any avenues that might lead to reduced sentences for their clients. Which was true. But Ramsey was very put out.

"They just want me to not only cop out but go in front of the media, standing next to the officer who killed my fucking friend, standing next to the commissioner of the police, and state that 'yes, I, Ramsey Orta, was guilty of a firearm that was on my possession,'" he seethed. "This is what they want me to do in the media."

As he talked about all of this on the phone, you could hear traffic on the Bronx streets rushing by.

"It's like, everywhere I go to get help, they're like, 'Well, our reputation's on the line,'" he said. "Or it's basically, 'Here, you got to take this deal.' So it's like, I don't know who to run to, who to go to.

"I just don't know who to trust."

Minutes later, Orta hung up and walked outside to head to a store. Almost immediately, at the intersection of Reverend James Polite Avenue and East 165th Street, police rushed him and threw him in a car. They'd keyed in on his cellphone, apparently.* By the time he made it to the Seventh Precinct, local news photographers were waiting for him. The local media knew he was busted before he did.

At any given time, on any list of the most miserable places in New York City, the downtown arraignments court at 100 Centre Street in Manhattan would have to rank pretty high. This grim little hall smells

---

* Ramsey had to wonder about me, too, after that phone call, given that he was arrested minutes after we hung up. For the record, I didn't turn him in.

like mold and features beat-up wooden pews for benches, and most of the action inside involves sending people nobody cares about to places the public will never see, down the toilet of the city's medieval jail system.

It's Saturday, the morning after Ramsey's arrest in the Bronx. While the rest of the city is sleeping in, a ragtag group of angry-looking lawyers, bailiffs, and defendants march one after another before an even surlier-sounding magistrate, Judge Patricia Nuñez. The honor of being a judge must feel a little muted when you're spending your weekends doing bail hearings for the kind of people you wouldn't even step over on a New York City sidewalk.

An African American man stands with his head bowed before Nuñez. He is charged with stealing soap. The city, ludicrously, is asking for five thousand dollars' bail.

"For a box of Dove soap," the man's attorney pleads. "I submit, Your Honor, that five thousand dollars is above and beyond the scope of this case."

Nuñez rolls her eyes and whacks her gavel.

"Bail is set at two hundred fifty dollars," she says, then sighs and looks with undisguised anguish at the sizable row of defendants waiting their turn.

In the next case, a defense lawyer stands up and tries to stammer out an argument that his client, another African American man, has insufficient funds to make bail. The accused supposedly stole a $769 leather jacket from a Gap store. He has nineteen failures to appear on his sheet. The guy is screwed, but his lawyer, juggling a pile of manila folders, gives it a college try.

"Your Honor, my client is of very limited means," he begins. "And bail at all is tantamount to remand . . ."

Nuñez, annoyed, whacks her gavel before he can finish. "Bail is set at ten thousand dollars," she says. "Next!"

Ten thousand! The Gap patron sags like he's taken a bullet, then shakes his head in rage. The bailiffs, sensing trouble, quickly move to take him away, but he struggles and shouts a string of obscenities at the judge on the way out.

Nuñez snaps awake.

"I heard that," she says. Then, slowly, so the court reporter can get all of it, she repeats the defendant's tirade.

"The defendant just said, 'I ain't pleading guilty to shit and this is fucking bullshit.'" She looks over at the man crossly and decides to throw a little judgeifying at him. "That increases his bail to twenty thousand dollars."

"Motherfucker!" the man hisses as the bailiffs drag him out.

A few minutes later, the monotony is broken when the hotshot lawyers Aronin and Perry appear. It's a bit of a surprise that they're here. The relationship between the two lawyers and their client has deteriorated to the point where it was unclear that they still represented him.

Late-night phone calls between Bella and the two men had not ended well, and whether or not Orta would even have a lawyer this morning had been in question until a few minutes before the hearing.

But once the two men showed up, nobody in the gallery would have guessed at any problems. They were the pros from Dover, and they acted like it.

Aronin is young, fit, has slick hair, and looks like an extra from a stockbroker-chic movie like *Wall Street* or *Boiler Room*.

Perry meanwhile has flowing silver hair that's thin on top, long in back, and kept in a faintly hippieish style. His look hints a little at famed countercultural activist lawyers like Bill Kunstler and J. Tony Serra.

Their client by then was famous enough that he was recognizable from a distance. Dressed in a trademark black ski hat and a black jacket, the lean, withdrawn-looking Orta, now twenty-four, sat glumly in the back of the courtroom. He looked like he expected an anvil to fall on his head at any moment. He certainly didn't look like he expected to get bail.

But he was wrong. After the DA finished a monotonous recitation of Orta's many misdeeds, ending with a Freudian flourish—"He, uh, threatened his knife, I mean his wife, uh, with a knife"—the judge asked Perry to respond.

Perry moved to the lectern.

"Let me address some of these factual allegations," he said, and plunged into an impressive impromptu speech.

"Since we have been representing him he has made every appearance," he said. He then turned to indicate Bella, who was sitting in the gallery. "We have been in touch with the plaintiff and her attorney, and she is in this courtroom today."

Bella waved.

"Your Honor, she has put a video online that describes what happened as an argument between newlyweds," continued Perry.

He switched gears and accused police of harassment. "Members of the warrant squad have made persistent threatening phone calls," he said. "He was very scared. There were further issues about articles in the press about unnamed police sources indicating he was suicidal. He is very active in the Black Lives Matter movement, Your Honor."

He gestured in the direction of the judge and smiled. It was unclear what effect the words "Black Lives Matter" had on the judge, but they certainly got her attention.

"Bail in this case is improper," Perry went on. "This case isn't going anywhere. It will disappear."

Nuñez looked at Perry and sighed. She did not appear to relish dealing with a case with this kind of profile. On the other hand, she didn't quite seem to buy Ramsey Orta as an innocent victim. She looked down at his file and shook her head.

"There's a lot of open cases," she said, raising an eyebrow.

Perry said nothing.

The judge went on: "And it's not unusual for the complainant of a domestic violence case to change her statement."

She looked over at Ramsey and his now-famous black hat for a moment, clearly not wanting this headache.

"Bail is set at ten thousand dollars," she said. "That's in light of the fact that the case will probably be discharged."

In the gallery, Bella smiled and jumped up and down in her seat, giddy. Ramsey said nothing and went back in the pen. He knew enough not to celebrate anything. He was getting out again, but for how long?

Just weeks after his arrest on domestic violence charges, Orta was arrested again, this time back at the Baruch Houses on the Lower East Side. He was out with Copwatch when police nabbed him for "interfering" with an arrest.

Orta hadn't moved back to the sidewalk as quickly as the police had wanted him to. He also handed a business card to the man being arrested. So they hit him with the usual pupu platter of legally vague/meaningless charges, including disorderly conduct and obstructing government administration.

This time, the judge just wrote Orta a desk appearance ticket and let him go, apparently unimpressed with the arrest.

When he got out, Orta and Bella had another argument and she took off for the West Coast to get away from him. He wondered if he should go after her to try to work things out. At the same time, he found himself increasingly perplexed by his situation. The mere fact that he could travel at all he found strange.

He was becoming exhausted and confused by this pattern of being arrested, then released to give interviews and travel the world, then arrested again, then released again, then arrested again, seemingly every few minutes.

"My rap sheet, the felonies that I copped out to before," he says. "Basically I should have never been home. I got six new cases and they keep letting me out on bail. If I'm such a criminal, I'm guilty, you got all this evidence against me, but why you keep giving me bail, though?"

Orta by then worked himself into such a state, he now wondered if this was some kind of weird cat-and-mouse game, like maybe the police enjoyed letting him out and hunting him down each time or something. He said he'd even taken grief for it inside.

"Even people in jail is looking at me like if I'm fucking snitching on people," he says. "Because they be like, 'How the fuck you keep coming home, nigga?'"

Things were so much simpler before.

"I don't want the fame, I don't even want to be Ramsey Orta," he said. "I don't want none of this shit no more."

Within a few weeks, Orta was giving in. The city was pressuring him to deal. A few years inside, they said, and all the cases go away.

On July 7, 2016, almost exactly two years after Eric Garner's death, Orta's saga came to an end. In Part Six of the Staten Island court, ironically before Judge Stephen Rooney, the original magistrate overseeing the Garner grand jury, Orta agreed to his plea deal. In yet another example of how chaotic and random the criminal justice system is, the deal wasn't settled until literally seconds before Orta stood before the judge.

Ramsey had decided to take the deal mainly because he had been told, in negotiations, that the case against his mother, Emily Mercado, would go away as soon as he pleaded out.

"They told me that if I copped, they'd drop her case," says Orta, minutes before his court hearing. Dressed in slacks and a plaid dress shirt, he was resigned to the years, but there was late news that had him worried.

"Now all of the sudden they're acting weird about that," he says. His mother, a quiet, sad-looking woman in her forties, sat next to her son, nodding. "They're telling me they have to review it or something."

A moment later, Orta disappeared into a conference room with Aronin and Perry, who'd just arrived. He came back shaking his head.

"They're telling me I've got to cop to weed, crack, or *heron*, but since weed isn't a felony, it's got to be crack or heron."

Orta shook his head. It was strange that it didn't matter which crime he did or didn't do; in the end, he just had to pick one that fit the sentencing guidelines in the right way. Which charge would he take?

"I'll take heron." He shrugged.

Meanwhile, there were conflicting reports about his mother's situation. At first the deal was five years' probation. When he and his mother went up to stand before the judge, the lawyers were still frantically whispering with one another. Not until a moment before Rooney began speaking did they settle on three years' probation for his mother.

Orta was sworn in. "Do you swear to tell the truth in all matters before this court?" he was asked.

"Yes," he said.

But then Rooney began asking him the usual boilerplate questions: is he mentally, physically and emotionally able to plead guilty today, is he on drugs or alcohol, does he understand the charges, etc.

Orta dutifully answered each question correctly. Then Rooney asked, "Has anyone offered you anything with regard to your plea deal today?"

Orta paused, mouth open. He looked at his lawyers. The true answer was yes. After all, he was offered a lower sentence for his mother.

"That's what I was thinking. I didn't know what I was supposed to say," he said later.

There was a heated exchange for a moment, and Judge Rooney looked miffed. Perry began to try to offer an explanation about the situation with Orta's mother, then cut himself off. You have to avoid literal truths sometimes in court. Finally Ramsey shook his head and just answered.

"No, Your Honor."

That was that. Four years in prison was the final tally, plus eighteen months to three years of postrelease supervision. Orta seemed exhausted and glad to be done with it.

His mother, Emily, seemed relieved, too. "I mean, it's not the ideal thing," she said. "But it's better than going to jail."

As he and his mother collected their thoughts on the sidewalk outside the Staten Island courthouse, the Internet was blowing up with the latest police videos.

A man named Alton Sterling had been shot to death by police in Baton Rouge while pinned to the ground, while a man named Philando Castile had been killed during a car stop while reaching for his documents.

By evening, the same bloody cycle that had marked the Garner case would have run its course, as a sniper in Dallas would shoot and kill five people, including four police, igniting a countermovement against Black Lives Matter. The stories stay the same, only the actors change.

Orta was about to disappear from the stage for a while.

"Crazy fucking system," he said.

FIFTEEN IBRAHIM

January 4, 2016. On a bench in the hallway of Staten Island's gleaming new courthouse building, Ibrahim Annan sits holding a cane between his knees. He looks up and around, casting a glance at the high ceiling.

This new Staten Island court had been under construction when Eric Garner was killed. Now completed, it's a gaudy, idiosyncratic piece of architecture, difficult to navigate but full of common space, curious angles, and sunlight. If you can imagine Frank Gehry designing a morgue, it might look something like this.

Annan scrolls through his phone. Someone has sent him the mug shot of Robert Lewis Dear, the fifty-seven-year-old white lunatic who shot up a Planned Parenthood clinic in Colorado Springs a little over a month before. Dear shot five cops and killed one, but the police conspicuously forgot to beat him after capture, a fact that didn't go unnoticed in Eric Garner's old neighborhood.

"Look at him. Not a mark on his face," Annan says, shaking his head.

Every court hearing involving the Eric Garner case has been a packed, media-filled affair, but this isn't typical of police brutality cases. Annan's situation is much more the norm. Cases like his, hundreds if not thousands of them every year, move through empty or near-empty courtrooms, heard by overworked judges who are often too exhausted to show any humanity.

In the courtroom of Judge Raymond Rodriguez, the island's first Hispanic judge, Annan and his lawyer are practically the only people in the room. They are present to witness the last stages of the preposterous game of legal chicken that marks a large portion of these less-famous brutality cases.

It's been almost two full calendar years since Annan was dragged from his car and beaten by a pair of Staten Island police officers, who left his leg broken in three places.

In that time he's been back and forth to court nearly a dozen times, playing out a macabre negotiation that has a lot more to do with a possible future brutality lawsuit than it does Annan's actual guilt or innocence.

To recap: Ibrahim Annan was parked in his car on private property on April 2, 2014, when two Staten Island cops, Dominick Raso and Joseph D'Albero, took him by surprise. Without warning they smashed his car window, yanked him from his seat (so forcefully he had to have his seat belt replaced), beat him with a police ASP (a telescoping metal wand), and threw him on the ground. There, says Annan, they handcuffed him, choked him, and stomped on his leg until it snapped in three places.

The ostensible probable cause for this arrest, as described by Officer Raso in the complaint, was that from his own seat inside his police cruiser, he somehow saw Annan in his own front seat waving around a bag of weed that was "open to public view."

Defense lawyers laugh about the probable cause excuses that police come up with in their reports. The "center console" phrase is a running joke. Another common literary device in police complaints is the suspect who drops his drugs on the ground as he flees police pursuit. Lawyers affectionately call these cases "dropsies."

In Annan's case, if Officers Raso and D'Albero had managed to avoid crippling their suspect, they'd probably have gotten a conviction. Even if what actually happened is that two cops barged into a parked car and committed a groping blind search on private property without any reason at all beyond Annan being black and in the wrong place, it likely would've worked.

But things went sideways, and the police not only beat the suspect but left him with undeniable injuries. Worse, they left him with an automatically compelling cause of action for a potentially expensive federal civil rights lawsuit. So what to do?

The three most common civil suits targeting law enforcement are for excessive force, malicious prosecution, and false arrest. Even a person found guilty of a crime can sue for excessive force. But as it happens, certain types of criminal convictions, even the most minor, obviate the possibility of federal lawsuits for false arrest or malicious prosecution.

Therefore when the authorities find themselves dealing with a case like Annan's, it becomes a math game almost immediately.

The DA usually gets behind the cops and piles charge upon charge on the defendant. In the beginning of the process, he or she then typically plays up the bad cop routine in court, representing that the state will go all out for a conviction and a maximum sentence.

In Annan's case, he was hit with a total of seven criminal charges as he recuperated in the hospital: assault in the second degree, assault in the third degree, obstructing government administration in the second degree, resisting arrest, criminal possession of a weapon in the fourth degree, criminal possession of marijuana in the fifth degree, and unlawful possession of marijuana.

The idea was to get Annan to plead to any one of these charges.

As time passes in these cases, the state becomes more and more flexible, and the offers get better and better. Suddenly, instead of real time and heavy fines, they're offering community service and a few days in jail.

In New York, they may even offer an ACD, or adjournment in contemplation of dismissal, which is basically a promise by the state to make the charge disappear if the defendant stays clean for a year or six months.

Most innocent people will hesitate to plead to any criminal offense, no matter how trivial, just to avoid having a record at all.

"What are you going to do," asks Joe Doyle, Eric Garner's Legal Aid attorney, "explain to your prospective employer the difference between criminal mischief in the second degree and criminal mischief in the third? A record is a record."

But an ACD is different. An ACD means that after a very short period of time, the whole thing goes away.

But taking an ACD kills your shot at a malicious prosecution suit. So if the police beat you up and they offer you an ACD—the law enforcement equivalent of a gift fruit basket—now you're in a no-win situation.

The criminal defense lawyer will want you to take the deal.

Your civil lawyer will want you to fight, to preserve the lawsuit.

Here's another twist. In a lot of these cases, the state will start off with a charge that sounds deadly serious, like a felony assault on a police officer. But then, four or five court appearances down the road, they may suddenly knock the charge down to B misdemeanor assault.

Why? Because felony cases are heard by juries. A B-level misdemeanor in New York goes to a bench trial.

In a place like Staten Island, the black defendant is suddenly faced with the possibility of taking on the unholy trinity of a district attorney, police witnesses, and a law enforcement–friendly judge.

Even if someone like Annan is completely innocent and there's no evidence to convict him, he's now got to put his fate in the hands of a system that has already proven itself at least somewhat corrupt by letting the case go toward trial in the first place.

"Pick your poison," is how one defense lawyer put it. "You can either plead to something small that you didn't do and kill your lawsuit, or you can draw a line in the sand, keep your lawsuit, and risk getting fucked in court."

After two agonizing years of wrangling, Annan and his smooth-talking, nattily dressed attorney, Gregory Watts, have managed to get almost all the way to the finish line with the chance at a lawsuit still intact. Watts, who's been doing this a long time, didn't flinch at any of the state's weak offers.

He and Ibrahim kept choosing to take their chances, and the state kept screwing up along the way.

The DA's behavior in the Annan case can only be described as a kind of arrogant incompetence. Prosecutors so routinely get away with so much that sometimes—and this case is one of them—they show up in court with nothing at all in hand and still expect judges to wave them through to trial anyway.

In Annan's case, the DA crucially called just one witness at a probable cause hearing: Officer D'Albero, who as it happened was the second officer on the scene.

It was eagle-eyed officer Dominick Raso, and not D'Albero, who allegedly spotted Annan waving his baggie of weed around for the world to see. That meant D'Albero was not able to tell the court what the probable cause was supposed to be for pulling Annan out of the car and beating the crap out of him.

Whatever their reasoning, the state's decision to bring in the useless witness D'Albero to make their case put the judge on the spot.

A short, carefully groomed man with glasses and a neatly trimmed goatee, Judge Rodriguez seems a smart, quick-witted, and fair jurist, a contrast to a lot of the splotchy, pinkening hacks on the New York bench.

Older judges will sometimes take their time in court and engage in weird and irrelevant discussions about sports, the weather, the attire of female jurists, whatever, because they know no matter how fast they go, the docket never clears. Try hard or don't, the system is always clogged.

Younger judges, however, occasionally seem annoyed while the lawyers standing before them babble on and drop piles of weak motions on the court. Rodriguez is one of these judges. In court, you can see his brain speeding up to amphetamine levels to hurry the participants along, often finishing the sentences of the lawyers.

This judge had more than a year to become exasperated by the Ibrahim Annan case. For one thing, he clearly grasped the brutality angle. At a hearing in the summer of 2015, Watts offhandedly mentioned that he planned on pursuing a suit against the county for breaking Annan's leg.

Rodriguez quipped, "I bet you will," and moved him along.

In subsequent hearings, the state made life tough on Rodriguez by giving him nothing to work with. Even if he wanted to be a good soldier and let the DA pressure Annan into submarining his lawsuit by pleading to something, the county tied his hands by handing him a nothingburger on the probable cause front.

After nearly two years, Rodriguez now explained that he had to kill six of the seven charges against Ibrahim.

"There is no detail of the probable cause for the seizure of Mr. Annan when he was in his car [at] a private residence," said the judge, throwing up his hands.

Rodriguez impatiently explained that if there was no legal reason to enter the car, then the DA couldn't introduce evidence of the alleged weapons (a lighter and an aerosol can that Raso claimed Ibrahim held up as he said, "If you open the window I'm going to burn you!") or the bag of weed. Since there was no legal arrest, he couldn't be charged with resisting it. And as for the omnipresent "obstructing government administration" charge, even that was a nonstarter in this case.

"The theory of obstructing government administration was Mr. Annan's alleged failure to obey a lawful order to exit his vehicle," the judge sighed. "But that has all been suppressed."

The judge stared forward and explained that all that was left was a single charge, Annan's alleged assault upon the officers as he was getting his ass kicked. "All that is left is the assault three," the judge explained.

The judge told the young female prosecutor that if the city wanted to proceed with the assault charge, they would have to do so without explaining the story of cops pulling Annan from his car, finding a baggie of weed, being threatened by a lighter and an aerosol can, the ostensible resisting of arrest, or anything else. The case would be a bizarre tale of a man suddenly and without context assaulting two officers on the streets of Staten Island shortly before having his leg broken in three places.

The judge stared, clearly hoping that the young ADA would drop the charges and remove this ridiculous, time-consuming, and incidentally quite plainly corrupt case from His Honor's docket.

The ADA said nothing.

Here Watts thought it might be worth chancing a word or two.

"Your Honor," he said. "In light of your rulings—this raises the question of whether the people can proceed . . ."

Rodriguez turned to Watts and flashed a sharp glare. Nice try, but he wasn't going to dismiss the case. "No, they can try," the judge said, nodding toward the prosecutor as if to say, It's their funeral.

Then Rodriguez suddenly turned to the ADA again and pointed. "Understand this, though," he said. "I'm not going to let you reduce this to a B misdemeanor. If you want to try this, it's going to have to be before [a jury of] men and women."

As plain as day, Rodriguez was telling the prosecutor that if she wanted to chance this weak case, she wasn't going to be able to pull the old "Let's get this to a bench trial so a Staten Island judge can rubber-stamp us out of our brutality beef" trick.

The ADA was mute. Rodriguez lectured onward. "If you want to try this case," he said, "you're going to have to think about this court's ruling."

Again the judge waited for the prosecutor to drop the case. She refused. She wanted him to set a trial date. The judge's eyes looked ready to burst out of his head. He asked when the prosecutors would be ready, a loaded question since the state had claimed not to be ready to produce witnesses over and over again for nearly two years.

"We can be ready in two weeks," the prosecutor said.

The judge glared once more. The idea that the state would be ready to go to a jury trial in two weeks on a case with no admissible evidence was total BS and everyone knew it. The only possible reason the state could want to set a trial date would be because it needed the extra time to try to pressure Ibrahim into a plea.

"You're not going to be ready in two weeks. When are you really going to be ready?" Rodriguez snapped. He pointed at Ibrahim. "This gentleman's been coming to court for nearly two years."

"We'll be ready in two weeks," she repeated.

The judge sighed, rolled his eyes, then shrugged. "Okay, then," he said, looking down at his calendar. "January nineteenth?"

The ADA nodded. "Yes, Your Honor."

He shook his head. "Trial set for January nineteenth."

In the hallway after the hearing, Watts shook his head in disbelief. Asked if it wasn't good news that Rodriguez had at least not allowed them to get a bench trial on the assault charge, he hedged.

"Well, yeah, sure. The judge was trying to do the right thing," he said. He nodded toward his client. "But on the other hand, a jury trial in Staten Island is no sure fucking thing either."

Ibrahim grabbed his cane and walked to the exit. He had a difficult decision. He could give up his lawsuit, or he could risk letting a Staten Island jury hear a white police officer tell a story about being attacked by a crazy black man. He had two more weeks to think about it.

Two weeks later it was more of the same, only with a twist. In October, Ibrahim had been pulled over and charged with driving without a license. The DA now tried to leverage the traffic case into a plea on the assault case: if Ibrahim took a plea on the latter, they'd make the former go away. Watts said no.

In court, the city once again told Judge Rodriguez they weren't ready to proceed on the assault case. Trouble with a witness, they said. He asked how long they'd need. "Two more days, Your Honor," was the answer.

The judge sighed and set yet another court date for a month later. In the hallway, Watts shrugged.

"It's just Staten Island," he said.

Finally, the next evening, on January 20, Ibrahim got some news. The city dropped the charges. He didn't harbor any illusions about the officers who broke his leg ever being disciplined, but he was at least finally free to sue the city.

He was back to even, down only a healthy leg. It had taken 658 days.

SIXTEEN ERICA

Throughout the year after her father's death, Erica increasingly found herself feeling depressed. The loss of her father weighed on her heavily.

Taking up his cause had forced her into a detective-like role, retracing the movements of his last months and days. This process kept him alive in her heart but also made her feel his absence more keenly. She would hear a story she'd never heard before, like him telling police "It's too hot" to go to jail on the day he heard of Eric Jr.'s scholarship, and she'd laugh with recognition, as though he were still there, just for a moment.

But he wasn't. He was gone.

As the year progressed, she watched as people all around her were pulled this way and that, while she remained focused on her father's case. People would say to her, "I just want to hurry up and get all of this done, so I can just move on with my life."

And she would be sitting there, screaming inside: "Move on from what?" There's no closure. This doesn't go away. It just is. She couldn't imagine what forgetting would even feel like. The idea frightened and offended her.

At times, thinking about all of this consumed her to the point where she felt like she needed help of some kind. Maybe she should go into therapy, she thought. But how?

Like Ramsey Orta, who often wondered if he was living the fugitive life intended for Daniel Pantaleo, Erica often compared her situation to that of her father's killer. Pantaleo, after all, still had public health insurance and twenty-four-hour police protection. If he was feeling sad, the state would pay for his counseling. How come the families of brutality victims had no access to mental health care?

Moreover, as the story continued to stay in the headlines, she found out the hard way how many other pitfalls there were to being in the middle of a high-profile case.

During one of her ferry protests in the heart of winter, an operative for Project Veritas, the media organ of reptilian right-wing activist James O'Keefe, braced Erica on the ferry and tried to ingratiate herself with her and other protesters.

The Veritas prankster, a white woman who called herself Laura Lewis, tried to demonstrate how down she was by showing around a picture of her "black boyfriend" on her phone and said her boyfriend had been the subject of police harassment.

She then started telling people she thought the murdered officers Liu and Ramos "got what they deserved," apparently hoping to score a "right on" from someone in the crowd.

Some people walked away from her, and Erica was certainly wary. At one point, "Laura" asked her what she thought of Al Sharpton, and Erica shrugged and rubbed two fingers together, as if to say, "He's all about the money."

The resulting video became a huge hit in conservative media, which relished the idea of the hated Reverend Al taking a haymaker from the sainted family member of a brutality victim.

Erica felt violated. She had somehow been sucked into a larger controversy between groups of people who always had and likely always would despise each other. A lot of energy was devoted to this nonsense, but increasingly, she saw, very little went toward the matter of getting any answers in her father's case.

She was surrounded by people who wanted a piece of her for one reason or another, but none of them wanted quite the same things that she did. There was always some larger cause that she was being recruited for, while the number of people helping out with her specific desire to get to the bottom of Daniel Pantaleo's past kept dwindling.

Throughout that winter, Dan Donovan's campaign slowly gathered momentum. In a preview of the polarizing politics that would grip the country's presidential election a year later, Donovan was passionately supported by white Staten Islanders who saw him as someone who'd stood up to "political correctness," Al Sharpton, and the idea that white Americans are racist.

March 22, at a Queens restaurant called Antun's, a sprawling middle-class banquet hall, the sort of place where young white kids from the outer boroughs hold wedding receptions for their starter marriages. On this date the Queens Village Republican Club holds its 140th annual Lincoln Dinner, raising money for party causes. The hundred-dollars-a-plate ceremony is supposed to feature conservative media personalities Steve Malzberg, Bill Kristol, and Donovan, whose upcoming election is a cause célèbre in local conservative politics.

A long line of speakers comes to the lectern, each one giving brief remarks before offering awards to local businessmen and police. Much of the content of these speeches is pure dog whistle. There's a lot of talk about liberal politicians lowering standards in schools to make life easier for an unnamed political constituency that apparently doesn't like to work hard.

"Diversity is always encouraged," says one speaker. "But we cannot achieve greatness by lowering standards."

David Lee, a conservative "education advocate," concurs. "Abraham Lincoln didn't go to school," he says. "He just worked hard. That work ethic is under attack."

The speakers go on to honor police officers, who "don't care about the race of the person, don't care about the gender of the person, they don't care about the class, they just try to save a life."

Late in the ceremony, Joseph Concannon takes the stage. The events of the last year have confirmed his every suspicion and fear about politicians like Bill de Blasio, Barack Obama, and Al Sharpton. His take on all of them is that they talk a big game about the problems of the inner city, but only from a distance. Bill de Blasio is the offspring of a bunch of Ivy League ancestors who grew up in Cambridge. Al Sharpton, he believes, lives in a gated community in New Jersey.

For them to rant and rave about communities that the police engaged every day "didn't play." Politicians were out of touch with the rank and file and used people like police officers as political props to get ahead. Concannon didn't believe people paid too much attention to Ramsey Orta's tape; he believed they paid too little attention to it. He believed that if people watched the whole tape, they'd see what he saw: disrespect for the law, contempt for society, a refusal to abide by the responsibilities of a civilized people.

Concannon explained all of this to the crowd, playacting a police call and reflecting upon the dangers that police face. He spoke to the assembled about law and order, "the very fabric that binds us together and makes us a civilized society." He pooh-poohed the Garner tape without mentioning it by name. "Some people like to pick apart an eight-second video," he said and went on to denounce politicians like de Blasio and Obama, against whom he would continue to fight.

"We will be out there until the dangerous and irresponsible rhetoric emanating from the mayor and the president stops," he said.

Not long after, Donovan himself came to the stage. In person he seems to have a long neck ending in a small blond head, like a yellow lollipop. He had this crowd on his side and decided not to make any waves, announcing only that he and his girlfriend Serena Stonick were about to have their first baby. "I say that to get women to vote for me," he quipped.

He looked over the crowd of loyal Queens Republicans who'd paid their hundred bucks for dinner and nodded in appreciation. "I know most of youse can't vote for me, but you can help," he said, to cheers.

He didn't need to say much else. The crowd knew who he was and what he was about.

The Donovan campaign brought the Garner story near its bizarre circular end. What began as a tragedy that momentarily forced even most white Americans to think about the dangers of overaggressive policing had flipped and become a cause for a significant percentage of white conservatives, who now cast themselves as victims in the story.

They saw themselves as a besieged minority, surrounded by a coalition of ivory-tower liberals, work-averse ethnic groups, and immigrants looking for handouts. They were tired of being called racists and were beginning to wonder why it was that only blacks and Latinos and Muslims and whoever else were allowed to have identity politics. What about us? Who looks out for our interests? Who fights for us? They were determined to elevate and protect the men—and it was mostly men—who put themselves on the line to maintain the system they'd come to know and their place at the top of it. They honored the ones who'd fight—and kill, if necessary—for that order.

On May 5, Donovan was elected to Congress. To Erica, this was another blow and convinced her of the virtually undisguised racism of Republican voters.

But, she noticed, it wasn't just conservatives who'd sent Donovan to Washington. After spending millions on Domenic Recchia's catastrophic bid to unseat Michael Grimm, national Democrats elected to pass on spending any money at all to defeat Donovan.

She'd hoped that on principle, the Democrats would want to make at least a symbolic effort at opposing Donovan's candidacy.

No such luck. The Democrat opposing Donovan ended up being Vincent Gentile, a genial, diminutive politician who was more believable as a U.S. congressman than, say, *Daily Show* punchline Domenic Recchia (although the *Daily News* called Gentile "not the sharpest knife in the Democratic drawer").

But the party gave Gentile no money at all, leaving the race for New York's Eleventh District one of the roughly 80 to 85 percent of congressional races in America that are essentially noncompetitive.

Gentile ended up raising about $200,000, about a third of the average for a losing congressional race. Donovan raised well over a million from supporters all over the country and cruised to victory, winning almost 60 percent of the vote. At his victory party, Donovan grinned and glad-handed supporters in his virtually all-white crowd, calling his election a "victory for America."

"The hardworking men and women of the middle class spoke loud and clear. You sent a message to President Obama, to Nancy Pelosi— and yes, even to Bill de Blasio—that their policies are wrong for our nation!" he said, to cheers.

During the campaign, he'd taunted the politicians and critics who pilloried the decision of his grand jury.

"I do not begrudge citizens who saw one video, heard none of the other evidence or saw any of the evidence, and heard a medical examiner use the word 'homicide,' to be confused," he said.

This, again, sounded like it made sense, except for one thing: If Donovan didn't believe there was a case, why had he presented one to a grand jury?

It didn't matter anymore. Donovan was off to Washington, and whatever questions anyone had for him would likely never be answered.

For Erica, the fact that Dan Donovan had been showered with campaign donations from around the country and sent to Congress, largely because he'd failed to do his job and prosecute her father's killer, was bad enough. Erica thought that the way people all over the country sent money to people like George Zimmerman and Darren Wilson, the policeman in Ferguson, was designed to send people like

her a message. But more dispiriting was the lack of support from
people she could have expected to be her friends.

For instance, there was the matter of who would replace Donovan
as district attorney. Legal experts had told her the next DA would
have the ability to refile Pantaleo's case to another grand jury, under
certain circumstances. So the matter of who succeeded Donovan was
of great importance to her.

When former Democratic congressman Mike McMahon threw his
hat in the ring as a candidate for the DA's office, that at first seemed
like good news to Erica.

Then she found out that McMahon had received and accepted the
endorsement of Pat Lynch, the hated police union chief who'd said
her father had killed himself by resisting arrest.

"I was like, he was endorsed by who?" she remembers. "I couldn't
believe it."

Moreover, it bothered her that city councilwoman Debi Rose, the
first black elected official in Staten Island's history, had thrown her
support behind McMahon even after Lynch's endorsement.

Erica began to suspect that all of these officials, behind closed
doors, had already agreed not to reopen the case. She didn't know
what to make of anything anymore.

Everything that had taken place, from the grand jury investigation,
to the court hearing to unseal the minutes of that grand jury, to her
failed effort that spring to get at Pantaleo's personnel file, convinced
her that while some politicians might say they were for doing this or
that thing on principle, in the end mostly what people in power
wanted to do was nothing at all, unless there was an immediate benefit in it for them.

Governor Cuomo, for instance, the son of a famous liberal, himself
a Democrat of some renown, had met with her family and in early
July 2015 approved a temporary plan to appoint an independent
prosecutor to investigate police-related killings. Cuomo got a nice
headline out of it and a photo op with Erica's grandmother, Gwen
Carr. But Erica was worried all the time that the policy wouldn't be
made permanent.

She began to feel alone, personally and politically.

. . .

In July 2015, Erica and several members of her family were stunned
to pick up the *Daily News* and see a troubling headline: "Eric Garner's Widow Rejects NYC's $5M Offer to Settle Wrongful Death Suit:
Source."

The paper reported that the family was holding out for more
money, against the advice of counsel:

> A $5 million settlement won't satisfy the heartbroken family of Eric
> Garner.
>
> A source familiar with ongoing negotiations between Controller
> Scott Stringer and the family of the Staten Island man killed by an
> NYPD cop say that his widow, Esaw Garner, turned down the hefty
> offer last week.
>
> The source said the Garner family's attorney, Jonathan Moore, is
> urging the family to accept the $5 million and then seek more
> money through a separate lawsuit against EMTs from Richmond
> University Medical Center.

The family was furious. There were only a few potential sources for
the story. And no matter what the source, the motive seemed quite
clearly to be to pressure the family into settling. The Garners were
convinced that it had come from Moore's firm. They held a family
meeting, along with Moore and the Reverend Sharpton, and things
got heated.

Erica remembers being struck by the fact that Sharpton kicked
Moore and his legal team out of the room at one point.

"I need everyone out the room. I need to talk with the Garner family," Sharpton said.

There was some hesitation. In Erica's account, Sharpton looked at
the lawyers and said, "This is some shady mess going on. I don't trust
you guys. Y'all guys got to go."

In Erica's telling, Moore hesitated, but Sharpton told him, "If
you're not family, you've got to go."

There are a number of ways to interpret this scene, but the family,
anyway, came out of the leak episode more wary than ever. They were
increasingly nervous about telling anyone anything. Moreover, they
learned that the size of the settlement contained hidden perils, from a
public relations standpoint and from a relationship standpoint. Once

that much money is involved, it tends to divide families. And the Garners were due a big settlement.

The next day, July 14, 2015, nearly a year to the day after Garner was killed, there was an announcement in the media. The City of New York had negotiated up with Moore and reached a deal to deliver $5.9 million to the family.

The size of the settlement, though actually modest compared with some other similar cases, drew outrage from the usual quarters.

In an op-ed in the *New York Post,* Ed Mullins, president of the New York City Sergeants Benevolent Association, called the settlement "obscene." He said the money was paid out to "placate outside political agendas."

Mullins implied that the taxpayers of New York had to pay for the fact that Eric Garner didn't provide for his family. "Although Mr. Garner did not provide his family with an abundance of wealth, it was clear from the outset that the Mayor's Office would," he wrote.

"Mr. Garner's family should not be rewarded simply because he repeatedly chose to break the law and resist arrest."

Erica's phone started ringing almost immediately from people offering congratulations. She was pleased, she guessed, at the money, but she also felt odd about the whole thing, like people were celebrating way too much. She wanted to stay focused on Daniel Pantaleo and keep every conceivable option open for bringing him to justice.

On the day of the settlement, she implored the Obama administration to pick up the ball. "We are calling for the Department of Justice and [Attorney General] Loretta Lynch to deliver justice for my father," she said.

Al Sharpton, who appeared at a press conference on the day of the settlement, looked pleased as well. He pledged to launch another rally in search of a federal civil rights indictment.

And those rallies happened, but not long after the settlement was done, Erica's fears came true. A silence fell over her case. The family began to splinter and fight with itself; the world moved on. In the police brutality playbook, the conclusion of the settlement tends to be the last stage of the story arc. In the end, the only people left still paying attention tend to be the family members. And even they get exhausted after a while.

. . .

In May 1964, less than a year after Martin Luther King's "I Have a Dream" speech, Lyndon Johnson announced a plan to build a "Great Society." It was to be a plan of unity and integration, finally fixing the inequities of American society, where "no child will go unfed, and no youngster will go unschooled."

The ensuing series of legislative programs passed included Medicare, Medicaid, the Civil Rights Act, the Voting Rights Act, the Food Stamp Act, even the Public Broadcasting Act that created PBS.

The Great Society was to domestic politics what the moon program was to the military-industrial complex, an audacious long shot. The very phrase "War on Poverty" conjured images of the unity and collective determination America had employed to defeat the Nazis.

These programs were never meant to be an expensive Band-Aid used to maintain a perpetual uncomfortable détente between rich and poor, black and white. They were designed to wipe out divisions and inequities and leave one prosperous, integrated people standing at war's end.

But almost immediately, in the years after the project was announced, Johnson began to get cold feet. So-called race riots in big cities were growing in size and frequency. Watts nearly burned to the ground. In Detroit in 1967, Johnson had to send in army airborne forces after police raided an unlicensed bar that was holding a party for two black servicemen returned from Vietnam, igniting the so-called Twelfth Street Riot.

In Newark that same year, a black cabdriver was arrested and roughed up for "tailgating," triggering five days of violence that ended with the arrival of three thousand National Guardsmen. Soon after, much of Newark's white population fled to the suburbs. To this day, those disturbances are called "the Newark riots" in white New Jersey and "the protests" in the city itself.

Johnson after his election in 1964 pledged to end the problems of America's cities. By the end of that term he was using federal troops to occupy them.

During the Detroit riots in 1967, Johnson ordered the creation of the Kerner Commission, the study cited by Meyerson when he concluded that "everything changes and nothing changes." LBJ installed one of his closest aides, David Ginsburg, as the executive director of the report on the causes of unrest in the cities. Johnson expected the commission to find that there was some kind of organized black power political conspiracy that had set out to cause all the mayhem.

One of the commission's stated goals was to discover the identity of "organizations or individuals dedicated to the incitement or encouragement of violence."

The commission included New York mayor John Lindsay, Massachusetts senator Ed Brooke, and NAACP director Roy Wilkins. It quickly came back to Johnson with some bad news. There was no conspiracy, just a lot of pissed-off black people.

The report basically said that the cities were blowing up because black America was tired of living in a racist country where there were no jobs.

Detailing extensive patterns of segregation, discrimination in the job and housing markets, and police brutality, the commission argued that the root of America's problems had to do with the failure to integrate white and black communities.

White people, the commission basically concluded, didn't want to live with black people. They preferred a segregated society and used complex discriminatory practices to enforce the distance.

Worse, the commission issued a warning. Unless we do something to encourage genuine integration, we'll end up with two completely separate societies.

"A rising proportion of Negroes may come to see in the deprivation and segregation they experience a justification for violent protest," the commission concluded. "Large-scale and continuing violence could result, followed by white retaliation, and, ultimately, the separation of the two communities in a garrison state."

The commission continued, using language that today seems prophetic:

To continue present policies is to make permanent the division of our country into two societies; one, largely Negro and poor, located in the central cities; the other, predominantly white and affluent, located in the suburbs and in outlying areas.

Johnson was furious when he received the report in February 1968. He couldn't have been happy with the headline in *The New York Times*: "Johnson Unit Assails Whites in Negro Riots."

LBJ recoiled from his own commission and rejected its conclusions. He also refused to implement any of its recommendations. Johnson was done with kumbaya utopianism. From then on it was less sociology, more police. If we can't fix it, let's at least keep it out of sight.

The Kerner predictions came true. By the mid-2010s, even after the election of a black man to the Oval Office, the country was almost completely segregated.

Statistics bore this dirty little secret out. At the conclusion of every census the country would sometimes even take a brief note of it, usually in the form of news stories buried somewhere in the back pages. Then the embarrassing issue would quickly be forgotten again.

From the proverbial thirty thousand feet, modern America has for some time now seemed integrated, especially the big cities. But if you take a closer look, walk from one block to the next, you'll discover that traditionally white enclaves like Lincoln, Nebraska, are actually more diverse, at the neighborhood level, than places like Chicago, New York, St. Louis, and Baltimore.

On close inspection, these great cities, not coincidentally all sites of horrific police brutality controversies in recent times, are actually just collections of tense racial archipelagoes where people of different races don't live near one another or socialize.

America, in other words, is a lot like Staten Island: white neighborhoods and black neighborhoods often separated by a physical border like the Mason-Dixon Line.

A half-century after Selma and Watts, three-quarters of white Americans don't have a single nonwhite friend. The average black person, a minority living in a majority white world, has eight white friends. He or she is also very likely to live in an exclusively black, heavily policed neighborhood.

The civil rights movement, legislation, and milestone court decisions of the 1950s and '60s produced remarkable changes and ended or ramped down centuries of explicit, statutory discrimination. But real integration was not one of the accomplishments.

The civil rights movement ended in a kind of negotiated compromise. Black Americans were granted legal equality, while white America was allowed to nurture and maintain an illusion of innocence, even as it continued to live in almost complete separation.

Black America always saw the continuing schism. But white America has traditionally been free to ignore and be untroubled by it and to believe it had reached the "postracial" stage of its otherwise proud history. That was until cellphones and the Internet came along.

When the murder of Eric Garner hit the headlines, it at first seemed to lift the veil on the ongoing violence of racism and discrimination. There was debate, controversy, furor, disgust, and a great deal of finger-pointing, even from the majority segment of white America, over what to do about the "unacceptable" problem.

But after a period of days or weeks, national media audiences exiled these red-hot stories to remote chambers of their memories. From there they become provincial tales, "black" controversies, troublesome things that happened once in a corner of society that still doesn't really concern most white Americans.

Huge portions of the country then wash their hands of the matter and leave others to deal with the things that sometimes happen in the places they don't think about. Baltimore. Ferguson. Staten Island.

This forgetting process is what police are for.

Aggressive policing maintains the reality of segregation in part by policing the borders separating poor black neighborhoods from affluent white ones.

But more important, it maintains the illusion of integration by allowing police officers to take the fall for policies driven by the white taxpayers on the other side of the blue wall.

Follow almost any of these police brutality cases to their logical conclusion and you will eventually work your way back to a monstrous truth. Most of this country is invested in perpetuating the nervous cease-fire of de facto segregation, with its "garrison state" of occupied ghettos that are carefully kept out of sight and mind.

Thanks to the ubiquity of cell technology and the instantaneous nature of modern media, those divisions became uglier and more visible after Eric Garner's death.

But the response to that increased visibility wasn't shame, embarrassment, and a national conversation about how to better integrate a broken society. Things went another way entirely.

Before 2015, Donald Trump was a fringe media curiosity, a rich loudmouth with the world's most elaborate comb-over who whored himself for ratings and Internet page views in the same waters as David Hasselhoff and Dramatic Chipmunk. Originally famous as a real estate magnate who obsessively pretended to be richer than he was and fumed over the media-created perception that he had short fingers, he was reduced in the late 2000s to trying his hand at reality TV, where weirdly enough America made him more famous than ever.

The Apprentice spoke to Middle America's most ghoulish masochistic fantasies about life in a world with no job security. In it, Trump played a vicious corporate tyrant firing unworthy losers over and over again in a revolting sadomasochistic ritual that millions for some reason found entertaining. Huge audiences got themselves worked up for the orgiastic "You're fired" climaxes, clearly enjoying the spectacle of being humiliated by the despotic rich.

But Trump wasn't satisfied. He wanted more. So he parlayed his *Apprentice* role into a new part in America's longest-running TV show, the presidential election, reinventing himself as a ludicrous caricature of a racist strongman.

It struck some people as odd that when America's white supremacist movement finally spilled out into plain view, it would be led not by a gap-toothed southerner but by a rich New Yorker in a power tie. But really it made perfect sense. For ages now New York has been at the center of every innovation in institutional racism, from redlining to blockbusting to the "war on crack" to mass incarceration to Broken Windows.

Somehow it always comes back to New York. And as a salesman for the first open revolution against the civil rights movement, Trump was perfect. He had money and education, but he spoke and wrote at a fourth-grade level. He shared a real bond with the Klansman in the Ozarks by having the same dumb reading habits.

Here, at last, was a member of the financial elite with a real link to the common man! But the link was that both consumed Internet conspiracy theories about Mexicans carrying diseases over the border or nice white people from the suburbs being butchered by minorities.

A terminal narcissist who flocked to crowds wherever they gathered, Trump unleashed a generation of suppressed hatreds simply by saying things he was too stupid to realize weren't just harmless personal opinions but political dynamite.

His boldest gambit was a proposal to build a wall separating Mexico and the United States, which he described as a protective measure necessary to keep America safe from the "rapists" across the border. He also pledged to ban all Muslims from entering the country until "we can figure out what's going on," a line that really resonated with people who loved the idea of a kind of racial cease-fire, a "temporary" stop to full integration.

Trump said little about black/white relations, but most everyone got his message all the same. On November 21, 2015, at a rally in Birmingham, Alabama, a black man who chanted "Black lives matter" at a Trump rally was kicked and punched by Trump supporters, who shouted back at him, "All lives matter!" On the same day, Trump promised surveillance of mosques.

The following day, Trump retweeted an Internet meme showing a dark-skinned man with a handgun and a set of data points, ostensibly about 2015:

Blacks killed by whites—2%
Blacks killed by police—1%
Whites killed by police—3%
Whites killed by whites—16%
Whites killed by blacks—81%
Blacks killed by blacks—97%

Trump's source was "Crime Statistics Bureau—San Francisco." One Google search would have revealed this bureau didn't exist. But Trump couldn't be bothered to look up the real numbers from the FBI, which showed all of his numbers were way off.

It didn't matter anyway. The issue wasn't that Trump had circulated the wrong numbers but that he'd circulated any numbers at all. The rhetoric about Mexican rapists and black crime rates resounded with Middle American audiences that wanted to hang on to long-forbidden beliefs about inherent racial differences.

The ideas we supposedly learned in the sixties, that people are people and what differences we have must be cultural and political, not racial, never quite stuck. Not really. And the incompleteness of that civil rights movement finally surfaced in the form of a national counterrevolt that seized every form of power in this country.

. . .

Bay Street, late December 2015. The Plexiglas box commemorating Eric Garner's difficult life and tragic death is now mostly unattended. It seems diminished, covered in scratches.

A pair of black police officers has been stationed on the block for most of the year now, and things are quieter, at least in terms of quality-of-life arrests and confrontations. But the failure to indict Daniel Pantaleo, the election of Dan Donovan, and the rise now of Donald Trump has left people on the block dispirited.

For James Knight, the death of his friend and the rise of Trump are linked. Just days after Trump's Alabama rally, he reflects on what it all means. Instead of providing a wake-up call, Garner's death might have just ended up driving hidden beliefs to the surface.

"You can see now how America really is." He sighs. "Most of the time, it was hidden, people didn't say things like they're saying now."

James sits on a stoop not far from where Garner had been killed, looks around, and shakes his head.

"But now you can see with Trump, the support he has behind him, how it's growing, you see what America is really feeling behind closed doors," he says.

"They're letting us know what they think of us."

Evening, December 4, 2015. Erica stands on the steps of the courthouse in Staten Island and addresses a small crowd of demonstrators. Her plan is to march through the St. George and Tompkinsville neighborhoods to commemorate a grim anniversary. It's a year and a day since Dan Donovan's grand jury elected not to indict her father's killer.

In the crowd stand representatives of a few rival protest organizations. Some of the Justice Leaguers, including Carmen and Rameen, are on hand. There are also demonstrators from groups like NYC Shut It Down, which have been holding weekly meetings and marches leading out of Grand Central station about this and other police incidents for some time.

The Shut It Down folks were younger and a little more hard-core, allied as they were with Black Lives Matter. They saw themselves as being much more grassroots and street oriented than other groups, and there were grumblings from the very start of the march, when some of the Justice Leaguers arrived in Staten Island in a brand-new Lincoln Navigator.

"Who the fuck comes to a street march in a *Navigator?*" groused one of the Shut It Downers.

Erica wasn't aware of the grumbling. She was instead trying to focus on keeping things together. Like Ramsey Orta, who went from being on the streets to trying to wear the activist hat virtually overnight, Erica had been thrust into the role of a political leader of sorts, without any training or guidance of any kind.

Unlike Ramsey, who seemed uncomfortable in the role, Erica took to it. She has a strong speaking voice and can be heard from a great distance. And she has a head for improvisation and a willingness to endure uncomfortable scenes and confrontations.

She stood by herself on the steps, surrounded by cameras. The Justice Leaguers were making a film about their involvement in the Garner case. So they rolled cameras as Erica gave a brief speech about the politicians in both parties who by then had walked away from the case.

She mentioned Governor Andrew Cuomo and his plan to create an independent prosecutor in police abuse cases, which would be in force for a year before it had to be renewed, by a Republican-dominated Assembly.

"I'm calling out Andrew Cuomo," she said. "He's throwing us scraps! Because he promised the family he would renew the executive order if the legislature didn't pass it. Why would corrupt Republicans pass it?"

The crowd shrugged. Only a few knew what she was talking about. She went on to talk about Democrat Mike McMahon, who had just won the DA race.

"I'm calling out Mike McMahon," she said. "The new acting DA of Staten Island. He has the power to reconvene a second grand jury. But he won't do it."

She mentioned again that McMahon had been endorsed by Pat Lynch. Then she paused and added, "I'm calling out Debi Rose, the only black elected official in Staten Island. She said to my face that my father's life matters. But she endorsed McMahon. And he's not gonna do anything.

"You know what they are?"

Liars! the crowd answered dutifully.

She went on to say they were there that night to demand answers and justice, to make sure that the idea of prosecuting Daniel Pantaleo remained alive. Then she led chants, which she'd apparently learned somewhere in the last year of leading these sometimes-lonely protests:

"No justice for the blacks! No justice for the browns! So what we gonna do?"

Shut it down, shut it down!

"When they say get back . . ."

We say fight back!

Then she began singing a poem her family had written. Most of the protesters knew it by heart:

I can hear my father crying, "I can't breathe"
Calling out the violence of the racist police
We ain't gonna stop, till the people are free
We ain't gonna stop, till the people are free

The crowd soon started walking through the St. George area, stopping periodically to lie down in front of traffic and block cars and buses. Erica was usually the first (and sometimes the only) person to lie down in traffic, and she would chant from time to time:

"Who's this for?"

Eric Garner!

"Say his name!"

Eric Garner!

She led the march through the projects, past Eric and Esaw's old apartment. Young men popped out of doorways and leaned out of windows and said things like, "He lived here!"

The marchers followed behind her, though conspicuously in different groups. There were whispers among some present that Erica was being goaded into lying down in front of traffic for the sake of the Justice League documentary. But Erica didn't hear any of it and kept on.

The police throughout the march had followed behind, seemingly not wanting to start a confrontation yet not wanting to let it go entirely either. At every major intersection there were bunches of police, who quietly let the group pass. There was a bit of eye rolling at the "die-ins" in front of traffic, but mostly the officers remained mute.

Finally, the crowd made it back to Bay Street, where Erica briefly addressed the group, asking them to hold hands in a circle around the spot where her father had died. Rameen, dressed in his trademark Orioles cap, stood beside Erica during this serene moment.

During this last address, in which she called for a moment of silence, word spread that police had massed around the corner, up the street at Victory Boulevard. And indeed, Victory was clogged with giant armored trucks belonging to Bill Bratton's much-ballyhooed Strategic Response Group, or SRG.

Surrounding the trucks were a bevy of specially trained riot police in Kevlar, some with machine guns. Given the small number of decidedly scraggly demonstrators, this giant battalion of muscle seemed comic and unnecessary.

"Oh, shit. SRGs are here," muttered James Woods, a cameraman filming the scene.

Some people took off to look at the scene around the corner, but the bulk of the demonstrators had remained on the spot on Bay Street next to the Plexiglas memorial at the spot where Eric Garner had died.

Tensions between the different groups of demonstrators finally boiled over and they were mostly all now standing there, split into two sides, pointing fingers and engaged in a ludicrous argument. The fighting-words moment had come when someone had accused someone else of being a fake, invoking the image of the Navigator car.

In response, one of the Justice Leaguers shouted back that having money didn't mean you weren't real. After all, the young man said, "Harry Belafonte led a revolution from a mansion!"

There was an outbreak of guffawing at this. A young woman shouted in response, "You did *not* just say that!"

While all of this was going on, Erica quietly wandered around the corner to walk up Victory and have a look at the gathered police force. Word had filtered back to her that there was an argument going on between the two protest groups at the memorial spot, which she would later say both angered and saddened her. She felt that her father's memory had been disrespected by the argument. It also left her with a not-insignificant logistical problem.

There must have been a hundred heavily armed officers standing on the street in front of her. Storefronts on both sides were lit up, reflecting the blinking red-and-blue siren lights. The sidewalks were cleared. The huge armored vehicles lined the sidewalks far up the street, like a caravan of elephants.

Erica rarely spoke of her father as a hero or a martyr. He was, she realized, "just a man," a single flawed person ground up by the power of the state.

Eric Garner was murdered by history. The motive was the secret sin of a divided society, a country frozen in time for more than fifty years, stopped one crucial step short of reconciliation and determined to stay there. Now the long line of armor and weaponry arrayed against a single grieving woman appeared as symbols of our desire to separate. Hatred can be organized, but only individuals love.

For a long moment Erica just stood in the middle of the street, staring at the preposterous show of force. The demonstrators were around the corner, still arguing. She was by herself.

EPILOGUE

On March 21, 2017, the site *ThinkProgress* published an exclusive: "The Disturbing History of the Officer Who Killed Eric Garner." The site, it seemed, had been contacted by "an anonymous source who said they [*sic*] worked at the Civilian Complaint Review Board (CCRB)."

This source unilaterally broke the court impasse between Legal Aid and New York City, which had refused to turn over even a partial list of officer Daniel Pantaleo's disciplinary records, by sending *Think-Progress* a list of Pantaleo's CCRB complaints: fourteen allegations, four of which were substantiated. The list showed that Pantaleo had an extensive enough history of complaints that his superiors probably should have intervened long before Eric Garner was killed.

The journey just to get this list out to the public had been an arduous one. Legal Aid, remember, had already successfully fought this issue in court, winning a judge's ruling that the city had to turn over a limited list of Pantaleo's disciplinary records.

But the city had appealed the judge's decision in the summer of 2016, arguing that Section 50-a of the state's civil rights code prohibited them from releasing any "personnel records used to evaluate performance." The bizarre thing about this excuse was that the city had, in the years prior to this case, freely released similar records on multiple occasions. The excuse for not doing so in the Garner case therefore amounted to an admission that the state had previously violated the law as a routine matter, only realizing in 2016 that they were prohibited from releasing such records.

In any case, one of the four substantiated complaints against Pantaleo was a "vehicle stop" on December 23, 2011. This was the same date of videographer Charles Roberson's fateful encounter with Pantaleo that led to a strip search in front of a laundromat. Roberson never knew it, but it appeared the department investigated his complaint, found it to be accurate, and even punished Pantaleo for it.

But the punishment, as *ThinkProgress* wrote, was not terribly rig-
orous:

> The documents indicate that the CCRB pushed for the harshest
> penalties it has the authority to recommend for all four substanti-
> ated allegations . . . But the NYPD, which is not required to heed
> the CCRB's recommendations, imposed the weakest disciplinary
> action for the vehicular incident: "instruction," or additional train-
> ing.

ThinkProgress characterized Pantaleo's record as a "chronic history" of abuse cases that would put him "among the worst on the
force." The stats backed up their analysis. Only about 5 percent of
police received eight or more complaints. Pantaleo had fourteen. And
only about 2 percent had as many as two substantiated complaints,
while Pantaleo had four.

Was this an accurate reflection of how bad Pantaleo was relative to
other officers? I heard anecdotally that Pantaleo, though an "ass-
hole," was far from the worst officer working that part of Staten Island. But it was certainly clear now that between Pantaleo's CCRB file
and his multiple lawsuits for strip-searching and "flaking," the NYPD
had had ample evidence before the Garner incident that he was a
problem cop.

Naturally, the response of the police union to the Pantaleo story
was outrage—at the leak. The always-in-character Pat Lynch had
never stopped being furious about the Garner case and showed it
when asked for comment by the *Daily News* about the leaked CCRB
list.

"The leak of such information is simply another demonstration of
the CCRB's inability to function in the fair and impartial manner pre-
scribed by the City Charter," Lynch said. "Their ineptness is well
documented."

Had this news come out in December 2014, when protesters filled
the streets, it might have rocked the city. But by March 2017, the
world's attention was focused elsewhere.

Around that same time, on March 20, the House Intelligence Com-
mittee in Washington had held dramatic hearings in which former FBI
director James Comey had announced the existence of an investiga-

tion into associates of Donald Trump's campaign and their possible ties to Russia. Trump had fueled the media furor associated with the hearings by denouncing the Russia story as "fake news."

The Trump story captivated the world and dominated the Internet and social media, obliterating everything else. Nobody cared about the Eric Garner case by then. Though Trump was a new variable, the rapid fading from memory of public outrage is a key part of the pattern of these police misconduct incidents.

When someone takes a beating or gets killed by police, city bureaucracies go into siege mode, reflexively stalling and delaying at every turn. The patience of complainants and their families is stretched to the limit. Embarrassing information, if it ever comes out, comes out years later, long after the streets have calmed down.

The quest for changes and reform tends to get dulled over time, especially if there's been a financial settlement in a case. That's usually because there are so few people left who can stay angry enough to keep the fight going.

Everyone just gets tired.

For Erica Garner, the *ThinkProgress* story was just an additional insult piled atop many others. "It doesn't tell us anything we didn't already know," she said. "He shouldn't have been out there on the streets."

The part that really bothered Erica was that Pantaleo even now was still on the police payroll. Even after his history came out, even after he'd killed someone—he was still police.

Pantaleo was still stowed away somewhere quietly pulling a salary. Meanwhile, Ramsey Orta went away to jail for four years, and over time, a host of other characters from the Bay Street neighborhood where Garner had died were arrested in stings and raids. The police in Staten Island were not amused by the attention the story had won them, and made sure that the people in Tompkinsville Park knew it.

Even outside of Staten Island, Garner's friends and acquaintances had a hard time over the years.

On February 20, 2016, John McCrae went to a little party in Edison, New Jersey. Just after midnight, he headed out of town, back toward Staten Island, driving a silver Dodge Durango. A white woman was in the passenger seat. Two Edison police officers named Joseph Palko and Daniel Hansson thought they saw a malfunctioning taillight and pulled McCrae over. They leaned in and started questioning McCrae, who was wearing a spiffy blue jacket.

"Man, that's some jacket," one of the cops said. "How much you pay for a jacket like that?"

McCrae, realizing right away he was being messed with, shrugged and said he didn't know.

"Well, that's quite a jacket," one of the two officers repeated. Then he shined a light at the girl in the passenger seat.

"How much did you pay for *her*?" the officer asked.

McCrae rolled his eyes.

"How much did I pay . . . man, that's a normal girl right there. We're friends!"

"Uh-huh," he was told. "Get out of the car, please?"

They asked him if they could search him. McCrae didn't think he had a choice and just shrugged and said yes. Going through his pockets, they found three little baggies of weed, worth a total of about thirty bucks. They arrested him and took him to the station to be questioned.

At the station house in Edison, they told him to take off his clothes so that he could be searched properly. He ended up stripped to his underwear, seated at a desk in the middle of the station for what seemed to him like a really long time.

"I was in there in my damn underpants," he later said. "And they started talking to me, like making jokes and shit. One of the guys there started asking me about cocktails, like what kinds of mixed drinks I liked. Like he was my friend or something. I'm like, 'Man, can I put my pants on?'"

Asked later if it was normal for police in Edison to interview arrestees in their underwear, the department released a statement:

> Officers Palko and Hansson transported McCrae, 52, of Staten Island, N.Y., to Edison Police Headquarters where—consistent with departmental arrest procedures—McCrae was thoroughly searched for other contraband that may have been concealed under his layers of winter clothing.

They did not find any more "contraband" and McCrae was ultimately allowed to dress and leave. He was charged with possession of marijuana under fifty grams, and possession with intent to distribute.

He was looking at six months in jail at first, but ultimately took an ACD and stayed free.

"Ain't going back to no motherfucking Edison," he said, shaking his head.

Doug Brinson was in Rahway, New Jersey, a few weeks later. He had a little stand out for his shirts and oils in a public square—unlicensed, he admits, but that wasn't the problem. Doug had a big, new pickup truck, a silver GMC that he cared for like a newborn child. He got back to his truck to find a police officer writing him a ticket for trespassing.

"For what?" Brinson asked.

"Trespassing," the officer said.

He offered some kind of explanation about how Doug's truck was obstructing a driveway by a few inches. Doug didn't quite get it and asked him to explain again. The officer, annoyed, looked Doug up and down.

"Say," he said finally. "Whose truck is this, anyway? Where'd you get it?"

Doug shook his head. "What does that have to do with anything?"

The officer at this point threw his hands back up over his head. "All right, all right!" he said, as if Doug had overreacted and needed to settle down.

At the sight of the cop's hands over his head, Doug froze.

"I thought maybe he thought I had a gun or something," he recounts. "I damn near had a heart attack when he put his hands up like that. I was like, 'Man, don't do that, you'll scare me to death.'"

Doug got a ticket for "defiant trespassing" and ended up having to pay more than $300.

Around the same time that Doug was getting ticketed, I found myself in the green room of a TV network, waiting to do a live interview. Ahead of me in line to go on the show was a prominent Democratic Party official. The official had a good reputation with progressives and was considered something of a strategic guru. He asked me what I was working on.

When I mentioned that I was looking at the Garner case, he nodded. "Oh, right," he said. "The thing about that case is—that's the unequivocal one."

I didn't say anything. I knew what he meant, of course. The significance of Eric Garner to a lot of politicians and pundits was that he was a "truly innocent" victim—in other words, not a menacing-looking young man like Michael Brown, who may or may not have robbed a store before his death.

This obsession with the individual guilt or innocence of victims among pundits and pols seemed to me to miss the entire point of the police brutality issue. The real villain in that story, I thought, was math and probability, and a community policing policy that was designed to massively amp up police confrontations in certain neighborhoods only. As was revealed in the Stop-and-Frisk lawsuit, the problem was that the policy pre-concluded that some people are more prone to crime than others. Simply looking a certain way became probable cause. That some of the people who ended up being searched and/or roughed up turned out to be criminals, and some didn't, seemed totally random and irrelevant to me. The real issue was that we employed the strategy in some places and not in others.

It was incredible to watch the reaction when a reporter named Dan Heyman was arrested in West Virginia in May 2017 for shouting a question at Trump's Health and Human Services secretary Tom Price. Heyman overnight became a martyr to the evil of Trump. The Twittersphere couldn't contain its outrage that such a thing could happen. This is America! What about free speech? The Constitution?

But Heyman's "crime"—"willful disruption of governmental processes"—is a charge that gets handed down in neighborhoods like the one where Eric Garner died virtually every day. It's a legal wild card, a bailout tool for cops who need leverage to search or detain people not obviously guilty of doing anything illegal. You'd be hard-pressed to find a person in Tompkinsville Park who hasn't received an "obstructing government administration" ticket at some point.

But beyond all that, my green-room encounter with the Democratic official who knew Eric Garner only as the "unequivocal case" bothered me on another level. I knew enough about Garner by then to be depressed that he was destined to be remembered only as a political symbol. If there's anything I hope *I Can't Breathe* can accomplish, it's to change that impression.

I'd first become interested in the case in December 2014, just after a grand jury voted not to indict Officer Daniel Pantaleo in the killing of Eric Garner. When the decision came down, I drove over to Staten Island to ask a few questions about the case.

I'd just finished writing a book called *The Divide,* which focused on law enforcement inequities. The book contrasted the negotiated, parlor-room approach to white-collar crime with the beatdown-based model of "community policing."

In the back of my mind, I thought maybe a magazine article about Garner would be a way to continue researching that world, given that Garner's case seemed from the outside like a textbook example of what happens when initiatives such as Stop-and-Frisk go south.

But when I got out to Bay Street and started asking about Garner, something odd happened. As I listened to stories about the man, all the policy issues faded from mind. More and more I found myself just asking about Garner the person. I liked him.

Garner in life had been a physically huge man, but he also had a sizable personality, so much so that even six months after his death, you could still sense him out there on that block. After a while, it got so that I could almost see him leaning up against the beauty salon window, or arguing sports with the chess players in the park, or chatting up girls in the doorway of the check-cash store. I could even see him lumbering back to his SUV (I remember being told that his car would sink almost to the curb when he stepped inside it) to go home at dusk.

I soon ignored the policy story completely and just started retracing Eric Garner's last years on the street. It was like chasing a ghost. It wasn't hard to get a measure of the man, because he was spoken of in much the same way by almost everyone who knew him.

An outsider entering a neighborhood that had experienced a world-shaking event like that might expect to hear stories of a saint and a martyr. But Garner's friends cared about him too much to slander him after death with false praise. Garner, I learned very early on, was a man who was loved by his friends and by his family members not in spite of his faults and not because of them, but because of the totality of who he was—the fullness of his imperfect humanity.

On the one hand, he was a flawed character and hard-luck case that trouble seemed to find with unerring regularity. Cursed with impeccably bad timing, Garner could be counted on to pick the wrong one almost every time he was faced with more than one option and a coin-flip chance for success. He got ripped off more than once, and the Bay Street crowd ribbed him for his runny nose, sloppy dress, and fat feet. But they loved him. There were a lot of slow hours in that park, and Garner's good nature and eccentricities kept everyone entertained.

He argued for hours over meaningless things such as sports statistics that didn't need to be argued at all, he was amazingly messy, and he ate in amounts that made jaws drop—the descriptions I heard of Garner folding a whole pizza in half and eating it like a taco were incredible. In short, he was the kind of character people would have been telling stories about on park benches and alleyways well into the future, even if this terrible thing had never happened to him.

I soon learned that beyond his caricature street persona there was another Garner. This was a more serious and thoughtful person, clever in his own way despite his clumsiness. This more serious man struggled to find a place for himself in a world full of confounding obstacles. The private Garner was flawed, too, but in a different way.

He wanted to be there for his family, but let them down early and often, repeatedly leaving them to go to jail—mostly for selling drugs, but once for a serious crime of violence, a beating of a neighbor that left Garner's family home looking like a murder scene.

Crime nearly cost him the love of his daughters, who eventually froze him out for leaving them to go to prison. He suffered terribly behind bars, and when he reemerged, Garner behaved like a man who finally understood where his priorities lay.

He organized his life around his love for his children. Though he sometimes pretended otherwise, acting like a mini-kingpin of Tompkinsville Park and boasting about how much money he made, really everything he did on the street was for his kids. Almost every dollar he made went to them. Even as his health failed, his weight ballooned, and the clothes on his back began to split into rags, Garner still marched to the corner every day to bank as much as he could.

An ex-athlete whose body had taken a beating through years of prison, untreated disease, and standing in rain and snow for hours on end to hustle quarters and dollar bills, Garner by his early forties had begun to fall apart physically.

Like so many middle-aged people, he had learned to truly appreciate what was important in life at the exact moment when his strength began to leave him. On one level, his was a profound and universal story, about how people—in ways that are simultaneously tragic and beautiful—inevitably fight with all their might to hold on to things they know deep inside can never last forever.

At heart, he was "just a man," as his daughter Erica said, trying like most of us to hold on to a little piece of something. This is a story anyone can understand, making the brutal ending that much more painful.

Of course, another part of Garner's story is not universal. His troubles with the police were of a character almost exclusively familiar to black and Hispanic men. As a white man I was poorly equipped to even guess what he might have thought or felt about any of this, and I knew that any story I tried to tell about Garner would therefore be lacking in important ways. All I could do was try to describe the incredible breadth of the institutional response to his life and death.

The lengths we went to as a society to crush someone of such modest ambitions—Garner's big dream was to someday sit down at work—were awesome to contemplate. What happened to Garner spoke to the increasing desperation of white America to avoid having to even see, much less speak to or live alongside, people like him.

Half a century after the civil rights movement, white Americans do not want to know this man. They don't want him walking in their neighborhoods. They want him moved off the corner. Even white liberals seem to, deep down inside, if the policies they advocate and the individual choices they make are any indication.

The police are blamed for these deaths, and often rightly so, but the highly confrontational, physically threatening strategies cops such as Daniel Pantaleo employ draw their power from the tacit approval of upscale white voters. Whether they admit it or not, many voters would rather that Eric Garner be dead and removed from view somewhere than living and eating Cheetos on the stoop next door.

Garner kept running headfirst into invisible walls. Each time he collided with law enforcement, this unspoken bureaucratic imperative to make him disappear threw him back into an ever-smaller pen. Even allowing him a few feet of sidewalk space was ultimately too much. His world got smaller and smaller until finally even his last breath of air was taken away from him. He was finally deemed greedy for wanting even that much.

Garner's real crime was being a conspicuous black man of slovenly appearance who just happened to spend his days standing on the street across from a string of new high-end condominium complexes. No white people I talked to would say it out loud, but Garner was just too visible for everyone's tastes. His raw presence threatened property values. Plus he was an easy bust, and so became a regular target of police mandated to make busts like clockwork.

Garner himself for a long time happily went along with this absurd charade. He accepted his "community policing" arrests as a business cost and trudged to court and to jail on command for years. He didn't begin to get truly wound up about his treatment by police until he felt the cops were breaking the unwritten rules of the game, busting him after hours as he did his laundry, vouchering his money over and over, and so on.

Then, on a day when he didn't even commit a crime, as he was still huffing and puffing and leaning up against a wall after breaking up a neighborhood fight, Garner made the critical mistake of refusing for once to be dragged out of sight. In a way that was somewhat out of character, he decided suddenly that he'd had enough. He stood up for himself, not with violence but merely in the most literal sense, standing up straight and refusing to bend.

This tiny act of defiance triggered not just a preposterous display of force but the mother of all disproportionate bureaucratic responses. The latter encompassed an apparent thrown case by the district attorney's office, months of grand jury sessions, multiple judges in multiple courts holding the line against inquiries, years of obstinate refusal by city officials to turn over records, a sweeping effort by police to target individuals on the block deemed responsible for the controversy, and countless other actions.

Garner's death launched the political career of the prosecutor who failed to indict the policeman who killed him. It even contributed to a national backlash political movement that eventually coalesced around a presidential candidate, Donald Trump, whose "Make America Great Again" platform drew from an old well of white resentment.

Once elected, Trump named as attorney general a man, Jeff Sessions, who made one of his first acts a decision to "pull back" on the federal civil rights investigations of corrupt local police departments. The gutting of federal authority to conduct civil rights cases rolled back decades of work by people such as James Meyerson, who sought to find a way to police the police. It also cut off what would have been one of the last possible avenues for justice in the Garner case.

Between the Bay Street tragedy and the onset of the Trump administration years later, America had essentially decided to start moving back in time, formally pushing back against the civil rights era. Garner's death, and the great distances that were traveled to protect his killer, now stand as testaments to America's pathological desire to avoid equal treatment under the law for its black population.

But Eric Garner isn't a symbol. He was a flesh-and-blood person—interesting, imperfect, funny, ambitious, and alive—who just happened to stumble into the thresher of America's reactionary racist insanity at exactly the wrong time. But his story—about how ethnic resentments can be manipulated politically to leave us vulnerable to the lawless violence of our own government—is not his alone. His bad luck has now become ours.

ACKNOWLEDGMENTS

This was a difficult and painful book to write, and it would not have been possible without the understanding and cooperation of the friends of Eric Garner and members of his family. First and foremost, I want to thank Erica Garner, daughter of Eric, who insisted upon telling all sides of her father's story, including those that were painful and uncomfortable. Erica's courage in telling both her story and the story of her family's ordeal was a continuing inspiration. Moreover, the fact that she and many family members and friends continued to go out on the streets and protest, often when there was no media around and there were only small crowds of supporters, spoke to a determination to find justice that sadly was matched only by the relentless ignorance and insensitivity of the city bureaucracy.

Erica's mother, Esaw Snipes, similarly told insightful and colorful stories about her husband's life as a young man and father, and I'm grateful to her especially for telling the story of how young Eric Garner met her and fell in love. Gwen Carr, Eric Garner's mother, was also generous with her time despite the obvious discomfort the retelling of her experiences caused her. The story of how she finished her shift driving a subway car en route to Coney Island on the day of her son's death is one of the most powerful in the book. Her husband, Ben Carr, whom I saw often on Bay Street, was also a great help and never hesitated to add perspective to the story—his tale of growing up in the South with the two-faced men is another image I'll never forget.

Jewel Miller, the mother of Eric Garner's last child, Legacy Garner, was an immense help with this story. Her painstakingly candid recollections helped paint a compelling picture of the complex but likable figure who was Eric Garner. I wish her nothing but the best and hope she and her children find happiness and peace.

The people with whom I spent the most time were in and around Tompkinsville Park in Staten Island, where Eric Garner worked every day in the years preceding his death. To people like James Knight,

John McCrae, DiDi, Ramsey Orta, and Doug Brinson I owe a tremendous debt of gratitude. The little stretch of Bay Street where Garner spent his days is a unique place, and they all welcomed me into it from the start.

This book really began with a bitter cold afternoon when John and James walked me through the essentials of the Garner story from their perspective, while we all stamped our feet on the sidewalk. The sections about Bay Street draw upon more than two years of visits in which I mostly just sat and listened to them tell stories. I couldn't be more grateful.

A great many lawyers helped me through the complicated second section of the book. Those include, first of all, James Meyerson of the NAACP, a compelling philosophical personality whose historical perspective was critical to helping me understand the legal battles that took place after Garner's death. Legal Aid Society lawyers Christopher Pisciotta (who runs the Staten Island office), Joe Doyle (Garner's personal lawyer), and Cynthia Conti-Cook (who handled the effort to unseal Daniel Pantaleo's history) were all a great help and very generous with their time.

Michael Colihan offered valuable perspective, as did Art Eisenberg of the NYCLU, Jen Levy (representing the public advocate's office), Ken Perry and Will Aronin (who represented Ramsey Orta), and numerous others. Richard Emery, named head of the CCRB just before Garner's death, is an old acquaintance who was gracious enough to pick up the phone when I called about this terrible story. Gregory Watts, who represented Ibrahim Annan, is another attorney who took time he probably didn't have to walk me through the vagaries of the New York criminal justice system.

Pedro Serrano, the whistleblower cop who helped defeat Stop-and-Frisk in court, was someone whose perspective from the police point of view was invaluable. There were other police officers with whom I spoke throughout the course of researching this book, many of whom I could not name, who all sounded the same theme: that policing is a difficult and thankless job that in the modern era has been compounded by "community policing" policies and statistical stressors that make it virtually impossible to avoid problem encounters on the job.

Even voices like ex-captain Joseph Concannon, who was so incensed by the Garner protests that he started pro-police protests of his own, offered important perspective on the difficulty of the job in the CompStat age.

George Kelling, the father of Broken Windows, is another person who was exceedingly generous with his time. Over the course of many conversations with George I came to believe that he was a misunderstood figure who may be unfairly maligned by history for having made a simple but brilliant observation about human behavior. I sense that Kelling himself feels that Broken Windows is a concept that evolved in directions he never foresaw, and that he's torn about its applications. On the one hand, he clearly believes in the efficacy of the concept as a policing tactic. But the mechanical or indiscriminate use of Broken Windows—what turned into "zero tolerance" policing—was to Kelling a bastardization of his ideas. I'm glad for his cooperation, and I hope readers will see him for the complex figure he is.

Ibrahim "Brian" Annan, whose brutal story provides the opening chapter of this book, is another figure who deserves recognition. Ibrahim kept me in the loop throughout his tortuous and ridiculous years-long court ordeal, and he took time out to help me re-create his experience through repeated trips to the scene.

Sam Roudman, who helped with research throughout, found countless facts and leads to pursue. He's an outstanding young journalist and I imagine he'll be writing his own books soon. Thank you, Sam, and sorry to drag you on all those trips across the Bay.

I owe a great deal to my editor, Chris Jackson, without whose help and guidance I would have been lost. Chris has been a great friend and mentor over the years and it's been an honor to work for him.

Joining Chris at Spiegel & Grau and Penguin Random House are countless others who helped along the way, but most notably Catherine Mikula, Nicole Counts, Barbara Fillon, and of course Cindy Spiegel and Julie Grau. Their support in taking on this difficult and controversial subject has been invaluable.

There are so many others to whom thanks are owed: Carmen Perez and the Justice Leaguers, Dennis Flores of Copwatch, Public Advocate Letitia James, and countless other unnamed sources helped with this book. I am grateful to everyone who took calls from Sam and me during these years.

As always I must thank my wife, Jeanne, for her love and support. Two of our children, Nate and Zeke, were born while this book was being written. My hope for them, and for my oldest son, Max, is that they grow up in a world that is better than the one described in these pages.

Lastly, I want to thank Miss Clementine Russ and her family for welcoming me into their home in Arkansas. Miss Clementine lost her husband, Carnell, to a brutal shooting nearly five decades ago. She told the story of her loss in the kitchen of the same home she shared with Carnell back in 1971. I remember listening to her describe how he used to come home after work and collapse from exhaustion in that very house, his work clothes beside the bed. I could almost hear him snoring in the bedroom a few yards away.

Until I visited, Miss Clementine had never been back to the scene of his death. That was an emotional experience, and I immediately felt a great sadness that there was not more I could do to bring attention to the continuing injustice of her case. I hope readers will take note of her story, and I have a faint hope that someone in Arkansas who sees her story told again might be inclined to take up her cause.

INDEX

Section 50-a of Civil Rights Law in, 241–42, 295
New York Times, 78, 81, 127, 146, 161, 171, 182, 185, 186, 284
Noerdlinger, Rachel, 145, 146–47, 186
Nuñez, Patricia, 262–64
NYC Shut It Down, 289–90
NY1, 171

Obama, Barack, 142, 146, 150, 163–64, 166, 277, 278, 279, 282
Office of Police Complaints, 234
Oliphant, Thomas, 226
O'Malley, Martin, 69
114th Precinct (Queens, N.Y.), 65, 224
120th Precinct (Staten Island), 6–9, 73, 91, 97, 110, 185, 229
  Sayon case and, 169–71
  see also New York Police Department
Orta, Ramsey, 102–5, 112, 114–15, 262, 263–64, 275, 297
  activism of, 191, 252–53, 255, 258, 259–60, 264, 290
  Bella incident and, 250, 260, 263–64
  celebrity of, 250, 251, 252–53, 255, 256, 258, 263, 265
  drug dealing bust of, 252, 253–54, 258
  Garner video filmed by, 114, 120, 122, 127, 137, 157, 231, 250, 251, 255, 258, 261, 277
  as hiding out from police, 250–51, 252, 256, 260, 261
  NYPD's alleged targeting of, 127, 251–58, 260, 261, 264–65
  shady plea deals offered to, 257–58, 260–61, 265–67
  in Spofford youth reform facility, 102–3
Ortiz, Chrissie, 252, 254
Owens, William, 35–36

Palko, Joseph, 297–98
Pantaleo, Daniel, 113–14, 134, 147, 153, 160, 162, 165, 166, 174, 181, 216, 222, 243, 245, 261, 280, 282, 289, 290–91, 303
  background of, 139, 231–32
  CCRB's petition for grand jury minutes of, 243–44, 245
  city as fiercely protecting privacy of, 231, 242, 244, 246, 248, 249, 295, 304
  in fatal Garner confrontation, 113, 114–15, 118–20, 121, 127

history of abuse complaints against, 229–31, 232, 233, 242, 246, 295–96, 297
  illegal chokehold used by, 120, 127, 138, 160–62, 168, 216, 223
  inappropriate groping and strip searches by, 229–31, 232, 242, 295, 296
  legal efforts to open personnel file of, 233–34, 241–43, 246, 249, 280, 295
  nonindictment and escape from punishment of, 162, 165–66, 174, 232, 254, 257, 275, 280, 282, 289, 290, 297, 300, 304–5
  planting of drugs by, 231, 232, 296
  twenty-four-hour police protection of, 257, 275
Party Line, 14–15
Patrolmen's Benevolent Association (PBA), 32–33, 195
People v. DiNapoli, 209, 214–15, 217, 227
Perez, Carmen, 174, 175, 176–77, 179, 180, 182, 188, 190, 195, 289
Perry, Ken, 256, 257–58, 260–61, 263–64, 266–67
Pink Houses, 222, 224–25
Pisciotta, Christopher, 158, 197–98, 208, 209, 213–14
Planned Parenthood shooting, 268
police, policing, 38, 42, 64–66, 68, 285, 297–98, 299, 303
  Black Codes and, 116, 117
  Broken Windows concept in, *see* Broken Windows theory
  CompStat system in, 65, 66–68, 185, 190
  fundamental role as defined in, 56, 57, 58–59
  growing feeling of alienation and betrayal in, 185, 190
  half-legal/illegal arrests in, 105–6, 222, 269, 272, 300
  Kelling's studies on automobile vs. foot patrols in, 56–57
  marches and demonstrations in favor of, 184, 185, 186, 225–26
  nonwhite resentment of, 88, 250
  rise of "zero-tolerance"/"community," 68, 69, 300; *see also* police field searches; Stop-and-Frisk program
  on subways, 61–64
  violence against, 66, 163, 182–84, 185, 186–87, 190, 192, 193, 194, 195, 267
  see also New York Police Department

ABOUT THE AUTHOR

MATT TAIBBI, author of the *New York Times* bestsellers *The Divide, Griftopia, The Great Derangement,* and *Insane Clown President,* is a contributing editor for *Rolling Stone* and winner of the 2008 National Magazine Award for columns and commentary.

Twitter: @mtaibbi